POLES in the 19th Century Southwest

To: Frank A. Nowak,

With deep respect for a fellow writer
Sto Lat!

Francis Casimir Kajencki
El Paso, Texas
March 14, 1994

Books by Francis Casimir Kajencki

Star on Many a Battlefield:
Brevet Brigadier General Joseph Kargé
in the American Civil War

1980

"Uncle Billy's War:"
General William T. Sherman's Changing Concept
of Military-Civilian Relations during the
Civil War — from Staunch Civilian Protector
to "Cruel Plunderer"

1989

Poles in the 19th Century Southwest

1990

POLES in the 19th Century Southwest

FRANCIS CASIMIR KAJENCKI

SOUTHWEST POLONIA PRESS

El Paso, Texas

Copyright 1990 by Francis Casimir Kajencki

Southwest Polonia Press
3308 Nairn Street
El Paso, Texas 79925

Cataloging in Publication Data

Kajencki, Francis Casimir
    Poles in the 19th Century Southwest

    Bibliography: p.
    Includes index

    1. United States – History – War with Mexico,
1846-1848 – Santa Fe Trace Battalion, 1847-1848 –
United States & Mexican boundary survey, 1849-1855
– Civil War in New Mexico, 1862 – Santa Fe Trail –
Territorial New Mexico. 2. United States – History
– Polish immigrants, 1834-1905 – Biography.
3. United States – History – Regular Army – First
U.S. Dragoons, 1841-1858 – Third U.S. Dragoons,
1847-1848 – Second U.S. Cavalry in Texas,
1856-1858.

Library of Congress Catalog Card Number: 90-61764

ISBN: 0-9627190-1-3

To the Memory of

CHARLES RADZIMIŃSKI

Polish Revolutionary, American Engineer and Soldier

Radzimiński Family Coat of Arms.
Courtesy of Library of Congress Photoduplication Service.

Preface

Historians have become aware of the influence of the West on American culture and history. Our experience on the frontier in the 19th Century has shaped the growth and character of the nation. But much of what our forebears have lived through remains to be researched and documented.

In 1977, this writer accidentally turned to facets of Western history, primarily in Territorial New Mexico. Earlier, I had devoted time to the Civil War. Upon my retirement from the U.S. Army in 1973, I wrote about the military service of Brevet Brigadier General Joseph Kargé and his 1st and 2d New Jersey Cavalry Regiments. This long-time effort, begun while I was still in the army, led to publication of *Star on Many a Battlefield* by Fairleigh Dickinson University Press in 1980.

While I was still occupied with the Civil War, El Paso artist Wanda de Turczynowicz Hermann told me that Ysela O'Malley's great grandfather, Louis William Geck, fought in the Civil War in New Mexico. Researching Geck, I found that this Polish immigrant was not a combatant but a merchant who traded with both the Union and Confederate forces. The pursuit of Geck's activities uncovered the names of several heretofore unknown Poles who intrigued me. Consequently, I turned my attention from the Civil War to Poles in the 19th Century Southwest. This effort yielded a series of essays published in historical journals on Geck, Martin Kozlowski, Alexander Grzelachowski, Charles Radzimiński, and Napoleon Kościalowski.

In addition to my principal subjects, Federal Census records for New Mexico disclosed the names of many other individuals who listed Poland as their birth place. They were primarily residents of mining towns and soldiers at military posts. Because of his medical profession, Francis L. Russ especially seems worthy of further research. He first appears on the 1860 census for Bernalillo County in the precinct of Albuquerque. He gave his age as 33 and occupation of farmer. Both he and his parents were born in Poland. (Russ, like many others, never said Russia, or Russian Poland, Austria, or Prussia, but simply "Poland," as if his native land were a viable country in the 19th Century). Ten years later the census taker found him a physician in the town of Bernalillo. By 1880, Russ had returned to Albuquerque. He was now 54, still single although listed as Head of Household of servants, and practicing medicine. He apparently left no offspring. Because few doctors were found on the frontier, their presence and knowledge were especially critical in the life of the region. I have not written about Russ, but perhaps some historian may yet document the contribution of Russ to the Territory.

—FRANCIS C. KAJENCKI
El Paso, Texas

Contents

List of Illustrations

Photographs and Documents

Maps

Polish Pronunciation Guide

Letters used in the book:

a — as in father.

c — "tse" as in tsar.

ć — similar to "tch" in hatch.

ch — "h" as in hot.

e — "short e" as in met.

ę — "nasal e" like French "in" in vin.

i — "ee" as in meet.

j — like "y".

ł — like "w" in water (note slanted line through "l"; it is not a "t").

ń — like "ni" before a vowel, as in companion.

o — "o" in democrat.

ó — "oo" in boot.

ś — similar to "she" in lashes.

w — like "v" in vane; sometimes like "f" before a voiceless consonant.

Phonetic Spelling of Surnames

Gajkowski	— Guy kof ' ski
Grzelachowski	— Gre ze la hof ' ski
Kościałowski	— Kosh cha wof ' ski
Kozłowski	— Koz wof ' ski
Radzimiński	— Ra dzi mean ' ski
Kajencki	— Ka yen ' tski

Analysis

and

Comparison

FOUR OF THE FIVE POLES

presented in this collection of essays were born in Warsaw: Geck, Kozlowski, Radzimiński, Kościalowski. The fifth, Grzelachowski, was a native of Gracina. (Though I have not been able to locate Gracina, I believe it is a small community in Eastern Poland that was forcibly taken by the Soviet Union in World War II. The name may have since been changed by the Soviets.)[1] Socially, Geck and Kozlowski were evidently of the middle class, while Grzelachowski, Radzimiński, and Kościalowski belonged to the gentry class in a country composed primarily of peasants. Grzelachowski, however, did not gain gentry status until 1845, when he was twenty-one. He and his brothers, Józef and Tomasz, were accorded the recognition on the basis of their father Franciszek's military rank of captain in the Polish army during the Napoleonic era. Like their father, Józef and Tomasz served in the army, but for the tsar.

In Poland, Radzimiński, Kościalowski, and Kozlowski fought as revolutionaries in the cause of Polish independence. The failed uprisings prompted a substantial political emigration to Western Europe and the United States. In the case of Radzimiński and Kościalowski, they took part in the November 1830 Uprising against Russian domination. Upon the collapse of the rebellion, the two escaped into Austria with their units. Subsequently, the Hapsburg monarch deported them to America with an initial group of 235 exiles in March of 1834. I believe that Geck, a sixteen-year-old lad, found himself among those exiles. As a minor and subject of the tsar, he was not listed on the passenger manifest. Contemporary Geck family tradition tends to corroborate my theory that young Geck arrived as a stowaway in his teens.

In 1848, Martin Kozlowski at age 21 joined the Polish rebellion against Prussia in the Poznań province. When the rebellion was crushed, he escaped to England, and two years later he emigrated to America.

Only Alexander Grzelachowski was not a revolutionary. As a newly-ordained priest of the Roman Catholic faith, he was recruited for the recently-established Diocese of Cleveland, Ohio. Less than a year after coming to Ohio, Grzelachowski accompanied Father Jean Lamy to New Mexico Territory, where Lamy was installed as the first American Bishop of the Diocese of Santa Fe.

Once in America, all five Poles saw military service. Geck and Kozlowski enlisted in the United States Dragoons. Radzimiński and Kościalowski volunteered for service in the War with Mexico. Grzelachowski became the chaplain of the Second New Mexico Volunteer Infantry Regiment in the Civil War. He played an indispensable role in the Battle of Glorieta Pass, March 28, 1862. Reverting to civilian life, Grzelachowski and Geck became successful merchants; Kościalowski and Radzimiński, civil engineers; and Kozlowski, rancher and innkeeper on the Santa Fe Trail.

Except for Radzimiński, who remained a bachelor, the other four took wives and raised families. Geck had four wives in succession, and thus he fathered several family branches, both of Hispanic and non-Hispanic heritage. Kościalowski's descendants are of Anglo stock. Although Grzelachowski took a Hispanic wife and favored the use of the Spanish language, his descendants are in the Hispanic and Anglo categories. Grzelachowski taught his children Polish, a capability that was passed on to some grandchildren. Kozlowski's offspring became Latinized through intermarriage, but the surname survived.

My first contact in New Mexico with the Kozlowski name occurred in 1960, when I examined the Albuquerque telephone directory. It listed about a dozen Kozlowskis, an unusually large number. After all, the city is not Chicago, Philadelphia, or Buffalo, where thousands of Polish Americans live. The given names, too, caught my attention – all in Spanish. I solved the mystery of the "Hispanic" Kozlowskis some twenty years later, when I researched the life of Martin Kozlowski.

Four of the five Poles maintained their Polish surnames, despite their difficult pronunciation for most Americans. Geck was the exception. His original surname was Gajkowski, according to granddaughter Lillian Weir Dukeminier. However, no documents have been found that would tie Geck to this name. When the 23-year-old Geck enlisted in the U.S. Army, he signed his name "William Geck." If he had landed at New York in 1834 with the two shiploads of Polish exiles, he would have been near sixteen, thus corroborating family tradition that William came to America in his teens. Furthermore, William was a man-servant, or striker, to Robert E. Lee, when the lieutenant served as army engineer at St. Louis in the period of 1837-1840. What brought Geck to St. Louis? We know that a number of the Polish exiles traveled west to Illinois in anticipation of receiving a land grant from the Andrew Jackson Administration. Thus, Antoni Gajkowski resided in Vandalia in 1838, and the state capital at that time lay only some sixty miles from St. Louis.[2] If William were the son of Antoni, he may have left to seek employment in St. Louis. Admittedly, the data are circumstantial, but at this time the only available information.

The Kościalowski surname disappeared. Son Paul Casimir did not marry and died quite young. His brother Philip Leon, born in Jacksonville, Illinois, in 1851, never knew his father, who left the family in 1853 to enlist in the U.S. Marine Corps. At age 19, Philip worked on Thomas Rhea's farm in New Berlin, Sangamon County. He became a lawyer and practiced his profession in San Francisco. Unfortunately, he changed his name to "Kaye," in deference to American unwillingness to spell and pronounce his name. Although married twice, Philip did not have children.[3]

Of the five, Radzimiński seems to have displayed his pride of origin the most. Whether as an engineer with the James River and Kanawha Company of Virginia, second lieutenant with the Third U.S. Dragoons in the Mexican War, surveyor and secretary of the U.S. Boundary Commission, and first lieutenant with the crack Second U.S. Cavalry on the Texas frontier, Radzimiński always signed his name with a slanted, diacritical mark over the "ń." It is the Polish spelling of the name, and he assiduously maintained it.

Collectively, the five Polish immigrants contributed significantly to the history of the Southwest. Geck soldiered with the First U.S. Dragoons for ten years, in pacifying the West and advancing

Drawing by Boundary Commissioner John Russell Bartlett, portraying the Commissioner's Quarters at Magoffinsville (El Paso), Texas. Charles Radzimiński arrived here on June 24, 1851. (Courtesy of John Carter Brown Library at Brown University, Providence, Rhode Island.)

American civilization. Upon being honorably discharged from the service in 1851, he remained in New Mexico Territory, where he began and operated a successful mercantile business for forty years. He rose to be the leading citizen of Doña Ana, contributing a civilizing influence to the frontier and promoting its growth.

Martin Kozlowski served with the First U.S. Dragoons in New Mexico and Arizona for five years. He, too, became enchanted with New Mexico and decided to stay. Buying a 600-acre ranch near Pecos in 1858, he became an innkeeper on the historic Santa Fe Trail. In the Civil War, his ranch served as the headquarters for the Union army under Colonel John P. Slough. The property possessed a plentiful supply of water for men and animals, as well as an excellent campsite strategically located with respect to Glorieta Pass. Kozlowski invited the Union soldiers to his ranch, cooperated with and assisted them materially. Thus, he contributed to the decisive Battle of Glorieta Pass, a Union victory that turned back the Confederate invasion of New Mexico.

Grzelachowski's single, most dramatic contribution to the history of New Mexico took place in the Civil War, when he served as Chaplain of the Second New Mexico Infantry Regiment. Grzelachowski joined Major John Chivington's raiders, who destroyed the Confederate supply train in Apache Canyon on March 28, 1862 (Battle of Glorieta Pass). Padre Polaco was the only individual in the command that could and did lead Chivington's men around the Confederates, in darkness, and through a trackless area to the safety of Kozlowski's Ranch. Beyond the fact that he saved some 400 Union soldiers from possible capture, Grzelachowski probably at the time did not appreciate the strategic result of his deed. However, by preserving Chivington's physical and psychological blow to the Confederates, Grzelachowski insured the collapse of General Henry Sibley's Army of the West.

An educated person blessed with a dynamic personality, Alexander Grzelachowski provided stability and character to his community and the society that evolved around him in east-central New Mexico for forty years. He left the priesthood due in large measure to boring pastoral duty at small, isolated communities. His boundless energy demanded challenges that the Church could not provide. Padre Polaco, undoubtedly, would have made an excellent Bishop of Santa Fe.

Although he arrived in America an unwilling immigrant, Napoleon Kościalowski nevertheless demonstrated loyalty and commitment to his adopted country. He volunteered to serve in the War with Mexico, 1846-1848, and he recruited a company of Missouri soldiers for the Santa Fe Trace Battalion. Under the command of Lieutenant Colonel William Gilpin, this indomitable unit marched more than 3,000 miles across the Plains for the protection of the vital Santa Fe Trail. As part of this unique but unheralded battalion, Kościalowski and his company of native-born Americans helped to carry out an important mission under the most difficult conditions.

Of the five Poles whose lives influenced the history of the 19th Century Southwest, I would rate Charles Radzimiński as first among equals. Radzimiński was educated, ambitious, dynamic, and very personable. It is clear from his accomplishments that he did not brood over his deportation to America in 1834, but sought to turn misfortune to advantage. He quickly mastered the English language, as evidenced by his correspondence. By 1840, he gained the responsible position of assistant engineer with the James River and Kanawha Company of Richmond, Virginia. And he enjoyed the confidence and friendship of the company president, Joseph C. Cabell. On one occasion in 1843, Radzimiński represented individual stockholders by proxy (10 votes) at a meeting of company stockholders.[4] Despite the satisfaction of his employment, he volunteered for service in the War with Mexico and was commissioned a second lieutenant. In the post-bellum period he continued his engineering work with the Northeast Boundary Commission, run by the Army Topographical Engineers. His impressive work led to the appointment of Principal Assistant Surveyor with the United States Boundary Commission. In this capacity, he surveyed more than 330 miles of the international boundary along the Rio Grande. As second-in-command and secretary of the Commission, he worked closely and harmoniously with Commissioner William H. Emory in the delineation of the Gadsden Treaty line. Although Radzimiński was of foreign birth, his exceptional ability led to his selection and appointment of First Lieutenant, Regular Army, by Secretary of War Jefferson Davis in 1855. The Pole served in the top-rated Second United States Cavalry Regiment in Texas with Robert E. Lee. Undoubtedly, Charles Radzimiński would have achieved a distinguished career in the Civil War if he had not died prematurely of tuberculosis in Memphis, Tennessee, August 18, 1858.

Louis William Geck

Soldier, Merchant, and Patriarch

of

Territorial New Mexico

Introduction

I DERIVED A SUBSTANTIAL AMOUNT
of primary source data from Geck's original documents in the possession of granddaughter Lillian Weir Dukeminier of El Paso, Texas. She inherited them from her mother, Caroline Geck Weir. These papers deal with Geck's military service, business activities, land transactions, citizenship, Civil War activities, treason trial by the Federal government, and military pension. During late 1978 and 1979, Mrs. Dukeminier graciously consented to allow me to examine the documents, some of which were reproduced for my research files.

Realizing the importance of the Geck documents, I asked Mrs. Dukeminier what she intended to do with them. She said she would give them to her children, although a county historical society had asked for them. Suggesting that the documents be entrusted to professional historians and archivists, I recommended the New Mexico State Records Center and Archives (NMSRCA) in Santa Fe.

Lillian Weir Dukeminier died on January 20, 1988, less than two weeks after husband Ray had passed away. Her remains were cremated. Son Gerald and daughter-in-law Christine Dukeminier of Albuquerque invited me to join the family at a memorial service at Restlawn Cemetery in El Paso on January 23, 1988. Prior to her death, Mrs. Dukeminier donated more than 100 Geck papers to NMSRCA. The packet included a copy of *Polish American Studies* (Autumn 1982), containing my essay on Geck. The NMSRCA identified the documents as the "Louis William Geck Papers."

Some descendants were unaware that Geck was of Polish descent even though Geck's daughter, Caroline Geck Weir, emphasized her father's Polish origin to a writer of the Federal Works Progress Administration in 1937. I mention the interview in my essay. Geck himself brought up his Polish birth periodically. On one occasion in 1874, he came to the attention of the editor of the *Las Animas Leader*, who referred to Geck as a "Polander from New Mexico." Geck drove into Las Animas, Colorado, with his wagons, heading east on the Santa Fe Trail for St. Louis. Staying overnight, he evidently did some drinking in the town saloons since a local law officer picked him up in an intoxicated state and found $1,000 cash on his person. The newspaper reported that, for Geck's own protection, he "was placed in the cooler to sober up and his money put in a town safe." The next morning Geck was let out of jail, received all of his greenbacks, and went happily on his way. How did the editor know that Geck was a Polander? Undoubtedly Geck told him so.[1]

As a member of the First U.S. Dragoons, Geck served at Fort Gibson, Indian Territory, located today near the city of Muskogee, Oklahoma. His Company H was commanded by Captain Nathan Boone, son of the famous frontiersman Daniel Boone. In 1843, the army ordered Boone's dragoons, augmented by Companies D and E, to make a reconnaissance in force of the prairies south of the Santa Fe Trail. Departing Fort Gibson with about ninety cavalrymen on May 14, Boone rode northwest into Kansas Territory, reaching the Santa Fe Trail at Walnut Creek. Here he met Captain P. St. George Cooke with two squadrons of dragoons from Forts Leavenworth and Scott. Cooke had the mission of protecting the annual caravan of traders along the Trail, from northwestern Missouri to the Mexican boundary of New Mexico. Taking leave of Cooke, Boone rode south into Indian Territory again and then east to Fort Gibson, which he reached on July 31.

The reconnaissance was a 69-day odyssey. The troopers rode over uncharted terrain inhabited by wildlife and roving Indians. Although they met Indians, who managed to steal from them, the dragoons experienced a peaceful march. They also enjoyed hunting the buffalo, but more from necessity to procure meat for the mess.[2]

It is logical to assume that Geck rode with Boone. Admittedly, the soldier could have been sick or remained on detail at Fort Gibson. Because the companies were habitually understrength, however, Boone would want every able-bodied dragoon for the mission. Therefore, Geck undoubtedly took part in this fascinating experience, conducted under the leadership of a skilled frontiersman.

In addition to *Polish American Studies*, two other publications printed a short version of my essay: *Perspectives* (January/February 1985), a Polish American Educational and Cultural Bi-Monthly of Washington, D.C., and *Gwiazda Polarna* (Polar Star), May 25, 1985, a Polish American newspaper in Stevens Point, Wisconsin.

Appreciation for Research Assistance

Louis William Geck's granddaughters Lillian Weir Dukeminier of El Paso, Texas, and Albina Geck Provencio and Josefina Geck of Anthony, New Mexico; Ysela O'Malley and Simeon H. (Bud) Newman of El Paso; Jess D. (Jay) Weir, Jr. of Las Cruces; Charles Geck and Gerald and Christine Dukeminier of Albuquerque.

Also, James H. Purdy and Donald R. Lavash of New Mexico State Records Center and Archives, Santa Fe; Dale E. Floyd, Elaine C. Everly, Charles A. Shaughnessy, and Robert G. Matchette, National Archives; Stanley L. Cuba, Denver; George J. Lerski, San Francisco; Marc Simmons, Cerrillos, New Mexico; Richard J. Sommers and John J. Slonaker, U.S. Army Military

History Institute, Carlisle Barracks, Pennsylvania; Beverly Bishop, Missouri Historical Society, St. Louis; and Julie Colombo, Catholic Archdiocese of St. Louis, Missouri.

My essay on Louis William Geck was first published in *Polish American Studies*, Vol. XXXIX, No. 2 (1982 Autumn), and I include it in this book through the courtesy of the Polish American Historical Association.

Essay

LOUIS WILLIAM GECK, a Polish immigrant who arrived in America as a stowaway, joined with fellow cavalrymen to establish sovereignty over newly-gained territory from Mexico. Later, as a pioneering merchant, he helped to transform New Mexico from a wild frontier into a developing state of the Union.

Geck was born in Warsaw, Kingdom of Poland, on June 4, 1818.[3] Almost nothing is known of his formative years since, according to family tradition, he emigrated as a ship's stowaway in his teens. His entry into the United States took place in the mid-1830s.[4]

Geck's descendants tell the story of young William as a man-servant to that famous Southerner, Robert E. Lee.[5] If true, Geck knew Lee prior to January 1841, the date of Geck's enlistment in the U.S. Army. We note from Lee's biography that the lieutenant of army engineers was assigned to St. Louis, Missouri, from August 1837 to October 1840, when he headed the project to control the river channel at that port.[6] The Geck family story, therefore, is plausible in time. Furthermore, Geck seemed to have an affinity for St. Louis. As a territorial entrepreneur, he favored that city in his business dealings and family affairs.

Louis William Geck of Doña Ana,
New Mexico Territory in 1887,
aged 69. (Courtesy of granddaughter
Josefina Geck, Anthony, New Mexico).

The documented biography of William Geck begins in 1841 when he was twenty-three years old. On January 12, he enlisted in the United States Army at Baltimore, Maryland. Captain F. Morris, recruiting officer, described him as five feet six inches tall, with dark eyes, dark brown hair, and of dark complexion. The recruit's signature reveals a bold handwriting that is clear and legible. He listed Poland as his place of birth.[7]

Geck was assigned to Company H, First United States Dragoons. Established by Act of Congress of March 2, 1833, the regiment was scattered over an immense area of the West.[8] He probably reported to Fort Leavenworth, Kansas, since the Regimental headquarters with Companies E, F, H, I, and K were located there at the close of 1840. The remaining five companies were assigned to Forts Gibson, Wayne, and Crawford.[9]

Geck's Company H was commanded by Captain Nathan Boone, the youngest son of the famous Daniel Boone of Kentucky. Although he was then about sixty years of age, Captain Boone was an experienced and still vigorous frontiersman. As a lad of fifteen, he had gone west across the Mississippi River with his father and remained there.[10]

In uniform Geck undoubtedly presented a colorful appearance. During the period of the Indian campaign in Florida and the War with Mexico, the dragoon wore a blue fatigue jacket, trimmed with yellow lace, and a flat forage cap with a wide yellow band. Of sky blue material, the trousers were reinforced with two yellow stripes up the outside seam.[11] Regimental practice called for designating the color of the horses of each company, and thus Geck rode a sorrel.[12]

In the five-year period of Geck's first enlistment, the companies of the regiment performed their usual detached service and carried out changes in station between Forts Leavenworth, Wayne, Crawford, and Towson. At the end of 1845, Geck was with his company at Dragoon Camp near Evansville, Arkansas, where he was honorably discharged on January 12, 1846. Less than a month later, he re-enlisted for another five years in St. Louis, Missouri, on February 6, 1846.[13] His bounty for re-enlisting was $24.00, a

Enlistment of William Geck, 23, in the Army of the United States for five years at Baltimore, Maryland, January 12, 1841. He re-enlisted for another five years at St. Louis, Missouri in 1846. (Courtesy of National Archives).

sum that equaled three months' pay. Again he was assigned to Company H.[14]

In the War with Mexico, 1846-48, five companies of the First Dragoons served with General Stephen W. Kearney's "Army of the West," which marched to New Mexico and then to California. Four additional companies saw action in Mexico, but Geck's Company H did not join the fighting. The unit remained at Dragoon Camp, Arkansas, for the protection of the Indian frontier. On October 18, 1846, the company was ordered to Fort Gibson and stayed there until July 17, 1848.[15]

While serving as a dragoon, Geck married a woman of German extraction. She is identified only by her first name, Mamie. It would appear that Geck married Mamie before the year 1848. The marriage may have occurred in St. Louis during his break of three weeks between enlistments. He brought his wife to Fort Gibson, located a few miles east of present Muskogee, Oklahoma. In the 1840s, the post served as a frontier base in Indian Territory. Situated on the banks of the Neosho River, the post overlooked an extensive prairie. Although the view from the fort was beautiful, service there was unhealthy. Malaria afflicted many members of the garrison. Lieutenant James H. Carleton, who served at Fort Gibson, called the place the "charnel house of the army."[16]

Mamie Geck bore a son, Charles, but soon suffered a tragic death when she accidentally fell into a well at the fort. Unable to care for his infant son, and probably forced to a decision by an impending movement of his company, Geck left the child with friends. Whether the separation was to be temporary or permanent is not known. Nonetheless, after leaving the army Geck returned to Fort Gibson to look for his son but found no trace of him or the foster parents.[17]

Following the end of the Mexican War, Company H departed Fort Gibson to serve in the territory acquired under the Treaty of Guadalupe-Hidalgo. At the time, the soldiers believed they were marching to join the fighting in Mexico as they were unaware that the treaty of peace had been signed. Hundreds of miles west of Fort Gibson, Company H met Colonel Sterling Price's regiment returning to Missouri. Price told the dragoons that the war was over. The company continued its march into New Mexico, reaching Santa Fe and later displacing south to Socorro. A detachment of twenty-five men moved on to the village of Doña Ana, a few miles north of Mesilla, on the east bank of the Rio Grande.[18] Geck arrived here in 1848 and would remain in Doña Ana until his death in 1890.[19]

The company entered the territory under the command of Brevet Captain Abraham Buford of Kentucky.[20] Captain Enoch Steen, who had distinguished himself at the Battle of Buena Vista, later relieved Buford.[21]

The soldiers were the visible presence of the United States Government in the Mexican Cession. They maintained the peace and safeguarded the citizens, especially against raids by Indians. On August 16, 1849, Steen led his dragoons in a fight with a party of Apaches at the San Diego Crossing on the Rio Grande, north of Doña Ana. Steen was severely wounded, but six months later he fought them again. On February 2, 1850, Steen's dragoons followed the tracks of an Apache party across the desert region known as "Journado del Muerto" (Journey of the Dead Man). After pursuing the Indians for many miles, Steen observed another group passing through a canyon above the San Diego Crossing. The dragoons could clearly see the Indians who were not more than a mile away. Steen decided to go after them, and a spirited chase began. The fleeing and pursuing parties galloped at full speed over a level plain for more than thirty miles. Toward the end, the troopers saw their quarry throw away blankets, provisions, and everything else but their weapons in order to make themselves light as possible. The chase was hard on Indians and soldiers alike, with Steen's horses becoming thoroughly broken down. Three of the best were left dead on the route, yet the Apaches still managed to elude the cavalry.[22]

A year later, Geck completed his enlistment and was honorably discharged at Doña Ana on February 6, 1851. Brevet Major Oliver L. Shepherd, Third U.S. Infantry, commanding the Post of Doña Ana, signed the discharge papers.[23] A civilian once again, Geck

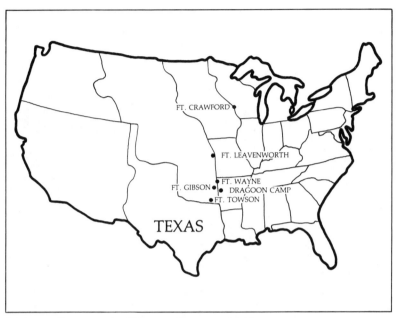

Military Posts on the Western Frontier, 1845.

applied immediately to the United States Commissioner of Pensions for a land bounty to which he was entitled. By letter of February 8, 1851, he forwarded his discharge to the commissioner, who acknowledged and approved Geck's claim on June 7, 1851.[24]

On land adjacent to the village of Doña Ana, the 33-year-old Geck built a large, solid adobe building that served as his home and trading post. He entered upon a life long career as a merchant.[25] He prospered and, in time, operated four stores – one in Doña Ana, one in Old Mesilla, and two in Las Cruces.[26]

Geck acquired land gradually. In 1852 he bought a house and lot in Doña Ana for $500 from Lieutenant John Trevitt, Third U.S. Infantry. Trevitt served at Fort Bliss, Doña Ana, and Fort Conrad in the period 1849-53. Writing to Geck from Fort Conrad, Trevitt said he would forward the deed through an intermediary, Lieutenant John C. McFerran. In the meantime, Trevitt authorized Geck to take possession of the property. The deal was consummated

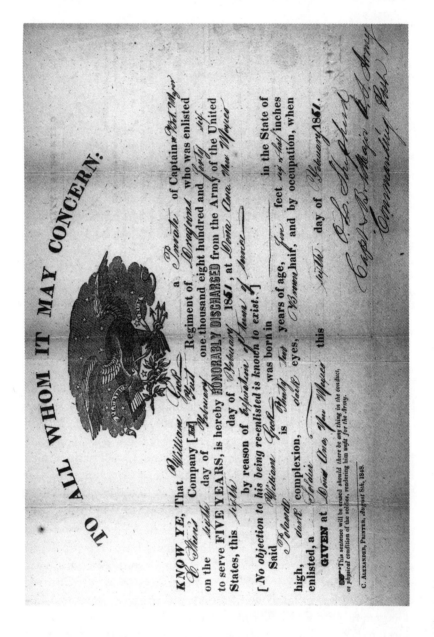

at Fort Fillmore, just south of Doña Ana, on October 4, 1852, when McFerran acknowledged receipt of Geck's $250 in cash and a note for $250, payable in six months.[27]

Trevitt's letter addressed Geck as "Don L. Geck." Shortly after establishing himself in Doña Ana, Geck took the additional name of Louis, or Luis in Spanish, and acquired the title "Don." In his receipt, however, McFerran refers to "Mr. Lewis W. Geck."

On October 21, 1854, Geck bought a house lot in Mesilla for $80. The front extended on the plaza for seventeen *varas* (aproximately fifty feet) and was fifty *varas* deep.[28] Four months later Geck obtained clear title to a piece of land just north of the town limits of Doña Ana. This land joined with Las Lomas on the northeast, with the limits of the town of Doña Ana on the southeast, with the property of Gregorio Dabalos on the southwest, and with the land of James W. Graves on the northwest. Earlier, on July 29, 1846, the Mexican government had given the land to a Guadalupe Olivares. Nine years later some twenty-three "owners" relinquished the property to Geck "for and in consideration of the title and claim presented to us by Luis Wm. Geck." The individuals conceded that this land was "settled by each of us through mistake and our ignorance." James A. Luey, county clerk of Las Cruces, certified to the authenticity of the document on February 28, 1855.[29]

Geck's landholdings demonstrated his intention of striking roots in New Mexico. He also sought the status of citizen of his adopted country. On November 18, 1852, Geck appeared before Thomas I. Bull, Clerk Pro Tem of the District Court of the United States of the Territory of New Mexico, County of Doña Ana. The court's document reads, in part: "…Luis William Geck who being duly sworn declares that it is his bona fide intention to become a

Private William Geck, Company H,
First Regiment of U.S Dragoons, is
honorably discharged from the Army
of the United States at Doña Ana,
New Mexico, on February 6, 1851.
(Courtesy of National Archives).

citizen of the United States and that he renounces all allegiances to every foreign prince, potentate, sovereignty and power, and more particularly to Nicholas Emperor of Russia whose subject he now is."

Two years later Geck was granted full rights of citizenship at naturalization proceedings before the Honorable Kirby Benedict, judge presiding in and for the Third Judicial District, County of Doña Ana. The action took place on "the first day of the November Term, A.D. 1854, of said Court." Richard Campbell and Charles H. Hopper testified as witnesses in Geck's behalf. They swore that Luis William Geck "has resided within the limits of the United States for the last five years and for more than two years in the Territory of New Mexico and that he has behaved as a man of good moral character, attached to the principles of the constitution and Government of the United States...." Vincent St. Vrain, Court Clerk, certified to an official transcript of Geck's naturalization proceedings on December 22, 1854.[30]

Even as he sought ownership of land and the status of citizenship, Geck wanted to be a family man. Upon his discharge from the army he married Margarita Severiana de Jesus Barrio, born in El Paso (Juarez), Mexico, on February 21, 1838. They were married by Padre Ynojos in Mesilla on April 24, 1851. She died two years later, while giving birth to her first child, Jesusita.[31] This daughter, of very proud bearing, later became the bride of Simeon H. Newman, who at age twenty came from St. Louis to New Mexico along the Santa Fe Trail.[32] After some time in the territory, including a stay at Las Cruces as editor of the *Thirty-Four*, a weekly newspaper, Newman moved to El Paso. In the early 1880s he became editor of the *Lone Star* newspaper. His crusade against vice

Entry in the family bible in William Geck's own hand. This Holy Bible was published by American Bible Society of New York in 1850. (Courtesy of Lillian Weir Dukeminier and New Mexico State Records Center and Archives, Santa Fe).

FAMILY RECORD.

I. I. F. William Geck was born on the 4th June 1818 in the City of Warszaw Kingdom of Poland. Got married on the 24th of April 1851. in the town of Mesilla Mexico by the Padre Inojos. my wife was born at Alpaso Mexico on the 21st February 1838. and died on the 12th day of July 1853 at one O'Clock in the morning with a Child in bed. her name was Margarita Severiana de Jesus Barrio her fathers name Franchisco Barrio her mother Dolores Contreras

my Child Jesusita Geck was born on the 12th July 1853 on Thuesday morning at one Oclick when in few minutes the mother Expired and prostitution upset the gamblers, who struck back through an advertising boycott by the town's merchants. As a consequence, the *Lone Star* went out of business.[33]

Jesusita's marriage to Simeon H. Newman in March, 1882, began one branch of the expanded family. Geck's third wife was Beatriz Aguirre, whom he married in 1854.[34] Yet once again his wife died in childbirth when William Cidroño Peter was born at Doña Ana on July 11, 1856.[35] The father sent young William to a Catholic elementary school in St. Charles, Missouri, in the 1860s. It was at St. Charles that the son received First Holy Communion in September, 1867.[36] Later he earned a college degree, a rare accomplishment in those days.[37]

W. C. P. Geck settled in Anthony, New Mexico, in 1902. He was active in the community, serving as a school board member and trustee, interpreter for the courts, and justice of the peace. The town went into mourning when he died on May 3, 1920. The schools and several businesses were closed on the day of his funeral. He and his wife, Beatriz Barrios, had seven children.[38]

Following the loss of his third wife, William Geck remained a widower for more than three years. However, on December 31, 1859, he married Sarah Aguirre, first cousin of the deceased Beatriz. The Reverend Justin Manuel Chavez performed the ceremony at Doña Ana. Sarah was a child bride, being not yet thirteen years of age.[39] The husband showed great sensitivity when he sent Sarah, along with daughter Jesusita, to a Catholic convent school in Missouri. Jesusita stayed to receive a twelfth grade education, but Sarah was home again before 1864.[40] She gave birth to a daughter, Beatrice, on April 9, 1864, but the child lived only nine days. Two years later a son, Samuel, was born on April 25, 1866. Another son, Marion Samuel, born in 1868, lived only sixteen months. William and Sarah had four more children, all daughters: Caroline in 1870, Wilhemina (Minnie) in 1872, Mary in 1874, and Sarah (Lillian) in 1879.[41]

The eldest daughter, Caroline, became the wife of Charles Weir. They had nine children, but two sons died shortly after birth. The family resided near Mesilla Park and at Organ, and later moved into the old Geck home in Doña Ana. When Caroline died in 1955, she was the last occupant of the Geck homestead. Her youngest son, Jess, became a prominent Las Cruces attorney.[42]

William Geck's four wives and his many children clearly displayed his proclivity for a large family. Long before the expansion of the family, however, Geck sought to establish himself as a successful merchant by advertising regularly in local newspapers. In 1861, the *Mesilla Times* carried his front page advertisement as follows: "Louis Wm. Geck, wholesale and retail dealer in all kinds of merchandise at Doña Ana, Arizona."[43] By the advent of the Civil War, Geck was well established. But this greatest of fratricidal conflicts, which tore families apart, also had its impact on Geck.

The southern part of New Mexico (called Arizona Territory in 1861) came under Confederate control for about one year when Colonel John R. Baylor's Texans marched into Arizona from Fort Bliss. Baylor captured Mesilla and quickly disposed of Federal troops opposing him. He took the initiative in organizing a military government with Mesilla as the capital and appointing himself as governor of the territory.[44]

Baylor announced a number of appointments for the organization of the Confederate territorial government. Of the seven justices of the peace, Louis William Geck was appointed for Doña Ana County.[45] In addition to his official position, Geck also sold goods to the Confederates.[46]

The following year General Henry H. Sibley's Confederates lost the decisive Battle of Glorieta Pass, March 26-28. Lack of supplies and reinforcements caused Sibley to abandon the territory and withdraw into Texas. Close on Sibley's heels, Colonel Edward R. S. Canby's Union forces reoccupied all of New Mexico. The Union army seized and confiscated much of Geck's property and goods in retaliation for his collaboration with the Confederates. One long list of confiscated merchandise was worth a total of $21,675.42. The items included 660 gallons of whiskey, 132 gallons of Old Cognac, eighty-eight gallons of New York Brandy, sundry grocery and household items, four complete wagons with twenty-two stock of cattle and one mule worth $3,000, and lastly one accordion.[47]

THE MESILLA TIMES.

VOL. I. | M. C. MURRAY & Co., Publishers. | MESILLA, ARIZONA, SATURDAY, JULY 27, 1861. | TERMS: $3 00 per Annum, in Advance. | NO. 41.

The Federal government also seized Geck's house and lot in Mesilla. Under the orders of Brigadier General Joseph R. West, commanding the District of Arizona, a company of soldiers occupied the house on July 20, 1862, and used it, the corral, and the auxiliary buildings until August 8, 1863.[48] Meanwhile, the Federal government indicted Geck for treason. He was imprisoned at Fort Craig, where the U.S. Marshal took $371.00 from his person. Later, authorities transferred Geck to the county jail in Albuquerque. Here, on Christmas Day, 1862, he petitioned General James H. Carleton, commanding the Department of New Mexico, for an interview with the general to explain his loyalty to the United States Government.[49]

It is not known whether Carleton granted Geck his wish, but the prisoner's case was placed on the docket of the February 1863 term of the Second Judicial District Court. One witness in Geck's behalf, Peter J. Dice (Deuz), was subpoenaed and summoned by the Court. Geck paid Dice the sum of $36 for travel expenses as a defense witness for eight days.[50]

Geck was apparently acquitted of the charge, since U.S. Marshal Abraham Cutler immediately ordered Francisco Fanio of Doña Ana to "turn over to Louis Geck all of the goods, chattels, effects, [and] stock hands seized from the said Geck and placed in your keeping by the Marshal of the United States."[51]

Geck believed that the Federal government had unjustly seized and abused his property. Hiring attorney Frank Higgins, he sought redress from the army. Higgins presented Geck's claim for $1,700 to Colonel George W. Bowie, commanding the District of Arizona

Louis William Geck advertised his merchandising business regularly in local newspapers. He operated four stores; one in Mesilla on the Plaza, two in Las Cruces, and his main trading post in the town of Doña Ana. In 1861, the southern part of New Mexico was called Arizona Territory. (Courtesy of Library of the University of Texas at El Paso).

at Franklin, Texas, on April 13, 1864. The sum represented compensation for the rental of the house and lot in Mesilla, for damages to the house, auxiliary buildings, and corral, for counters and shelving taken from the house, and for 200 damaged lime stones appropriated for government use.[52]

Colonel Bowie responded by appointing a commission of three officers, who met at Las Cruces on May 2, 1864, to inquire into and report on the facts relative to the claim. The board made a favorable recommendation, and Bowie forwarded the matter to Headquarters, Department of New Mexico, in Santa Fe. Major John C. McFerran, the chief quartermaster, advised the commander that the board had failed to consider a crucial question: Was Geck a loyal citizen? If he was loyal, the claim should be paid. If disloyal, the claim should not be paid.[53] Accordingly, Bowie appointed another board of officers, who were scheduled to meet at Las Cruces on December 5, 1864, to inquire and report whether Geck "has been loyal during the Rebellion, or gave aid and countenance to the rebels upon their invasion of New Mexico."[54]

It appears doubtful whether the board ever met. An extract copy of the orders for Geck was not received by his attorney until December 7, 1864, two days after the board had been scheduled to meet. Higgins wrote the president of the board, Major Joseph Smith, asking about the status of the proceedings.[55] Meanwhile, on December 8, 1864, General Carleton abolished the District of Arizona. All units of the former district were instructed to report directly to Santa Fe.[56] While the general's order did not invalidate outstanding administrative actions of the District of Arizona, the abolishing of Colonel Bowie's command tended to cause a degree of confusion. Some pending activities would fall victim to the consolidation.

Geck undoubtedly became apprehensive when the issue of loyalty was raised once again. Uncertainty over the board's ruling probably made him less willing to press his claim. He now risked losing a great deal more if the United States Army should confiscate his property again. In view of the absence of government records that the board met and deliberated a decision, it is likely that Geck quietly dropped the matter.[57]

Having worked hard to make his business successful, Geck became a merchant of considerable standing. His legal battles with the army attest to a determined character – one that would not tolerate an injustice whether actual or perceived. The substantial sum of $21,000 for his goods that were temporarily confiscated by the U.S. Marshal in 1862 indicated the volume of his business.

Geck's main suppliers were trading companies in St. Louis and Kansas City, Missouri, although he also traded with other merchants in New Mexico and undoubtedly in the Mexican state of Chihuahua. Consequently, all of his merchandise had to be hauled in overland for great distances.

In St. Louis, he dealt with J & J Beakey, wholesale dealers in tin, sheet ironware, stoves, hollow-ware, and castings. Chase & Brother sold him boots and shoes. Heincke & Estil provided Geck with china, glass mirrors, and solar lamps. Another wholesaler, H. O. Pearce & Co., sold him clothing such as hats, caps, ladies' furs, shaker hoods, ruches, and artificial flowers.

In Kansas City, the W. H. Chick & Co. sold groceries, household products, and whiskey. Geck usually bought the merchandise in substantial amounts. A bill of lading from W. H. Chick & Co., dated August 16, 1861, shows a purchase of more than 21,000 pounds, consisting of such items as coffee, sugar, soap, tobacco, tomato catsup, and a good deal of whiskey. Anacleto Aguirre, Geck's agent, signed for the merchandise. Before the era of railroads, all goods were loaded and transported in wagons. Aguirre moved this merchandise to Doña Ana in five wagons.[58] Descendants said that Geck freighted supplies from St. Louis by ox and mule teams. A six-wagon caravan made two round trips over the Santa Fe Trail yearly, with each wagon carrying about 4,000 pounds of goods.[59]

In the early years Geck risked his wagon trains to Indian raids. Recalling some of his grandfather's stories, Charles C. Geck said that "when a shipment of merchandise was ordered, the merchants never knew when they were going to receive it, if at all, for the Indians would ambush the pack trains and wagons, murder the drivers, rob the caravans, and burn the wagons."[60]

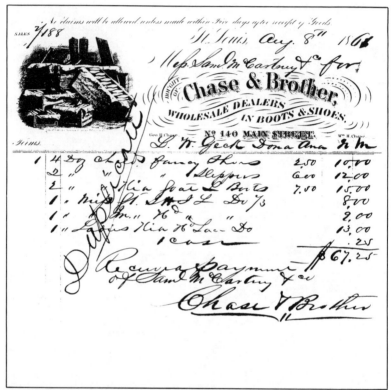

*Bill of Sale from Chase & Brother, Wholesale Dealers
in Boots and Shoes, St. Louis, Missouri, to Louis William
Geck of Doña Ana, New Mexico, August 8, 1861.
(Courtesy of Lillian Weir Dukeminier of El Paso, Texas).*

Geck also bought personal items for his family. One piece of fine
furniture was an organ-like piano, called a "Melodian," manufactured by S. D. and H. W. Smith of Boston. This wind instrument
was furnished with an ivory keyboard and leather bellows that were
pumped with the feet. Geck bought the melodian in St. Louis for his
wife Sarah and hauled it to Dona Ana by wagon. The melodian was
in the possession of Sarah's granddaughter, Lillian Weir Dukeminier,
who treasured it for its cultural and historical value.[61]

Living in a frontier environment that allowed but few of the amenities of life, Geck sought educational and cultural advantages for his wife and children. He also built a large, comfortable home for them. The great adobe house of Don Luis Geck was once the showplace of Doña Ana. Geck built the house in the form of a *murallo*, a Spanish word meaning a square building surrounding a patio. The adobe walls were two feet thick. Inside the house the rooms had high ceilings which were adorned with and supported by *vigas*. In addition to the living quarters, the structure housed a general store, a liquor store, and a pool hall. Stables for Geck's teams and wagons, and outside walls, completed the enclosure. The front of the house extended for a distance of seventy-five feet, and it was set off by a porch sixty feet long.

Members of the Geck family occupied the house for a century, the last occupant being Caroline Geck Weir, one of the seven children of Don Luis and Sarah. She finally left the old house to live her remaining years with daughter Lillian in Santa Fe, where she died in 1955 at age 85.[62] The abandoned structure was torn down in the 1960s.[63]

In 1888, when Geck was 70 years old, he applied for a Mexican War pension which the Congress had established on January 29, 1887. If granted, he would have received $8 per month. In his Declaration of Survivor for Pension, Geck said that since 1880 he was dependent on his children to take care of him because he was nearly blind and could barely walk. He listed old age as the reason for his disability.[64] The government rejected the claim on the grounds that Geck's unit, Company H of the First U.S. Dragoons, "was not in Mexico, en route thereto, or on the frontier thereof during the war." The Pension Office informed Geck of its decision on June 18, 1888. Notwithstanding, Simeon H. Newman, now Geck's legal guardian, wrote his congressman, S. W. T. Lanham, that he ask the Commissioner of Pensions to reconsider the claim. The commissioner answered Newman directly. "There is therefore nothing in the claim to warrant its reconsideration," the commissioner concluded, "and the rejection of same is adhered to on the ground originally stated."[65]

Geck lived for two more years. He died of heart disease at Doña Ana on June 9, 1890. The funeral took place from the family residence the next day at 7:00 a.m. He was buried in the family cemetery located some 200 feet east of the old homestead. The Rev. Pedro Lassaigne of St. Genevieve's Roman Catholic Church in Las Cruces performed the burial service. Geck's gravesite lies between those of wives Margarita Severiana and Beatriz. He had reserved the center plot for himself and requested that he be buried there.[66] Many years later a standard United States government headstone was placed on the grave. It bears the inscription: "Louis W. Geck, Co. H., 1st U.S. Dragoons."[67]

The year following her husband's death, Sarah filed a "Declaration of Widow for Pension." George Fulton and George Ackenback of Doña Ana, and Conrad Aubel of Las Cruces, testified on behalf of Sarah's declaration. The three friends had served with Geck in Company H. The Pension Office rejected Sarah's claim for the same reason that it had denied her husband's claim.[68]

In 1893, a board of examiners was investigating claims of war veterans in New Mexico. On behalf of Sarah, Simeon H. Newman wrote the Commissioner of Pensions in Washington requesting that William Geck's prior claim be thoroughly investigated when the board came to Doña Ana County. Hearing nothing from Washington, Newman wrote Isaac D. Laferty, Special Pension Examiner, then in Las Vegas, New Mexico. Newman told Laferty that Geck's claim had been unjustly rejected. Newman stated: "Three members of same Co., enlisted at same time and discharged at same time and serving side-by-side with him during the whole term of enlistment are receiving pensions and this one is denied."[69] Meanwhile, Commissioner William Lochren informed Newman that "the bureau does not deem it advisable to submit the above noted claim for special investigation."[70] The family made no further claims.

Sarah continued to live her golden years in the great adobe house in Doña Ana, where she died on December 18, 1924, aged 76. A funeral Mass was said the next day at the Catholic Church of Our Lady of Purification in Doña Ana.[71] She lies buried with her husband and his two previous wives in the family cemetery.[72]

William Cidroño Peter Geck, age 25.
(Courtesy of daughter Josefina Geck).

Sarah's son Samuel, the only surviving male of the marriage, took over the merchandising business. But Samuel showed little enthusiasm for the role of merchant. In a matter of time, the enterprise withered away.[73] Samuel died in Los Angeles in 1944, aged 78.[74] His wife Carlota, who proceeded him in death in 1909, is buried at Doña Ana.

What can be said about William Geck the man? He possessed a pioneering spirit. The development of his character was undoubtedly influenced by his military service on the Great Plains and the desert environment of the Southwest. On being discharged in early 1851, Geck could have gone either to St. Louis, Chicago, or the East Coast. Instead, he chose to stay in New Mexico Territory and face the challenges of the frontier.

Having served his adopted country as a soldier for ten years, he further demonstrated his commitment to America. As soon as he could, he applied for and was granted citizenship. He valued his rights as a citizen and the opportunities these rights gave him.

Geck was ambitious. He set out to own a thriving mercantile business and he succeeded. In gaining his objective, Geck displayed an indomitable spirit. He fought with the military authorities in the courts over violations of his rights as a citizen when soldiers trespassed or abused his property.[75] He also took delinquent civilian creditors to court. Geck did not seek quick retribution through lawless means, although he lived in an era when some men resorted to such practices. Instead, as a law-abiding citizen, he employed judicial measures.

Geck was very family-oriented. His many children from his last three marriages attest to that characteristic. At a time when educating the young was a difficult thing, he sent his children to established schools in Missouri at substantial cost and effort. He built a large, comfortable home in Doña Ana, and his financial success lent an aura of prestige to the family.

Geck respected the traditions and culture of ethnic groups. Perhaps as a recent immigrant, he felt more comfortable with the Hispanic than the Anglo[76] element in the territory. Yet, he seems to have mixed well in both groups. Three wives were of Hispanic descent, but two daughters married Anglos and other descendants did likewise. Religious belief may also have influenced him in his choice of wives.

Geck learned to speak Spanish fluently. In time, he seems to have become bi-cultural. Geck also spoke German, which he may have learned in St. Louis, if, as suspected, he had lived there for several years. In the 1830s St. Louis attracted increasing numbers of German immigrants. Geck also served with German-born soldiers in the U.S. Dragoons. During the nineteenth century the army recruited substantial numbers of foreign-born men such as the English, Irish, Germans, and Poles.[77] Geck's army comrades George Ackenbach and Conrad Aubel also settled in the Las Cruces area. William C. P. Geck, recalling incidents about his early years in Doña Ana, told his children that at times grandfather entertained friends who "spoke in a strange tongue."[78]

Geck's use of the German language may have led some to the impression that he was of German origin. Caroline Geck Weir commented on this point in 1937. She said: "Some of our family seem to think that Lewis William Geck was a German, but he was not. He came from Poland."[79]

It is natural to assume that Geck lost the ability to speak Polish, although he may have retained some expressions that had impressed themselves on his mind. It is clear, though, that he never forgot his Polish birth. Notwithstanding the fact that the Russian tsar abolished the Kingdom of Poland in 1831, Geck continued to list his country of origin as Poland on military and federal census records, and other legal documents, except during his naturalization proceedings, when he had to be technically correct in renouncing allegiance to the tsar.

It is revealing that he wrote the city of his birth the Polish way, *Warszawa*. However, in trying to conform to the English version of Warsaw, he simply dropped the final "a." Geck never changed his feelings about his birthplace, even after more than fifty years in America. Recall that in 1888 he applied for a Mexican War pension. Conrad Aubel supported his friend's claim with an affidavit in which he listed "Russia" as Geck's country of birth. Aubel was correct. On that same occasion, however, William Geck wrote "Poland" in his application.[80] Geck's position reflected that of Polish émigrés from the Uprising of 1830 and the 1848 Revolution. They never recognized the Partitions and the foreign rule of Poland, and they always referred to their native land as a viable state.

Geck's descendants from three marriages are legion. They live primarily in New Mexico, Texas, and Southern California. Others settled throughout the country. Many rose to prominent positions in their communities.

Descendants of the crusading editor Simeon H. Newman and Geck's daughter Jesusita contributed to the development of El Paso in such fields as medicine, real estate, music, education, and history.

William Cidroño Peter, the only child of Geck's wife Beatriz Aguirre, began another branch of the family which includes school teachers, well-to-do farmers, an artist-painter, and military officers, one of whom is a graduate of the United States Military Academy.

The offspring of Sarah Aguirre and William Geck are perhaps the most numerous. They appear in almost all fields of endeavor, including law, real estate, and politics. One served as a district judge in El Paso.

It is intriguing to speculate about the possible descendants of Geck's first son Charles, from his marriage with Mamie while he served in the army. Known descendants raise the possibility of a

Our Lady of Purification Church in Doña Ana, New Mexico, where the Geck family worshipped. Six children of Sarah Aguirre Geck were baptized here, and when she died in 1924, the Mass of Christian Burial was said here. In 1986, the parish erected a new church on adjacent ground. (Photo by Sterling Trantham of Las Cruces, New Mexico).

relationship with a Charles Geck family in the East. Genealogical research could perhaps solve the mystery of this first child.

The remains of Louis William Geck lie in a private cemetery in the little-known village of Doña Ana, New Mexico. Yet, the spirit of this immigrant Pole hovers over a large area of a nation that he adopted as his own and in which his descendants live to pursue happiness and enjoy the blessings of liberty.

Martin Kozlowski

Role

in

New Mexico History

Introduction

THE FOLLOWING ESSAY WAS PUBLISHED
in *Polish Heritage* (Winter 1986), a quarterly publication of the
American Council of Polish Cultural Clubs. Editor Wallace M.
West featured the essay by allocating the entire front page to the
opening paragraphs. This published essay, however, does not include the shooting incident that caused Martin Kozlowski to be
jailed for two years. At that time the available details were so sketchy and confusing that I needed time for additional research.
Uncertain of the duration of the research, I decided to go ahead
with the publication of the essay without the shooting incident. I
believed that Kozlowski's contribution to New Mexico history was
too significant to go unheralded any longer.

With regard to the missing episode, District Court records at
the State Records Center and Archives do not provide the circumstances that led to the tragedy. However, I was able to glean
enough facts from the English-language press to form a fairly clear
picture. As part of my research, though, I tried to locate Spanish-
language newspapers published in the period of 1878-1879. I believe

that Hispanic newspapers may have reported the incident more fully. According to Porter A. Stratton's *The Territorial Press of New Mexico, 1842-1912*, J. H. Koogler and Louis Hommel published the Spanish-language *Gaceta* in Las Vegas, New Mexico from March 1877 through December 1878. (The Kozlowski shooting occurred in this time period, on January 28, 1878). But were any copies preserved and, if so, what institution could claim this distinction? The reference librarian at New Mexico State University Library at Las Cruces informed me that the *Gaceta* is listed in the private William A. Keleher Collection (based on *New Mexico Newspapers, 1975*). Accordingly, I contacted Michael L. Keleher, grandson. Despite the demands of his law practice in Albuquerque, Keleher responded cooperatively. He asked his daughter, Anne B. Keleher, to make a search of the grandfather's newspaper files. She found several brief stories in the *Las Vegas Gazette*, which were forwarded to me. But, her search produced no copies of the *Gaceta*. I am indebted to Michael L. Keleher and his daughter Anne for their gracious help.

The ownership of the old Kozlowski Ranch reverted to the Federal government. In my essay published in 1986, I wrote that E. E. Fogelson bought the property in 1938 and added it to his larger Forked Lightning Ranch. He died on December 1, 1987, leaving the ranch to his widow, actress Greer Garson. Newspaper reports surfaced that Garson seemed disposed to sell the property, and some prominent New Mexicans became concerned when they learned that a Florida developer sought to purchase the ranch for the construction of a major resort and residential area. The New Mexicans urged the Federal government to buy the Forked Lightning Ranch, merge it with the nearby Pecos National Monument, and create a national park. In my opinion the creation of the national park would maintain the character of the Kozlowski Ranch. Private funds rescued the Garson property from developers. The Mellon Foundation provided the money to buy the ranch and turn it over to the U.S. government. Thus, the 5,556-acre Forked Lightning Ranch became a part of the new Pecos National Historical Park.[1]

Appreciation for Research Assistance

I wish to express my appreciation to the following additional individuals and institutions for their material assistance: Historians Donald R. Lavash, James H. Purdy, Stanley M. Hordes, and J. Richard Salazar of the New Mexico State Records Center and Archives, Santa Fe; Kozlowski's great grandchildren, Lena Baca, Joseph M. Kozlowski, Jennie Kozlowski of Albuquerque, and Josie K. Woodlief of San Leandro, California; historian Marc Simmons of Cerrillos, New Mexico; Wallace M. West, Pinellas Park, Florida; Mike Disimone, Dallas, Texas; Isabel Gutierrez and Marion M. Coleman, Albuquerque; Katherine Engel, Colorado Historical Society; Juliette H. Lukas, Milton Historical Society, Wisconsin; Dale E. Floyd, National Archives; Arthur L. Olivas, Museum of New Mexico, Santa Fe; and Sister Cecile Feldhaus and Leonard Cde Baca of St. Anthony's Parish, Pecos, New Mexico.

Essay

MARTIN KOZLOWSKI, A PIONEER
settler of the Territory of New Mexico, played a significant supporting role in the decisive Union victory over Confederates forces at the Battle of Glorieta Pass, March 26-28, 1862. Called the "Gettysburg of the West," this Civil War battle saved New Mexico for the Union. More important, the victory thwarted the Confederate goal for the conquest of Arizona, Colorado, and California with its prized gold fields.

Kozlowski's Ranch, located on the Santa Fe Trail near Pecos, became the field headquarters for the Union forces commanded by Colonel John P. Slough. The ranch had the only adequate supply of fresh water in the area. Beneath a grove of cottonwood trees, a spring flowed copiously through crevices in the sandstone rock. To the rear of the ranch house, a rise of ground covered with scrub cedar provided an excellent encampment.[2]

As a former member of the First U.S. Dragoons, Kozlowski welcomed the Federal soldiers. He sold them horses and mules at cost. He converted his tavern into a hospital for wounded soldiers, and it served this purpose for more than two months after the battle. Kozlowski's Ranch also became a place of interrogation for captured Confederates, before they were evacuated to the rear. Loyal to the old flag, the Polish immigrant sought to aid his adopted country.

The importance of Kozlowski's Ranch emerges from the play of events in the New Mexico campaign. In 1861, Brigadier General Henry H. Sibley's Confederate Army marched north into the territory from Fort Bliss, Texas. Upon the Rio Grande at the Battle of Valverde, February 21-22, 1862, Sibley defeated the Union forces, which retreated to the protection of nearby Fort Craig. Bypassing them, Sibley continued to Albuquerque and Santa Fe, which he occupied on March 23. He immediately ordered units to advance east against Fort Union, the guardian of the Santa Fe Trail. The fort also held large quantities of military supplies that the Confederates needed badly. Meanwhile, the First Colorado Volunteer Infantry Regiment, reinforced by U.S. Army regulars and New Mexico militia, moved westward from Fort Union to oppose the rebels.[3] (See map on p. 111).

At Bernal Springs, on March 25, 1862, Colonel Slough ordered Major John M. Chivington to raid Santa Fe. Chivington, a Methodist minister turned soldier, set out at once with about 400 cavalry and infantry. By midnight he reached Kozlowski's Ranch, some twenty-seven miles east of Santa Fe. Welcoming the Union soldiers, Kozlowski cautioned the major about the presence of Confederate pickets in the neighborhood. The Pole invited the Federal troops to encamp on his ranch. Part of Chivington's command – elements of Companies D and G, First U.S. Cavalry – were members of Kozlowski's former unit. Chivington set up camp to the rear of the ranch buildings. The soldiers named it Camp Lewis in honor of Captain William H. Lewis, U.S. Fifth Infantry.[4]

The next morning, reconnaissance parties captured four Confederate pickets near Pigeon's Ranch, five miles west on the Santa Fe Trail. Chivington's men escorted the prisoners to Kozlowski's where Chivington questioned them. Learning that a sizable body of Texans was nearby, he discarded the plan to raid Santa Fe and instead decided to engage the enemy.

Moving west through the canyon beyond Pigeon's Ranch, Chivington surprised and captured the enemy's advance party. He entered Apache Canyon, where he sighted the main body of Texans, led by Major Charles L. Pyron. The two forces clashed. The

Enlistment of Martin Kozlowski in the Army of the
United States for five years at New York City,
March 2, 1853. (Courtesy of National Archives).

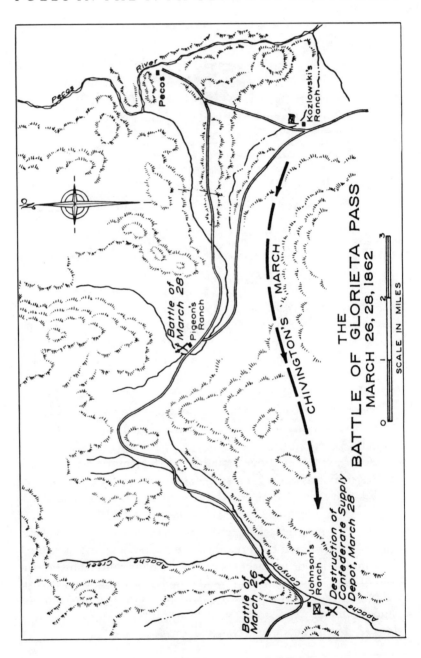

THE
BATTLE OF GLORIETA PASS
MARCH 26, 28, 1862

Union soldiers defeated the Texans, who retreated to their former camp at Johnson's Ranch. As it was sundown, Chivington did not pursue, and he camped overnight at Pigeon's. The water supply, however, was not sufficient for both men and horses, and Chivington fell back to Kozlowski's Ranch. In the custody of a company of cavalry, some seventy captured Confederates were evacuated to Fort Union. Meanwhile, Colonel Slough arrived at Kozlowski's with the remaining portion of his command.[5]

The main body of Confederates was some distance away. Lieutenant Colonel William R. Scurry led the elements of four regiments, some 700 soldiers of Sibley's Army of New Mexico. Reaching the village of Galisteo, south of Santa Fe on March 26, Scurry received word that Pyron had fought the Federals at Apache Canyon. Although he rushed to Pyron's aid, Scurry arrived after the battle. He assumed overall command for the expected engagement with the Union force.

On the Federal side, Colonel Slough planned to attack with a two-column movement from Kozlowski's. He marched 900 men along the Santa Fe Trail towards the Confederate camp at Johnson's Ranch, while Chivington and about 450 men followed a mountain trail to the high ground overlooking the ranch. Both columns were to converge on the enemy.

Becoming impatient, Scurry moved down the Glorieta Pass for about six miles to near Pigeon's Ranch, where he collided with Slough. An exhausting fight of six hours took place. Although the Confederates finally drove Slough's troops from the field of battle, their victory was temporary, since Chivington struck a devastating blow in their rear. He surprised the Confederate train, loaded with ammunition, clothing, commissary items, medical supplies, and forage. His men attacked and destroyed some sixty to eighty wagons. Chivington then rejoined the main command at Kozlowski's after a detour in darkness over a pathless route. The destruction of the Confederate train made the Battle of Glorieta Pass the decisive action of the New Mexico campaign. Left without supplies, Sibley became completely discouraged. His army retreated to Texas, never to threaten New Mexico again.[6]

The fortunes of war had thrust Kozlowski's Ranch into a base for the Union forces, and the owner helped them in every possible way. The soldiers' good behavior drew his praise: "When they camped on my place," Kozlowski said, "and while they made my tavern their hospital for over two months after their battles in the canyon, they never robbed me of anything, not even a chicken."[7] It was a high compliment for rowdy Coloradoans. One writer described them as "wild, gay, rollicking, tempestuous sons of the frontier, hard drinkers and hard fighters." They had looted chicken coops and smoke houses in Denver, and they were prone to burglarize the regiment's civilian sutler of his canned fruit, oysters, and wine. The volunteer soldiers had responded well to Kozlowski's hospitality.[8]

Martin Kozlowski was born in Warsaw, Poland. At the time of his birth, April 24, 1827, his native land was partitioned among Prussia, Austria, and Russia. There are no data on his early years. In 1848 Kozlowski joined his countrymen in an armed insurrection against Prussia. The uprising was part of the revolutionary fervor that shook Europe in what has been called the "Spring of Nations." The Polish bid for independence, however, was put down by the Prussians, and the 21-year-old Martin fled to England, where he remained a refugee for two years. Before leaving for America, he married an Irish woman in her early twenties, Elena Celenan (perhaps Callanan or Callahan).[9]

At New York, on March 2, 1853, Kozlowski enlisted in the Army of the United States for a period of five years. Brevet Major William N. Grier, the recruiting officer, described him as five feet seven and one-half inches tall, with blue eyes, brown hair, and fair complexion. Martin was then twenty-five years old. He listed his occupation as laborer.[10]

Following a course in cavalry training at Carlisle Barracks, Pennsylvania, Kozlowski was assigned to the First Regiment, United States Dragoons, which he joined in August 1853. Colonel Thomas T. Fauntleroy, a Virginian and veteran of the War with Mexico, commanded the regiment. Kozlowski probably reported first to Fort

Leavenworth, Kansas, and may have remained there for some time while waiting to accompany a train of supplies and replacements bound for the western posts. He was further assigned to Company G, commanded by Captain Richard S. Ewell, who became a Confederate general in the Civil War. Kozlowski joined the company at Los Lunas, New Mexico, some twenty miles south of Albuquerque.[11]

Ewell's dragoons, armed with the Sharp's carbine, fought the Apache Indians at various times. On January 18, 1855, Ewell engaged the Mescalero Apaches on the Peñasco River, which rises in the Guadalupe Mountains of southern New Mexico and empties into the Pecos River. He led a small force of 110 dragoons and fifty soldiers against the Indians who had been harassing his command the day before. He stopped for the night at an abandoned Indian camp. To insure his security, he directed Captain Henry W. Stanton to reconnoiter a valley some 500 yards distant. Stanton made the search; but, while returning, the Apaches ambushed his party in a narrow point of the valley. Stanton defended the escape of his men, whom he had directed to bring help. In the exchange of gunfire, an Indian shot Stanton in the head and killed him instantly. Ewell rushed a relief force under Lieutenant Davis Moore, whereupon the Apaches scattered into the mountains.[12]

In late 1856, the War Department relocated Company G to Fort Buchanan, Arizona Territory. Originally called Camp Moore, the post was located south of Tucson near the Mexican border. It was built in 1856 as one of the military forts between the Rio Grande and Colorado River to control the Indians and protect the white settlers. Although Fort Buchanan served an essential mission, its slovenly appearance belied its importance. The stables, huts, and corrals were constructed of old timbers covered with mud. The inhabited rooms were narrow, with low ceilings, dirt floors, and no ventilation.[13]

In addition to Company G, three other companies of dragoons were stationed at Fort Buchanan. In 1857, the dragoons pursued hostile Indians during the Gila Expedition from April 16 to September 16. In June the cavalry defeated a band of Coyotero and Mogollon Apaches. Captain Ewell was among the officers

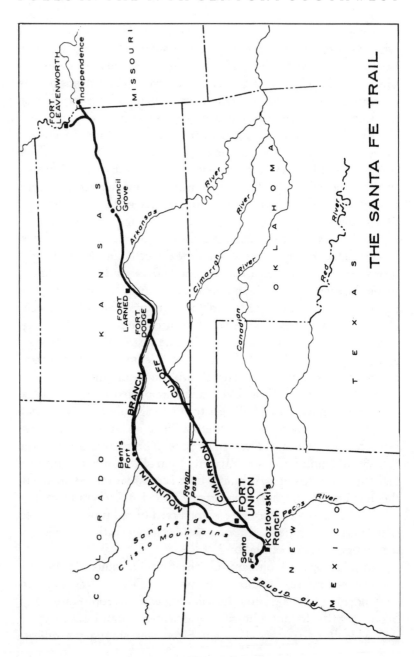

who distinguished themselves. Military records show that Kozlowski was present with his company during March and April of 1857, but he was at Fort Buchanan on detached service from May 3. Consquently, he may have missed the spirited fighting on June 27. However, he was present with his unit from July through the remaining time of the expedition.[14]

In the fall of 1857, Captain Ewell commanded Fort Buchanan. Nicknamed "Old Baldy" by his soldiers, Ewell drilled them daily and supervised the training in person. When the drill did not go well, the captain bawled out the slow learners. Nonetheless, they all respected him because he looked after them with a fatherly concern. Ewell also encouraged the troops to cultivate gardens of fresh vegetables with which to supplement the army ration.[15]

Despite the activities of Indian fighting, drilling, and gardening, the primitive life at Fort Buchanan provoked some bored soldiers to ride off with a stolen horse and desert. Ewell pursued them relentlessly and severely punished those whom he caught. Court martials handed down some or all of the following punishment: Fifty lashes on the bare back, six months of hard labor in irons, shaving of the head, and drumming out of the service with a dishonorable discharge and the letter "D" branded on the forehead.[16]

Having completed his enlistment, Kozlowski was honorably discharged on March 2, 1858. He remained in the Southwest and purchased a 600-acre ranch on the Santa Fe Trail and located two miles east of the ruins of the Pecos Pueblo. Constructed of adobe, the ranch buildings stood on the right bank of a stream that empties into the Pecos River. An abundant supply of pure spring water furnished the reason for locating the principal structures at this site. An instrument of transfer (in Spanish) that Kozlowski executed on June 27, 1861, describes the extent of the land. The property limits are defined loosely, in the manner of the times:

> The boundaries of the land being: to the north, the embankment of the Arroyo Pecos; to the south, the embankment of the same arroyo; to the east, the outlet of the arroyo into the river (beyond which point no land is included); and to the west, the fence which still stands.[17]

Kozlowski purchased the ranch from a Johan Pizer. It appears that Kozlowski gave his government bounty land warrant of 160 acres to Pizer in payment for the ranch.[18]

Kozlowski had the ranch barely two years when the Civil War began. Fearful that the Confederates might invade New Mexico and confiscate his property, the Pole transferred the ownership to his wife on June 27, 1861, less than one month before the invasion. He offered the following reason in the transfer document: "Given that the money used for said purchase originally belonged to my wife, Elena Celenan, she alone has the right to peacefully use and enjoy the property." The Confederates became a threat in March 1862 when General Sibley's army reached Santa Fe. The arrival of Major John Chivington's force of Coloradoans at his ranch on March 25 was undoubtedly a relief to the Pole.[19]

Kozlowski did not take part in the Battle of Glorieta Pass, but a compatriot, Alexander Grzelachowski, did. Grzelachowski was the Chaplain of the Second New Mexico Infantry Volunteers and was with Major Chivington on his bold strike at the Confederate supply train in Apache Canyon. Following the destruction of the rebel supplies, Chivington could not return to Camp Lewis along the mountain trail he had used on the approach. The Confederates had occupied the trail. It was dusk, and Chivington faced a dilemma. At this point, Grzelachowski rode up on his horse and offered to lead the soldiers on a pathless route through the mountains. Chivington accepted the offer. Over rugged ground and in intense darkness, Grzelachowski conducted the column of soldiers around the Confederates and to the safety of the main Union command at Kozlowski's Ranch.[20]

> Report of the Battle of Glorieta Pass, New Mexico, datelined "Kozlowski's Ranch," where Union forces made their field headquarters in the Civil War. (Extracted from Official Records of the Rebellion, IX, 533).

No. 1.

Reports of Col. John P. Slough, First Colorado Infantry.

KOZLOWSKI'S RANCH, *March* 29, 1862.

COLONEL : Learning from our spies that the enemy, about 1,000 strong, were in the Apache Cañon and at Johnson's Ranch beyond, I concluded to reconnoiter in force, with a view of ascertaining the position of the enemy and of harassing them as much as possible ; hence left this place with my command, nearly 1,300 strong, at 8 o'clock yesterday morning. To facilitate the reconnaissance I sent Maj. J. M. Chivington, First Regiment Colorado Volunteers, by a road running to the left of the cañon and nearly parallel thereto, with about 430 officers and picked men, with instructions to push forward to Johnson's. With the remainder of the command I entered the cañon, and had attained but a short distance when our pickets announced that the enemy was near and had taken position in a thick grove of trees, with their line extending from mesa to mesa across the cañon, and their battery, consisting of four pieces, placed in position. I at once detailed a considerable force of flankers, placed the batteries in position, and placed the cavalry—nearly all dismounted—and the remainder of the infantry in position to support the batteries.

Before the arrangement of my forces was completed the enemy opened fire upon us. The action began about 10 o'clock and continued until after 4 p. m. The character of the country was such as to make the engagement of the bushwhacking kind. Hearing of the success of Major Chivington's command, and the object of our movement being successful, we fell back in order to our camp. Our loss in killed was probably 20, including Lieutenant Baker of Company I, Colorado Volunteers; in wounded probably 50, including Lieutenant Chambers, of Company C, Colorado Volunteers, and Lieutenant McGrath, U. S. Army, who was serving with Captain Ritter's battery; in missing probably 30. The enemy's loss is in killed from 40 to 60 and wounded probably over 100. In addition we took some 25 prisoners and rendered unfit for service three pieces of their artillery. We took and destroyed their train of about 60 wagons, with their contents, consisting of ammunition, subsistence, forage, clothing, officers' baggage, &c. Among the killed of the enemy 2 majors, 2 captains and among the prisoners are 2 captains and 1 lieutenant. During the engagement the enemy made three attempts to take our batteries and were repelled in each with severe loss.

The strength of the enemy, as received from spies and prisoners, in the cañon was altogether some 1,200 or 1,300, some 200 of whom were at or near Johnson's Ranch, and were engaged by Major Chivington's command.

The officers and men behaved nobly. My thanks are due to my staff officers for the courage and ability with which they assisted me in conducting the engagement.

As soon as all the details are ascertained I will send an official report of the engagement.

Very respectfully,

JNO. P. SLOUGH,
Colonel, Commanding Northern Division, Army of New Mexico.

Col. E. R. S. CANBY,
Commanding Department of New Mexico.

The two Poles contributed significantly to the decisive battle of the Civil War in New Mexico. If they did not know each other before the battle, they met at the ranch with the arrival of the Colorado volunteers and the New Mexico militia.

As an innkeeper on the Santa Fe Trail, Kozlowski became associated with a famous road that ran through America's heartland to the fabulous Southwest. The trail stretched 800 miles from Independence, Missouri, westward across Kansas to Santa Fe, New Mexico. From its opening in 1821 to its close in 1880, this great transcontinental highway served as the principal artery for thousands of merchants, soldiers, gold-seekers, adventurers, and settlers.

A trip by stagecoach from Missouri to Santa Fe took two weeks. Heavy rains and Indian attacks added delays of several days. The journey was fatiguing since the stage continued day and night. Passengers caught some sleep as best they could, while sitting upright in a moving carriage. The stage stopped at stations located from ten to fifty miles apart. Here the horses and drivers were changed, and the passengers gulped down some food. Most of the time the company-owned stations served unappetizing meals of hardtack, bacon, and vile-tasting coffee. However, when the stagecoach reached New Mexico Territory, conditions improved. Passengers could buy such delicacies as brook trout, venison of deer, elk, bear, and other game that was plentiful in this region. The cost of the meal was one dollar.

Kozlowski's Ranch was one of the favorite taverns on the Santa Fe Trail. Travelers were always sure of good food prepared by Elena Kozlowski. Colonel Henry Inman, who had traveled much along the trail during his military service, recalled those tasty dishes, "the main feature of which," he wrote, "was the delicious brook trout, which were caught out of the stream which ran near the door, while you were washing the dust out of your eyes and ears." Inman described the stop as the "well-known Kosloskie's [sic] Ranch, a picturesque cabin at the foot of the Glorieta Mountains."

At first the stage ran once a month. One coach started from each end of the route at the same time. The frequency was increased until the early 1860s, when daily stages operated on the trail. A coach transported eleven passengers. If going the full distance, the passenger paid $250. The daily stages brought a steady flow of passengers. In 1866 Kozlowski's Ranch became a main stop for the Barlow, Sanderson and Company, when this stage line began operations.[21]

The Kozlowskis prospered. The family grew too. By 1870, Martin and Elena had six children: Joseph, Thomas, William, John, Carlos, and daughter Juana, aged 12. The oldest was Joseph, 16, and the youngest, Carlos, 2. The older children assisted with the chores of the ranch. Nevertheless, the responsibilities for a large family and the managing of the tavern prompted Martin to hire some help. He employed a washerwoman, Josefa Martinez, and two domestic servants, Juan Benavidez and Santiago Roibal. While the Kozlowskis catered to travelers on the stage lines, they always fed and helped some poor Hispanic, who happened to come their way.[22]

Like Colonel Inman, another traveler recorded Kozlowski's Ranch in his travelogue. James E. Meline rode 2,000 miles on horseback from Missouri to Santa Fe and back. Every few days he wrote about his travels and impressions. On July 18, 1866, he was the guest of the Kozlowskis. While at the ranch, he penned one of his many letters, in which he described the historic location of the ranch. "Ascending a hill before reaching Kosloski's," he wrote, "you have a beautiful view of the Pecos Valley, in the midst of which stands a natural elevation surrounded and partially covered by two remarkable ruins—the Pueblo village, and the ancient Catholic church, built by the Spanish Franciscans in the last century."

Meline reported the climate as admirable and the valley as "one of the most beautiful pastoral countries the eye ever rested upon." He noted that two crops a year are often harvested, and cattle and sheep can graze on the land the year round. Meline added that Kozlowski "now has about him wife, children, flocks, herds, and lands."[23]

With time there were changes, and for the Kozlowskis the year 1880 spelled disaster, for on February 9 the first train of the Atchison, Topeka, and Santa Fe Railroad made its maiden run to

Santa Fe. The old road vanished as a highway of commerce. Colonel Inman related how the event brought hard times to the Kozlowskis. Following a visit in 1883, he wrote:

The old Pole was absent, but his wife was there; and, although I had not seen her for fifteen years, she remembered me well, and at once began to deplore the changed conditions of the country since the advent of the railroad, declaring it had ruined their family with many others. I could not disagree with her view of the matter, as I looked on the debris of a former relative greatness all around me.[24]

Perhaps Kozlowski should have anticipated the decline of his business on the Trail and gone into ranching or another endeavor. However, tragedy struck the family two years earlier, when Martin killed a man by accident. The shooting occurred in San Miguel County, probably at the tavern, on January 28, 1878. Kozlowski's single bullet pierced the victim's face below the left eye and killed him instantly. As tragic and unfortunate as the manslaughter was, it nevertheless brought out Kozlowski's character. He did not run out of the Territory to escape justice. On the contrary, he accepted responsibility for the tragedy without question and acted in a forthright manner. He sent his son Thomas to report the shooting to the Justice of the Peace, Manuel Varela. The next day, when Kozlowski himself appeared before this official, he confessed that he, indeed, fired the round that killed Jose Dolores Archuleta, "without there being any bad feelings between them at that time or any other time."[25]

Available court records do not disclose the specific circumstances that led to the shooting. Sketchy details in a Santa Fe newspaper, however, indicate that Archuleta engaged in a heated argument with Kozlowski's sons Thomas and Joseph. The *Weekly New*

Martin Kozlowski, in front of his former stage line tavern on the historic Santa Fe Trail near Pecos, New Mexico Territory, circa 1899. (Courtesy Colorado Historical Society).

Mexican identified the victim as a young man. Circumstances also indicate that Thomas assaulted Archuleta, as evidenced by a case in the District Court in July 1878, when Thomas Kominsky [*sic*] pleaded guilty to a charge of assault and was fined $10 and costs. Kozlowski, too, may have become emotionally involved in the young men's argument. He had been drinking; and, believing his sons were threatened by Archuleta, fired a wild shot in the dark.[26]

On March 13, 1878, Samuel C. Parks, Associate Justice of the Territorial Supreme Court and Presiding Judge of the First Judicial District Court, ordered the sheriff to bring Kozlowski to court. Grand Jurors of the March 1878 Term found him guilty as alleged. For reasons unknown, however, the case was delayed and again referred to Grand Jurors of the August 1878 Term. They, too, found that "the said Martin Kozlowski, the said Jose Dolores Archuleta in manner and form aforesaid, unlawfully, willfully, feloniously, maliciously...and from a premeditated design to effect the death of him the said Jose Dolores Archuleta did kill and murder..." William Breeden, attorney general for the Territory of New Mexico, signed the indictment.[27]

The case of Martin Kozlowski excited much public interest and prompted great sympathy for him. His friends and acquaintances recalled his long and reputable residence in San Miguel County and brought up his advanced age. Many rushed to help him with money for his defense. They also petitioned the court with a long list of signatures, asking for the lightest punishment.[28]

Martin's trial was held during the March 1879 Term of the District Court of San Miguel County. Judge L. Bradford Prince presided and Henry L. Waldo represented the Territory. After the prosecution had presented its evidence, Kozlowski withdrew his initial plea of Not Guilty and pleaded Guilty to the lesser charge of murder in the 4th degree. Judge Prince handed down a relatively mild sentence, confining Kozlowski for two years in the county jail and imposing a fine of $109.20 in court costs. The Federal Census of 1880 lists Kozlowski an inmate of San Miguel County jail in Las Vegas, under the supervision of jailer John J. Webb.[29]

After two years, Sheriff Hilario Romero released Kozlowski from jail, March 11, 1881, but not before Martin paid the $109.20 that he still owed the court. The Santa Fe *Daily New Mexican* gave credit for providing the money to William Breeden and W. Scott Morse, who were present in Las Vegas for Kozlowski's release. In addition, the two lawyers gave the Pole $8.50 for the cost of transportation to his ranch.[30]

It seems strange that two prominent and much sought after attorneys would have the time for a charity case. But, Breeden was Alexander Grzelachowski's attorney and handled many of the merchant's court battles against delinquent creditors. Coincidentally, the Las Vegas *Daily Optic* mentioned on March 8, three days before Kozlowski's release, that "A. Grzelachowski, the leading citizen of Puerto de Luna, is in town." More than likely Grzelachowski supplied the money through the lawyers to insure Kozlowski's freedom. Martin would have been too proud and embarrassed to have accepted the money from his fellow countryman.[31]

Kozlowski's imprisonment had dealt him a psychological blow. And, during his absence, his business on the Santa Fe Trail collapsed with the advent of the railroad. He returned home to face a bleak future. The Kozlowskis never recovered from the double shock, but life went on. The children were reaching maturity, entering marriage, and leaving home to live on their own. Seeking employment, the young Kozlowskis were attracted to the growing city of Albuquerque. Thomas settled there in 1892. He had married Merijilda Roybal in 1884, and at the time of his move he had three children: Josefa, Joseph L., and Patrick. Son Raymond followed two years later.[32]

Kozlowski's son Joseph was the first to marry. In 1880, during his father's confinement, he and wife Eutimia Ruis lived with Elena at the ranch. They had two children: Juan and Caroline. Kozlowski's only daughter, Juana, became the wife of José Garcia of Rowe, New Mexico. She cared for the mother during her last years. Elena had been ailing and died in Albuquerque on August 10, 1895. Martin continued to occupy the ranch until 1898, when he left to join sons Thomas, William, and Charles in Albuquerque.[33]

The Kozlowskis settled in the Barelas area, along the east bank of the Rio Grande and south of Sacred Heart Roman Catholic Church, which became their parish. The Federal Census of 1900 records Martin as living with Charles. The family included wife Matilde (Esquibel) and three young daughters: Maria, Elena, and Antonia. They resided on Barelas Road, south of Huning. At the time, Charles was employed by the Santa Fe Railroad.[34]

In 1902, at age 75, Kozlowski applied to the government for a pension under the Acts of July 27, 1892 and June 27, 1902 (Survivor of Indian Wars). The Commissioner of Pensions granted him the pension of eight dollars a month, and he continued to receive it until his death on November 15, 1905. He was buried in accordance with Catholic ritual in "Barelas," as records of Sacred Heart Church show. Although this notation could mean Santa Barbara Cemetery, it is more likely to refer to San Jose Cemetery (Edith and Torreon Avenue), for here were later buried son Thomas, grandson Joseph L., and grandson Raymond's wife, Amalia Kozlowski. If markers had been erected over the graves of Martin and Thomas, they have not survived.[35]

The family surname survived, although it was recorded in many forms. The Colorado soldier Ovando J. Hollister spelled the name "Coslosky." Colonel Inman wrote it "Kosloskie." Colonel Slough used the name correctly, "Kozlowski." Martin's handwriting may have misled people to write "s" instead of "z." The Pole wrote the letter "z" the Polish way, like a printed "Z," which when scripted leans into an "s."[36]

Documents at St. Anthony's Church in Pecos, New Mexico, where the family worshipped for many years, provide some interesting variations. Pastors spelled the name in different ways when they recorded baptisms and marriages, from Koslosky – Kosloski – Koslowski – to Kozlowski. At one baptism in 1894, Father Maximo Mayeux wrote the name in phonetic Spanish as "Collosque". By 1915, the Kozlowski name re-emerged in its original form.[37]

After Martin's death the ranch remained in the possession of the family. The last owner was Thomas. About 1924 he lost the

The Kozlowski Ranch in 1925, about the time that
son Thomas lost the property for non-payment of taxes.
(Courtesy Museum of New Mexico, Santa Fe).

property for not paying the taxes. Tex Austin bought the land for
a summer recreational ranch and built a guest house in 1927. The
old Kozlowski structure above the creek bed, meanwhile, served as
a residence for Austin's employees. During the Great Depression
Austin lost the ranch to the Federal government. About 1938, E.
E. Fogelson bought the land from the Reconstruction Finance
Corporation and added it to his larger holdings that extend from
the town of Pecos south to Rowe. The expanded property was an
active cattle ranch, called Forked Lightning.[38]

Kozlowski's Ranch disappeared with time. Inman lamented
the changing scene: "The trout have vacated the Pecos; the ranch
is a ruin, and stands in grim contrast with the old temple and
church on the hill; and both are monuments of civilizations that
will never come again." Nonetheless, Kozlowski's Ranch remains a
part of the history of the Civil War in New Mexico.

Most historians make only a brief reference to Kozlowski in their narratives of the Battle of Glorieta Pass. However, historian William Clarke Whitford brings out more fully the significance of Kozlowski's contribution to that decisive battle. Whitford, educator, author, editor, and president of Milton College in Wisconsin, wrote *Colorado Volunteers in the Civil War: The New Mexico Campaign in 1862*. He conducted research during several visits to New Mexico. He tramped over the battlefield and interviewed participants and eyewitnesses who accompanied him on his surveys.[39]

Whitford also interviewed Kozlowski in the approximate period 1898-1900. The author photographed the site of Camp Lewis on the ranch, where the Union soldiers encamped in March 1862. He photographed that abundant source of spring water in the bank of the creek that flowed behind the ranch house. Perhaps most important, he took a picture of Kozlowski. The photo reveals a trim, military-looking figure, even though Kozlowski was more than seventy years old. His legs are slightly bowed, resulting perhaps from the many years in the saddle as a cavalryman and rancher. The occasion for the photograph was a proud moment for Martin, and he wore formal clothes, including a frock coat, white shirt with bow tie, and a Western-style hat. The photographs are part of Whitford's excellent book, published by the Colorado Historical Society in 1906. In recognizing Kozlowski's contribution to the Civil War, Whitford included some biographical data about the Pole. It was a fortunate decision since these data are the only facts known about Kozlowski's earlier period.[40]

During his lifetime Kozlowski had known the joys of prosperity and the despair of financial disaster. He had experienced happiness and tragedy. In his declining years he found himself penniless and dependent on his children for support. Whitford's historical project elevated Kozlowski to the position of a contributor to events that shape the history of a nation. Martin Kozlowski, Polish revolutionary, American soldier, and innkeeper on the Old Santa Fe Trail, is a part of that history.

Alexander Grzelachowski

New Mexico's "Padre Polaco"

and

Pioneer Merchant

Introduction

ALEXANDER GRZELACHOWSKI
was one of the earliest members of the Historical Society of New
Mexico, which was founded in 1859. The Society received his application for membership at the seventh regular meeting in Santa
Fe on July 30, 1860. At the next meeting on August 27, he was
elected a member. An excerpt from the Minutes of the Eighth
Regular Meeting reads: "Rev. A. Geralaschowski [sic]. L. W. Ash-
ley, Esq., Capt. D.H. Maury, and Mess. Solomon Beuthner and
Samson Beuthner were elected members of the Society."[1]

Leaving the Church, Grzelachowski became a successful merchant, cattle and sheep rancher, and spokesman for the Hispanic
community. He was a close associate of Charles Ilfeld, the Territory's foremost merchant. He dealt with John S. Chisum, New
Mexico's cattle baron. And he hired some of the most prominent
lawyers: Thomas B. Catron and William Breeden, both of whom
figured prominently in New Mexico's history. In fact, Grzelachowski became a leading personality of east-central New Mexico in the
19th Century. Notwithstanding, except for brief mention in books
on Billy the Kid and William Parish's *The Charles Ilfeld Company*,
Grzelachowski's contribution to New Mexico Territorial history
was almost unknown. Parish himself emphasizes this strange omission: "A. Grzelachowski receives far less attention than he deserves
in written New Mexico history."[2]

Historians are gratified to unearth previously unknown facts about their subjects. I, too, experienced the joys of discovering gems of data as well as deep regret over material lost irretrievably. In 1982, I interviewed granddaughter Oma Gallegos of Las Vegas, New Mexico. She had inherited letters that her aunt, Amelia Sofia Grzelachowski Clancy, received from her cousin in Poland, Barbara Grzelachowski. When the Gallegos family was relocating from Santa Fe to Las Vegas, Felix Gallegos persuaded his wife that the letters had no value. She could not read Polish. Why keep them? So they burned forty years of correspondence that Amelia had lovingly kept in a special wicker basket. Not quite all correspondence was destroyed — Oma Gallegos saved one special letter, from Joseph Grzelachowski to brother Alexander, written in 1883. She did not know the contents of the letter, never having it translated. She let me read the letter, and I offered a quick translation. She also allowed me to take the letter for reproduction, and I returned it with a full English translation. Surprisingly, this one letter disclosed many facts about the Grzelachowski family, and I make it a part of this account.

Grandson Charles C. Grzelachowski also was very helpful. Among his contributions, he provided a photograph of his grandfather. Another grandson, named after his grandfather, was Oscar Grzelachowski's son. I searched for him for several years. Granddaughter Florentina Flores of Santa Rosa, New Mexico, told me that Alexander had moved to California, but no relative in New Mexico seemed to have his address or telephone number. Unexpectedly, I made contact with grandson Alexander through the help of Paul R. Kintzinger of Puerto de Luna. In August 1984, Kintzinger sent me a clipping (photo) from the *Albuquerque Journal*, which showed a traffic victim being attended to by a paramedic. The injured person was identified as Carmen Grzelachowski, and her address was stated in the caption. I wrote her immediately. She did not answer, but her father-in-law did, Alexander Grzelachowski, who telephoned me. He gave me a good deal of information about himself and the family. Father Oscar, he told me, attended St. Michael's College in Santa Fe. He married Ramonita

Olivas of Sapello, New Mexico. They had one son, Alexander, born in the Grzelachowski home in Puerto de Luna on September 12, 1925. Oscar left Puerto de Luna for Ricardo in De Baca County, where he took up ranching. He died of a heart attack in the Fort Sumner hospital on November 17, 1947 and is buried in the cemetery there. In World War II, grandson Alexander served in the U.S. Army from 1942 to 1946. After being discharged he joined the Air Force but left when his father died. Alexander married and raised a sizable family of three sons – John, Jerry, Anthony – and five daughters – Irene, Patricia Ann, Mary Lou, Angela, and Ruby. In 1984, he was serving as a minister of the Assembly of God Church.[3]

Overseas at the end of World War II, Alexander Grzelachowski attended a dance for American soldiers in Munich, Germany, where he met a young Polish woman, Emilia Grzelachowska. They talked excitedly all evening, trying to establish a family tie. He came away convinced that Emilia is, indeed, a cousin. Unfortunately, in the tumultuous post-war period, Alexander lost track of her.

The story intrigued me. "In what language did you converse?" I asked. "Polish," Alexander answered. "My father spoke Polish and taught me. When I met Emilia, I was able to conduct a tolerable conversation." My interview of Alexander Grzelachowski indicates that grandfather Alexander taught his children, in addition to English and Spanish, the Polish language to a more fluent level than I hint at in my original essay, published in *Arizona and the West* (Autumn 1984).

Appreciation for Research Assistance

Alexander Grzelachowski's descendants: Charles C. Grzelachowski of Fort Worth, Texas, Alexander Grzelachowski and Irene Chavez Herrera of Albuquerque, Oma Gallegos of Las Vegas, and

POLES IN THE 19TH CENTURY SOUTHWEST

Florentina Flores of Santa Rosa; Donald R. Lavash and James H. Purdy of New Mexico State Records Center and Archives; Charles Meketa of Corrales, New Mexico; Harwood P. Hinton, Tucson, Arizona; Catherine Engel, Colorado Historical Society, Denver; Paul R. Kintzinger of Puerto de Luna; Estelle Rebec, Bancroft Library, California; Robert B. Matchette, National Archives; Christine L. Kroesel, Catholic Diocese of Cleveland, Ohio; Rev. Philip Herndon, Pecos, New Mexico; and the Archives of the Catholic Archdiocese of Santa Fe.

Józef Grzelachowski's letter in Polish to brother Alexander, March 24, 1883, follows on the next four pages. A translation is found on page 77.

Carskie – Sinto dnia 12 Marca 1888r 24.

Kochany Bracie Aleksandrze!

List Twój datowany 21ª Februari od-
rzymałem 17 Marca. — Wielce mnie
uradowałeś swojem pismem, bo
tęskno mi już było, że tak dawno
od Ciebie drogi Bracie i od Tomasza
nie miałem wiadomości — cho-
ciaż Tomasz w ostatnim liście
swojem obiecał, że do mnie wkrótce przyjedzie, jednak do dziś,
ani przyjazdu, ani wiedzieć o
sobie nie daje — Pewno jest chory,
a przytem jeszcze, jak pisał po-
przednio ma wielki ambaras
ze swemi dłużnikami, — gdyż
miał troche grosza i rozpoży-
czył swojem znajomym — i teraz
jedni nie chcą mu oddać dru-
dzy zbankrotowali i rozumie
się do go bardzo, jak widać mar-
twi. — Zaraz po otrzymaniu
Twego listu pisałem do niego

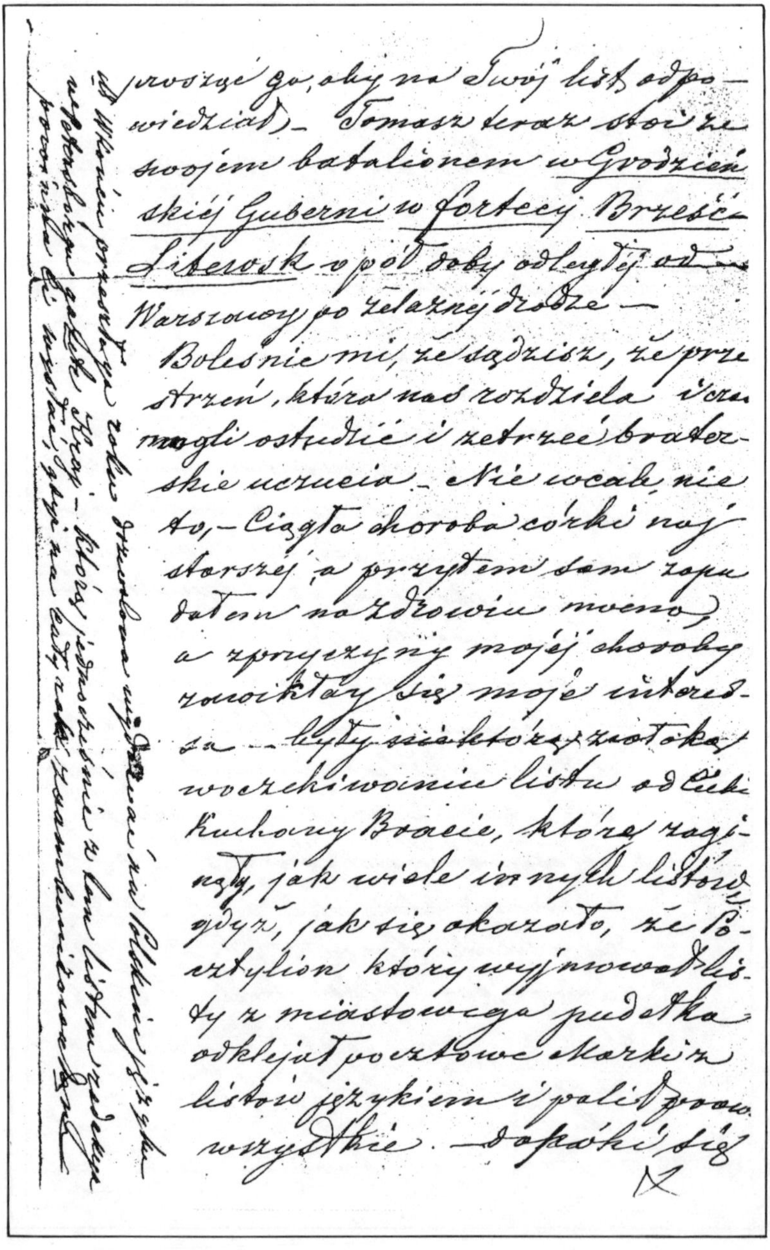

proszę go, aby na Twój list odpo-
wiedział. – Tomasz teraz stoi ze
swoim batalionem w Grodzień-
skiej Guberni w fortecy Brześć
Litewski o pół doby odległej od
Warszawy po żelaznej drodze –
Boleśnie mi, że sądzisz, że prze-
strzeń, która nas rozdziela i cza-
s mogli ostudzić i zetrzeć brater-
skie uczucia. – Nie wcale, nie
to, – Ciągła choroba córki naj-
starszej, a przytem sam zapa-
dałem na zdrowiu mocno,
a z przyczyny mojej choroby
zaniedbały się moje interes-
sa – były niektóre zwłoka
w oczekiwaniu listu od Ciebie
Kochany Bracie, które zagi-
nęły, jak wiele innych listów
gdyż, jak się okazało, że Po-
cztylion który wyjmował listy z miastowego pudełka
odklejał pocztowe marki z
listów językiem i palił pra-
wie wszystkie. – dopóki się

to niewykryta i teraz na ta
zwrócona uwagę — I teraz jestem
więcej pewny, że moje listy bę-
dą akuratnie dochodzić rąk Twoich
i to mi sprawia wielką przy-
jemność, kiedy prowadzę z
Tobą drogi bracie Korespondencyą a listy Twoje zawsze
otrzymuję z wielką radością
i upragnieniem. — Córka
moja najstarsza Barbara będąc
w przeszłym roku w Trouville
na kąpielach, jak ci pisałem
poznajomiła się z Księdzem
tamecznym w którem i teraz
prowadzi Korespondencyą i
ten ksiądz przysyła jej książ-
ki na francuzkiem języku
do czytania. — Perona i w tym
roku pojedzie znów do Trouville
gdyż będzie tam na kąpielach
dobrze się czuła na zdrowiu
Po powrocie w Paryżu znów za-
chorowała i teraz w Petersbórgu
najlepszy ją doktor kuruje, ale
zdrowie jest bardzo wątłe —

*Jak będzie wyjeżdżać to Ci napiszę.
Syn Jan skończył już komercyjną
szkołę i z powodu słabego zdrowia
siedzi w domu. — Córka najmłodsza
Józefina także skończyła naukę
i w domu mieszka — i już panna
na wydaniu — wyglądam tylko
poczciwego człowieka — Brat Tomasz, już wkrótce kończy termin
wysługi na Generała i pewno wyj-
dzie do dymisyi, gdyż już wysłu-
żył Emeryturę i w randze Generał
będzie otrzymywać nie złą pensyę.
Ja zaś muszę jeszcze się jużż
Służbę do późki nie ustalę dzieci.
Posyłam Ci moją fotografię
ż tym liście, z której się jeżeli
poznasz, jak prędko zestarzałem
się ale i nie dziw, gdyż i nam
pod 60 lat. — w przyszłym liście
przyślę Ci fotografję młodszej
córki Józefiny — ale bardzo Cię
proszę i swoją mi nadeślesz.
A teraz ściskam Cię serdecznie
i podpisuję rury, jako kochający brat
Józef Grzelachowski*

Translation:

Carskie Sioło   Day of $\frac{12}{24}$ March 1883 year
(Tsarist Hamlet)

My dear brother Alexander:

I received your letter dated 21 February on 17 March. I was greatly overjoyed with your correspondence, because I became concerned when I didn't hear from you, dear brother, or from Thomas for such a long time, although Thomas promised in his last letter that shortly he would visit me; yet to this day he has not come nor has he sent any news about himself. Surely he is ill; and, in addition, as he wrote before, he is embarrassed by his debtors, — since he had a little money and loaned it to his acquaintances — and now some don't want to repay him — others are bankrupt, and understandably and noticeably the matter worries him — Immediately after receiving your letter, I wrote to him and requested that he answer your letter — Thomas now is stationed with his battalion in the Grodno Province at the fort of Brest-Litovsk, about twelve hours travel distance from Warsaw along the iron road.

It pains me that you believe the great distance and time that separate us could cool and erase our brotherly feelings. No, not at all — The continual illness of my oldest daughter, and at the same time I fell ill seriously myself, and because of my sickness my affairs got tangled up — these were some of the delays. In awaiting letters from you, dear brother, some got lost, like many others, since, as it became evident, the postman who picked up the mail from the city box licked the stamps off with his tongue and burned almost all of them — until the practice was discovered, and now it is guarded against, — I am more confident now that my letters will surely be delivered into your hands, and this thought gives me great satisfaction when I carry on correspondence with you. Dear brother, I always receive your letters with longing and great joy. My oldest daughter Barbara, having been in Tronville for health baths last year, as I wrote you, became acquainted with a local priest, with whom she carries on a correspondence, and this priest sent her French-language books to read. Surely she'll go again to Tronville this year. After returning from Paris she again fell ill, and now the best physician in St. Petersburg treats her, but her health is very fragile. When she leaves, I'll write you.

My son John has already completed the commercial school and, due to poor health, remains at home. — My youngest daughter Josephine completed her schooling and lives at home and is ready for marriage — I'm looking for a good man — Brother Thomas shortly will complete his time of eligibility for a general's rank and no doubt will be retired, since he has served the required time; and, in the rank of general, he'll receive a fairly good pension. However, I must continue my service, until I get my children settled.

I'm sending you my photograph with this letter, and it will convince you how quickly I have aged, but don't be surprised since I'm more than 60 years old — In a future letter I'll send you a photograph of my younger [sic] daughter Josephine — but I earnestly ask you to send me yours. Now I hug you dearly a thousand times, as a loving brother.

JÓZEF GRZELACHOWSKI

(Postscript on margin):
At the end of the previous year, the publication of a Polish-language newspaper Kraj [Country] was allowed. Simultaneously with my letter, the editor should begin sending you issues, since I paid the subscription for an entire year.

Essay

IN THE 19TH CENTURY,
New Mexico Territory formed part of the wild American West.
The times were adventurous. Cavalrymen fought the Apaches.
Mounted gunmen roamed the ranges. The six-shooter seemed to
be the law, and Billy the Kid typified the era. No stagecoach was
safe from, or town bank immune to, a holdup by masked bandits.
Even peaceful cattle and sheep men warred on each other for the
right to grazing land. The 19th Century in New Mexico saw the
cattle baron, the cowboy, and the rustler. It was a time when mining communities mushroomed and quickly faded into ghost towns.

During this tumultuous period lived an individual with character, leadership, and a willingness to adapt to the times – Alexander Grzelachowski. The Pole was described as a "powerful,
energetic man with a great flowing beard and flashing black eyes,
and a booming voice that commanded fluent Spanish."[4]

Grzelachowski is linked historically to Puerto de Luna in east-
central New Mexico. His large, imposing stone house in that once
thriving community served as his general store, as well. Billy the
Kid and Sheriff Pat Garrett never failed to stop in Puerto de Luna
and call on Padre Polaco, as he affectionately was called. Grzelachowski knew how to deal with the Kid, instructing his clerks to
give the young gunman unlimited credit. Captured by Garrett in
December 1880, and while in his custody, Billy ate his last Christmas dinner at Grzelachowski's.

Grzelachowski came to the Territory in 1851 as a young Roman Catholic priest in the company of Jean Baptiste Lamy, the future Archbishop of Santa Fe. The Reverend Grzelachowski served a number of parishes and pueblos. After the Civil War, however, he gave up the priesthood for a layman's life, becoming a successful merchant, rancher, and civic official.

Grzelachowski was born of well-to-do parents in Gracina, Poland, in 1824.[5] Although family data are meager, some recorded facts show that in 1812, during the Napoleonic era, his father Franciszek served in the Polish army. The mother's maiden name was Maryanna Szapska. The Grzelachowskis had three sons: Aleksander Jan, Tomasz Romuald, and Józef Franciszek. On the basis of their father's rank of captain, the sons were recognized as Polish gentry in 1845.[6]

Tomasz and Józef became soldiers in the Tsarist army, serving as officers and gaining the rank of general before retirement. In 1883, Tomasz commanded a battalion at *Brześć Litewski*, some 100 miles east of Warsaw. At that time, Józef served in Russia proper, residing with his family at an exclusive settlement called in Polish *Carskie Sioło* (Tsarist Hamlet) and located near the capital of St. Petersburg (now Leningrad).[7]

Aleksander took up the religious life. He may have prepared himself in a French seminary, since the family was affluent enough to allow members to travel abroad. It is believed that Grzelachowski was in France in 1848 or 1849 and that he was recruited for the Cleveland, Ohio, Diocese by the Rev. Jean Lamy or Bishop Louis Amadeus Rappé.

Lamy had come to America in 1839 and served in the Cincinnati Diocese. In May 1848 he returned to France on a visit. Before his departure, Bishop Rappé asked him to find three or four young priests for his diocese.[8] It is not known whether Lamy happened to meet with Grzelachowski. The following year the Bishop himself left for Europe to recruit priests and sisters.[9] It is assumed that either the Lamy or Rappé visits proved fruitful, for the young Pole was in the Cleveland Diocese in 1850. He became the first resident pastor of French Creek, now St. Mary's Church in Avon, Lorain

Alexander Grzelachowski
Puerto de Luna, New Mexico Territory.
(Courtesy of grandson Charles C. Grzelachowski).

County, from August through December 1850. He also tended to the mission churches of St. Teresa in nearby Sheffield and Holy Trinity Church in Avon.[10] At this time Lamy's close friend Rev. Joseph Machebeuf served at Sandusky, which also was in the Cleveland Diocese.[11]

If perchance Grzelachowski and Lamy had not met earlier in France, they came to know each other in Ohio, well enough for Lamy to ask Grzelachowski to volunteer for service in the Southwest. Lamy needed priests. He had been designated vicar general of New Mexico Territory by Pope Pius IX. The Frenchman's responsibilities extended over a vast area that included Arizona, most of Colorado, as well as New Mexico.[12] Lamy asked Grzelachowski and Machebeuf to accompany him to Santa Fe.[13]

Lamy took a roundabout route. Instead of traveling overland along the Santa Fe Trail to New Mexico, he and his party followed the longer route via New Orleans. From there they sailed to Galveston and Indianola, Texas, and by land to San Antonio. Lamy had gone ahead by himself, but they were together for the grueling part of the journey.

To insure their safety against bands of Comanches in West Texas, the priests joined a U.S. Army caravan of some 225 wagons guarded by a company of cavalry. In mid-May of 1851, the caravan moved west across 675 miles of desert. The travelers reached El Paso del Norte (now Juarez) in six weeks. It was the only Mexican town they saw, and Machebeuf observed that El Paso "was not worthy of any special notice." They rested for several days. Father Ramon Ortiz, local pastor, offered them every hospitality, but they were eager to go on. The last leg of the journey led them north along the Rio Grande for some 350 miles. In the company of Lamy, Grzelachowski reached Santa Fe on August 9, 1851, and witnessed the triumphal welcome accorded the vicar general by civil, military, and church authorities.[14]

Bishop Lamy assigned Father Grzelachowski to San Felipe Indian Pueblo the very next month, September 1851, but immediately thereafter he transferred the Pole to St. Michael the Archangel Church in San Miguel del Vado.[15] Located on the Santa Fe Trail,

San Miguel in 1851 was one of the principal towns of New Mexico. It boasted a population of between two and four thousand inhabitants, thus making it (after Santa Fe) the second or third largest town. Today the church of St. Michael's stands as a commanding edifice, but San Miguel del Vado is only a shell of its former self.[16]

Grzelachowski's parishioners were Spanish-speaking natives who had been Mexican nationals just four years earlier. The War with Mexico, 1846-48, had changed their status. Padre Polaco, a natural linguist, mastered Spanish quickly. As pastor at St. Michael's, he recorded baptisms in that language.[17]

After a stay of five months at St. Michael's (November 1851-March 1852), Grzelachowski became the pastor of Our Lady of Sorrows Parish in Las Vegas. The modest adobe church was located on the Old Town Plaza.[18] Built in the form of a cross, about twenty-five by seventy-five feet, it stood one and one-half stories high. From the shingle roof rose a diminutive steeple, surmounted by a small wooden cross. A visitor to Las Vegas in 1862 described the unpretentious structure as "decidedly the most civilized looking object in town."[19]

In 1850, between one and two thousand residents were in Las Vegas.[20] The town's focal point was the plaza, which extended over an acre of ground. The streets were quite regular and straight. Corrals occupied the vacant portions of squares. The town was practically devoid of grass, shrubs, and trees. Padre Polaco served in Las Vegas for nineteen months, from April 1852 to October 1853.[21] He would return to this frontier town in the role of merchant.

Grzelachowski next ministered to the needs of three Indian communities within a short distance of each other: Cochiti, Santo Domingo, and San Felipe (located west of Santa Fe and then part of Santa Ana County).[22] During his ministry of four years at the three pueblos, he may have lived in the county seat of Peña Blanca, a beautiful village of neat Mexican houses belonging to prominent families.[23]

While in Peña Blanca, Grzelachowski applied for his naturalization as a citizen of the United States. He appeared before the Santa Ana County District Court on October 11, 1855. The Court recognized the five-year period since his first application in Lorain County, Ohio. The Court granted the citizenship, after he renounced forever all allegiances and fidelity to any foreign power, "and particularly to Alexander II, emperor of Russia, whose subject he was."[24]

In November 1857, Padre Polaco moved to Our Lady of Sorrows Church in Manzano, some fifty miles southeast of Albuquerque.[25] The pastoral duty at Manzano for one year appears to have been his last formal assignment. He began to lean toward a secular life. In 1859 he bought land, measuring 150 by 100 yards, in Las Vegas.[26] In 1860 he resided in Las Vegas, according to the Federal Census. To the census taker, he gave his occupation as a Roman Catholic clergyman, aged 36. He listed his real estate at $400 and his personal estate at $18,000.

The outbreak of the Civil War in 1861 delayed Grzelachowski's transition to a layman's role. Volunteering his services as a military chaplain, he joined the Second Regiment, New Mexico Infantry (Union), which was organized at Santa Fe in July and August of 1861. For some unknown reason, Grzelachowski did not receive a formal appointment but served nevertheless.[27] Eight companies of the Second Regiment took part in the Battle of Valverde, February 21, 1862, when the Confederates under Brigadier General Henry H. Sibley defeated the Union forces of Colonel Edward R. S. Canby.[28]

Whether Chaplain Grzelachowski was present at Valverde is not known, but he participated in the Battle of Glorieta Pass, near Pecos, on March 26-28, 1862. New Mexico volunteers and army regulars, led by the First Colorado Regiment of Volunteers, opposed the advance of Sibley's Texans on the military bastion of Fort Union. The key action became the envelopment of the Confederate rear at Apache Canyon by Major John Chivington's force of 400 men. They attacked and destroyed Sibley's supply train of some eighty wagons.[29] This strike dramatically reversed the Confederate hopes for the conquest of the Southwest. Without ammunition, rations, clothing, Sibley gave up his invasion of New Mexico and retreated to Texas.[30]

On the nineteenth anniversary of the battle, the *Las Vegas Daily Optic* on March 14, 1881 gave Grzelachowski the credit for guiding Chivington's men through the mountains to hit the Confederate train. No other historical accounts mention Grzelachowski. Nevertheless, Padre Polaco played a critical role in the decisive battle of the Civil War in New Mexico.[31]

Although Grzelachowski's Second Regiment had been organized for a three-year period, it was disbanded after nine months on May 31, 1862. Those officers and men retained were consolidated with members of the First, Fourth, and Fifth Regiments of Infantry to form the First New Mexico Cavalry Regiment.[32] Grzelachowski did not serve with the cavalry, but apparently joined the garrison at Fort Union as chaplain.[33]

Following the war, Grzelachowski became a merchant in the new settlement of Sapello, located about twenty miles north of Las Vegas.[34] He seemed to do well, as evidenced by sales invoices, but he sold his business to Henry Göke (Gorke) and moved to Las Vegas.[35] Before relocating to the larger town, he bought a lot on the Plaza for $5,000 from John Dold, a well-known merchant, on September 30, 1867.[36]

Grzelachowski also sought to do business with the U.S. Army. In 1868 he obtained a contract for transporting supplies by wagon from Fort Union, or other army depots in the Territory, to posts in the interior of New Mexico, Arizona, and Texas west of longitude 105°. The Army Quartermaster paid him $1.235 per 100 pounds per 100 miles. The rate was an increase of twenty cents over the previous year when the contractor was George Berg of Mora, New Mexico. Known as Route No. 3 of the Military Division of the Missouri, Grzelachowski's contract extended to March 31, 1870.[37] Grzelachowski subcontracted some, perhaps all, of his freightage. In August 1869, he paid Juan A. Sarracino of Valencia County the sum of $1,013.93 in credit for transporting 37,553 pounds of supplies from Fort Union to Fort Wingate in western New Mexico, a distance of 270 miles. He paid Sarracino at the rate of $1.00 per 100 pounds per 100 miles.[38]

Puerto de Luna, New Mexico Territory, at time
of Lincoln County War (1877-79). Alexander
Grzelachowski's general store on left. Man
wearing derby hat (second from right) is
believed to be Grzelachowski. (Courtesy of
granddaughter Oma Gallegos).

Grzelachowski prospered in Las Vegas. His store on the north
side of the plaza was near the Exchange Hotel, where traders and
ranchers stayed. On one occasion, April 23, 1868, he took a pro-
missory note for a period of eighty days from Louis Badreaud in
the sum of $957.17 for various and sundry goods.[39] Badreaud
defaulted, but Grzelachowski waited for eight years before suing
him in the First Judicial District Court of New Mexico.[40] The
Federal Census of 1870 reflects his growing financial success. To
the census taker, Grzelachowski described himself as a dealer in
general merchandise, with $11,400 in real estate and $35,791 in
personal property.[41]

Grzelachowski handled a gamut of articles. He sold dry goods,
clothing, notions, boots, shoes; drugs and medicines, paints, oils,

and varnishes; hardware, crockery, and tinware, and not to mention iron, nails, and glass. He dispensed such basic needs as groceries, liquors, tobacco and cigars, as well as lumber, wagon parts, and outfitters' goods for ranch hands.[42]

On the plaza, Grzelachowski was a next-door neighbor of the young and ambitious entrepreneur, Charles Ilfeld, who was a partner in the firm of A. Letcher and Company. In 1874, the 27-year-old Ilfeld bought out Letcher and built his merchandising business into one of the most successful in the territory. The Charles Ilfeld Company came to exemplify mercantile capitalism in New Mexico. Grzelachowski and Ilfeld became friends and business associates.[43]

About 1874 Grzelachowski moved to the town of Puerto de Luna on the Pecos River (located today eleven miles south of Santa Rosa in Guadalupe County). Historically, the town bridge across the Pecos is believed to be on the same site where the Spanish explorer Francisco Vasquez de Coronado built a wooden span in 1541 for his army to cross enroute to the land of Texas.[44]

From Puerto de Luna, Grzelachowski soon began a flow of supplies to Las Vegas. Mule trains carried wool, hides, firewood, goods, and other merchandise.[45] Grzelachowski also branched out into ranching. He acquired herds of cattle and bands of sheep, and bred fine horses. He operated several small spreads around Puerto de Luna, but his main ranch was at Rincon del Alamo Gordo, some twenty miles east of Puerto de Luna.[46]

Grzelachowski built for himself an architecturally imposing, single-story, L-shaped building. With flower gardens and orchards, it became the showplace of Puerto de Luna. The building housed a store at the south end, a warehouse in the "L" extension to the rear, with a basement and fireplace beneath the warehouse, and residential rooms at the north end. Each room had its own fireplace enhanced with wood trim. A massive veranda covered the entire front of the building. Grzelachowski laid a corrugated iron roof over the original some years later. His building typified a village commercial structure of the period 1870-1900 in east-central New Mexico. Towns were changing during that era from agrarian to mercantile centers, based on sheep raising as a large-scale industry.[47] In April 1970, the State of New Mexico recognized the Grzelachowski house as a cultural property and placed it on the State Register.[48]

Although Grzelachowski had moved to Puerto de Luna, he continued to operate the store in Las Vegas through a partner, Richard Dunn. A tall, well-educated individual, Dunn was a native of Nova Scotia but had spent some time in Maine. In the spring of 1878, Dunn sold all the stock to Charles Ilfeld and on June 1 leased the property to Ilfeld's friend Marcus Brunswick. Dunn moved to Puerto de Luna and continued his partnership with Grzelachowski. The three cooperated to each other's mutual advantage. Grzelachowski regularly sold his wool to Ilfeld. In turn, the young merchant acted as Grzelachowski's purchasing agent for goods from the East.[49]

The Catholic Pole and the German Jew developed a close business relationship. Ilfeld trusted Grzelachowski implicitly.[50] On one occasion Ilfeld attempted to collect money due him from a prominent rancher, August Klein, of Roswell and Lincoln. Klein, unwilling to pay in cash, preferred to pay in cattle. Since Ilfeld was not able to travel to Klein's ranch to look over the animals and determine their price, he wrote Klein: "I would like to ask you to deliver 20 cows from 3-6 years old to Padre Polaco in Puerto de Luna for my account." In a second letter, he added that "the price that you and the padre will agree upon, I shall be glad to credit to your account."[51]

Much later, when Ilfeld passed the managing of the company to his brother-in-law, Max Nordhaus, Grzelachowski's integrity and influence among the people continued to be highly regarded. In July 1893, Nordhaus lost a substantial amount of anticipated cash when a Colorado buyer cancelled a sale of a large number of sheep. Unable to pay for his orders, Nordhaus begged Grzelachowski to persuade the sheepmen in the Puerto de Luna region to accept payment in goods.[52]

As a properous merchant, Grzelachowski frequently had dealings with New Mexico's prominent citizens. However, one case turned sour, that with New Mexico's "Cattle Baron," John Simpson

Chisum of Lincoln County. In 1875, territorial newspapers boasted that Chisum employed some 100 cowboys on his Pecos Valley ranges to oversee 80,000 head of cattle and that he could on short notice carry out an order for 40,000 head of cattle.[53]

On August 1, 1873, Chisum, together with Fort Sumner rancher Peter Maxwell and Grzelachowski, endorsed a $5,000 promissory note drawn by Reed Bros. & Company, a cattle firm in the Seven Rivers area of the Pecos Valley. The Second National Bank located in Santa Fe loaned the money to the Reeds for a three-month period. The note carried a penalty of 18 percent per annum for late payment.[54]

Reed Brothers (or Chisum) made a late payment on December 22, 1873, and another on March 2, 1874. The two payments of principal and interest totaled $2,766.05. The Second National Bank refused to wait any longer for the balance and sued the indorsers: Chisum, Maxwell, and Grzelachowski. The court rendered a judgment against them of $3,340.00, including court costs. Chisum asked Grzelachowski in a gentleman's agreement to advance the money on a promise of repayment. Grzelachowski did, but Chisum reneged on his promise. Hiring lawyers William Breeden and Louis Sulzbacher, Grzelachowski brought suit against Chisum in the District Court in Las Vegas on March 3, 1876.[55]

Chisum's refusal to repay Grzelachowski may have been influenced by events that followed the bank loan. No sooner had Reed Bros. & Company obtained the $5,000 than Buck & Sam Stanton sued the company in Lincoln County. The local sheriff entered Doña Ana County and seized the company's cattle and other property there. Chisum, believing the attachment to be invalid, proposed to Grzelachowski that they post the $30,000 bond required by the sheriff and take possession of the impounded cattle. Chisum conveyed his proposal through a Captain Ford, who represented the Puerto de Luna rancher.[56] Grzelachowski declined, thinking the sum of money and the risk were too high. Chisum, therefore, put up the bond himself. He took the cattle and other property out of the hands of the sheriff. He also asked for and obtained a bill of sale from Reed Bros. & Company. As Chisum had expected, the court decided against the Stantons and released Chisum from the bond. He now legally owned the Reed herd.

Chisum showed a spirit of generosity toward the Reeds. They not only owed the Second National Bank but earlier had borrowed $4,800 from him and $3,700 from Grzelachowski. Chisum decided to liquidate the debt owed the padre, using the Reeds' cattle. He took the following actions. First, he placed his own brand on fifty-eight head to cover the expense of holding the herd under bond. Second, in the fall of 1874, he instructed his ranch hands to drive 580 head from Lincoln County some 140 miles north to Grzelachowski's ranch at Puerto de Luna. There, Padre Polaco received 364 head worth $3,700 at the prevailing market price. He marked these cattle with the A.G. brand. As for the remaining 216 cattle, Chisum asked Grzelachowski to keep them until spring, when he would call for them. Later, according to Chisum, Grzelachowski refused to deliver these animals, saying that some had been stolen, some had died, and others had wandered off. Now, two years later, Chisum struck back at Grzelachowski by refusing to comply with the gentleman's agreement. Then, too, Chisum looked upon Grzelachowski's lawyers as members of the powerful "Santa Fe Ring," a group of politicians and businessmen who, Chisum believed, were bent on causing him trouble. Nevertheless, Grzelachowski's legal action proved successful. The court rendered judgment against Chisum for $3,340 on August 17, 1876.[57]

To win a court decision was one thing, but to collect the money from Chisum was another. In the fall of 1875, Chisum had publicly conveyed all of his livestock to Hunter & Evans, beef commission merchants in St. Louis, and now he claimed to have no resources to pay his debts. Refusing to be outmaneuvered, Grzelachowski and eight other claimants obtained an injunction in the District Court on January 3, 1878. The order enjoined and restrained Chisum from assigning, transferring, or making any other disposition of real estate, personal property, bank deposits, debts owed him, and all other possible assets. Thomas B. Catron and William Breeden represented the plaintiffs. The litigation dragged on for several years, and the attorneys finally settled the claims after Chisum's death in 1884.[58]

One of Grzelachowski's unusual acquaintances was that Western character, Billy the Kid, also known as Henry McCarty. Billy liked to frequent the Grzelachowski store; it was one of his favorite hangouts. Since the merchant spoke several languages, Billy often pressed him to say something in Latin, Polish, or Greek. Padre Polaco obliged the young man, who was intrigued by Grzelachowski's command of languages, as well as by tales of distant Europe.[59]

The Kid was a special customer, and the merchant instructed his clerks not to deny Billy any ammunition and supplies. On one occasion, when clerk Frank N. Page was alone in the store, Billy came in and helped himself to ammunition. Seeing him stuffing his pockets, Page scolded Billy for stealing from a man who often had befriended him. Billy replaced the goods.[60]

Dances also attracted Billy to Puerto de Luna. Andres Coronado, a friend, sometimes took away the Kid's pistol, when he began to act unruly at dances. Cleto Chavez, a strong man, wrestled Billy for a championship belt that Grzelachowski offered as a prize. Sometimes Billy demonstrated his skill with a six-shooter or engaged in a spontaneous firing spree. Bullets imbedded in Grzelachowski's building attested to these wild affairs.[61]

Billy the Kid's nemesis, Sheriff Pat Garrett of Lincoln County, often stopped in Puerto de Luna to chat and have dinner with the Pole. In December 1880 Garrett fought a gun battle in front of Grzelachowski's store with a local badman. About a week later, the lawman and three deputies arrived in Puerto de Luna with four prisoners. Despite bitterly cold weather, he had captured Billy the Kid and three others near Taiban, east of Fort Sumner, and was heading for Las Vegas. On Christmas Day he and his party arrived in front of Grzelachowski's at about 2 p.m. A biographer of Billy the Kid describes the scene:

> An immense wild turkey with all the trimmings was about to be served to the big family, and the visitors were assured there was plenty for all. The Pole, who years before had changed his priest's robe for a rancher's

outfit, was a hearty, forgiving soul, and he joked with
Billy about what the young outlaw had done with that
latest haul of eight of his prize horses. Maybe the boy
would leave him alone from now on. While he plagued
him he saw that Billy's plate was kept well filled. He
could have used such a boy.[62]

At four o'clock the sheriff led his prisoners into the wagon and
departed. The feast with the Grzelachowski family was the last
Christmas dinner Billy had. On July 14, 1881, Garrett killed him
at Fort Sumner.[63]

Living the life of a layman, Grzelachowski took a wife and
fathered a family. While merchandising in Las Vegas, he boarded
at the home of Andrea Cde Baca, located in the San Antonio
district. Here he met the landlady's young daughter, Secundina,
and he fell in love with her. She bore him nine childen. The first
child, daughter Adelina (born 1870) was followed by son Adolph
and two daughters, Amelia Sofia and Emilia. They had five more
children: son Oscar and daughters Leticia, Celina, Emma, and
Florentina.[64]

Grzelachowski was a good father. He showed the same concern for his family as he had for his parishioners. Never abandon-
ing his devotion to the Roman Catholic faith, the father brought
up the children in that religion. The town lacked a suitable place
of worship until Our Lady of Refuge Church was dedicated in
1882.[65]

Son Adolph acquired much of his keen business sense from his
father, who often took him on visits to Las Vegas, eighty miles
away.[66] Adolph also maintained close ties with the Charles Ilfeld
Company. In 1906, he was named manager of Ilfeld's Pintada
Trading Corporation at Pastura, New Mexico. The operation dealt
with the wool industry, in which he had considerable experience.
Upon taking charge at Pintada, Adolph sold his Terreros Ranch in
the Puerto de Luna area to the Company for $11,000 in stock. He
remained as manager only until September 1908, when he resigned. The Company then leased the ranch back to Adolph for
$100 a month.[67]

Adolph P. Grzelachowski (1872-1949), son of Alexander, and wife Camille Moore Grzelachowski (1877-1954). (Courtesy of son Charles C. Grzelachowski).

Daughter Leticia became the wife of A. J. Padilla, who taught school in Puerto de Luna for twenty-one years and lived there for more than sixty-five years.[68] Daughter Amelia Sofia married John J. Clancy, son of J. G. Clancy, a retired sea captain. In 1877, Captain Clancy drove 3,000 head of sheep overland from California to New Mexico. He also brought $50,000 in gold coin, which he had placed in ordinary metal containers. Upon arriving in Puerto de Luna, Clancy arranged to secure the gold in Grzelachowski's large, store safe, the only one of its kind in New Mexico Territory.[69]

Grzelachowski was the leading citizen of Puerto de Luna for more than twenty years. People sought and valued his advice on various matters. Respectfully they addressed him as "Don Alejandro."[70] Assuming civic responsibilities willingly, Grzelachowski served as the town postmaster for ten years, from December 4, 1876 to July 22, 1886. Later daughter Leticia became the postmaster on January 8, 1910.[71]

Grandson Charles C. Grzelachowski, born in store-house
in Puerto de Luna, New Mexico, 1914, photo taken 1972.
(Courtesy of Charles, son of Adolph Grzelachowski).

    Grzelachowski's leadership extended beyond Puerto de Luna
into east-central New Mexico in matters that affected the social,
economic, and political life of the region. He led the fight for irriga-
tion projects along the Pecos River, and he succeeded in helping to
establish the people's water rights in the area.[72]

In the mid-1880s Grzelachowski bought additional land around Puerto de Luna for an expansion of his cattle business. Like most cattlemen and merchants of his time, he was plagued by a lack of cash. He resorted to borrowing from wealthy friends, including Henry L. Waldo, former Chief Justice of the Supreme Court of the Territory, and Robert H. Longwill, a prominent Santa Fe physician. In the doctor's case, Longwill loaned the merchant the sum of $7,000. On September 15, 1886, Grzelachowski and wife Secundina signed a note that called for repayment in one year, with interest at eleven and one-half percent per annum. Frank N. Page, former store clerk, witnessed the signature of the Grzelachowskis. Although loans were often made to friends in a loose, gentlemanly fashion, Longwill struck a hard bargain. He demanded and got security for his money in the form of an indenture on Grzelachowski's property. The document gave Longwill the right to seize and sell the property at public auction should the Grzelachowskis default.[73]

The property listed in the indenture included a substantial, if not a major, portion of Grzelachowski's land. Two pieces were located near Las Vegas. One tract was 1,000 varas wide, and the other, 150 varas wide (a Spanish vara equaled nearly one yard). Both tracts were bounded on the west by the Gallinas River. At La Singuijuela, near Sapello, there were two tracts. The first, 1,000 varas wide, and the second, 640 varas. The boundaries were fully described. In the Puerto de Luna area, two tracts of land of 160 acres each were mortgaged. The lands held 250 fruit trees and 3,000 vines. In addition to this extensive acreage, Grzelachowski's imposing dwelling and lot were also included in the indenture. One hundred yards wide, the homesite extended westward to the Pecos River.[74]

Grzelachowski apparently felt confident that he could repay the loan with interest in one year, but he did not. In August 1889, Longwill renewed the loan, and again in August 1890, as well as in June 1893, when the outstanding principal was $5,000. Grzelachowski sought to repay the loan, but he was buffeted by hard times as New Mexico entered "the depression years of the 1890s."

The Pole's financial problems reached a crisis in 1893, the year the United States suffered a nationwide recession.[75]

By now Longwill's patience had worn thin. He had been put off by his lawyer-friend, Louis Sulzbacher, and especially by Charles Ilfeld, who had interceded repeatedly on behalf of Grzelachowski.[76] In early December 1893, Sulzbacher told Grzelachowski: "Dr. Longwill has written to me that he received a letter from Ilfeld, pleading that he wait for the money until you sell your cattle. All that the doctor wants is his money." Ilfeld had been prompting Grzelachowski to sell some, if not all, of his cattle to repay loans. Sulzbacher had this impression when he wrote Grzelachowski: "Without doubt the cattle are on the road to this place." He advised the merchant to instruct the foreman in charge of the cattle drive to bring the money from the sale directly to him in Kansas City, Missouri. The lawyer added that he would wait for the money until December 20. He closed with a warning: "I know positively that the doctor will not wait."[77]

Sulzbacher deluded himself about the cattle drive. There was none. The cattle business was the pride and keystone of Grzelachowski's enterprises, and he was reluctant to give it up. In addition, he had acquired a partner, Frank Page. Any reduction of the herd would adversely affect Page too. Nonetheless, the pressure mounted on Grzelachowski to come to a hard decision.[78]

On December 19, 1893, Ilfeld's general manager, Max Nordhaus, complained to his brother-in-law that Grzelachowski defaulted on a contract to provide sheep to the Charles Ilfeld Company. Grzelachowski told Nordhaus during a visit to Las Vegas that he could not deliver the 1,500 sheep because he had moved them to grazing ranges in the Capitan Mountains of Lincoln County. Nordhaus urged Ilfeld to get after the padre. "Write him to start those sheep at once towards Las Vegas," he stressed, and "have a distinct understanding at once, as this is not the first time he has failed to come to time on a contract."[79]

Although Grzelachowski owed money to wealthy individuals, he was indebted to Ilfeld more than to the others. Notwithstanding, Ilfeld waited for Grzelachowski to better his financial standing,

Alexander Grzelachowski's former general store and home in Puerto de Luna, New Mexico, in 1970. View from the southeast, showing the warehouse in the L-extension. Used as a storehouse, the structure is rapidly succumbing to the ravages of time. (Photo courtesy of New Mexico State Records Center and Archives, Santa Fe).

and he attempted to persuade the others to do likewise. Ilfeld, too, experienced acute shortages of cash. He resorted to borrowing large sums from friends in New Mexico and from Jewish merchants in New York. Whereas he managed to obtain loans at rates of from six to eight percent, Grzelachowski had to agree to Longwill's terms of eleven and one-half percent.[80]

Padre Polaco keenly felt his obligation to the Las Vegas merchant, and he did an unusual thing, about which he told Sulzbacher. Surprised, the lawyer wrote Ilfeld on December 22, 1893: "Here I find a letter from Padre Grzelachowski, in which he writes me that you have authority to sell his property and *his cattle.*" Sulzbacher then reviewed his efforts since April to persuade

Longwill and Waldo to be patient, and to Grzelachowski to repay the two creditors. "J. Waldo and the Doctor acceded to my numerous requests to wait," Sulzbacher wrote, "but as nothing in this world lasts forever, I hardly think that I can make these people give further indulgence..." The lawyer pleaded with Ilfeld to use his influence with the doctor and the judge. He wrote:

> You can do it better than I, for if you state to them the existing facts; namely, that he owes you $15,000, for which you don't ever ask a security, that you are willing to wait on him for 2 or 3 years without interest, thereby giving the Padre a chance to use the proceeds of his wool and sheep and cattle to build himself up, your generosity may touch a tender spot with them, which I cannot do, in cases like this, when a party has made so many promises and not complied with any, and is not even paying his taxes.[81]

A few days later Sulzbacher received another of Longwill's letters. This time the doctor decided to foreclose on Grzelachowski's property.[82]

On January 15, 1894, the Honorable Thomas Smith, Chief Justice of the Supreme Court and Judge of the Fourth Judicial District Court, issued a subpoena to Alexander and Secundina Grzelachowski for them to appear in the District Court, in chancery, for the County of Guadalupe, on the first Monday of March 1894, to answer a bill filed against them by Robert H. Longwill. Louis Sulzbacher and H. L. Waldo represented the complainant.[83]

The Court met and Smith gave his decision on April 2, 1894. He decreed that the Grzelachowskis owed the sum of $6,175 in principal and interest, and attorneys' and solicitors' fees. He further decreed that the mortgaged property be sold at public auction at the front door of the San Miguel County Court House in Las Vegas not earlier than August 1, 1894. Furthermore, if the proceeds from the sale were insufficient to cover the indebtedness and court costs, the Grzelachowskis would be liable for the difference with interest at twelve percent. Lastly, the decree contained a grace period of ninety days "for redemption, payment of the decree and the discharge of the mortgage, and to avoid the sale, as required by law."[84]

There was no sale of Grzelachowski's mortgaged property. Notices of the auction, which were required to be published in the local press for twenty days beforehand, did not appear.[85] Moreover, the tax assessment rolls for the following year, 1895, show that Grzelachowski still possessed his land.[86]

Charles Ilfeld had come to the rescue of his friend. But there was a price — Grzelachowski had to sell his cattle, and this painful decision adversely affected his partner, Frank Page, as well. Ilfeld, Marcus Brunswick, and Page made a deal to dispose of Grzelachowski's cattle. One sale netted $4,000. In a letter addressed to "Max Nordhaus, Esq., Trustee," Page asked that this money be credited "on the renewal of Chat[tel] Mort[gage] at Puerto de Luna." The selling, however, did not proceed smoothly. Page believed that Ilfeld demanded more from him than he was liable for. His feelings surfaced when Ilfeld sent him a bill owed by Grzelachowski. The sum involved a mere $350, but the demand was the proverbial last straw. "I do not owe it," Page retorted, "but Mr. G does." Then Page released his bitterness: "I have lost enough and think I should not lose the 350 and interest and the old man should pay it." He asked Ilfeld to send him a copy of the note to Amarillo, Texas, where he had arrived with a herd of cattle.[87]

Ilfeld acknowledged Page's letter but did not forward the note. Page became upset and wrote back immediately: "It's not my intention to push Mr. G, but I wish to protect myself, as it was never my intention to pay this account — but that I was giving the note to cover part of expenses and taxes to be advanced." He accused Ilfeld of pressuring him to sell at a disadvantage to Ilfeld's friend, Wilson Waddingham, called the "Cow King of the Canadian River." Page wrote Ilfeld: "I would call your attention to the fact that I drove out in round numbers 650 head [of] cattle under the Mor[tgage] deed and have returned to you more than 9.00 net per head at which price you did your best to force me to sell to [the] Waddingham outfit." Page, no doubt, looked forward to completing his part of the agreement with Ilfeld and Brunswick. He told Ilfeld: "Coming season I hope to pay you up in full...." He met with Ilfeld and Brunswick in the office of Brown and Manzanares Company in Las Vegas on April 13, 1896. Page received $75.00, which he acknowledged as payment "in full of all claims and demands which I now have against the said Charles Ilfeld and Brown and Manzanares Co."[88]

While the liquidation of his cattle business went on for nearly a two-year period, Grzelachowski devoted himself to civic duties in Puerto de Luna. Son Adolph, now in his twenties, managed the general store. Although Grzelachowski retained possession of his house and store, the property remained mortgaged. Adolph occupied the homestead with his family until about the time of World War I, followed by brother Oscar's family. The building continued to serve as a residence until 1970. Since then the building that Grzelachowski designed with architectural flair has been used as a mere storehouse. It is succumbing to the ravages of time.[89]

During his nearly fifty years in New Mexico, Grzelachowski contributed to the mingling of Indian, Hispanic, and European cultures. His Polish background, pastoral duties in the pueblos, and business activities in an area of strong Hispanic character facilitated an accommodation of the diverse cultures in New Mexico. Wife Secundina's Hispanic origin exerted an influence on the family. The children learned Spanish, English, and even some Polish. Daughter Amelia always referred to her father as *Tata*, the Polish for Daddy. *Tata* was a kind and indulgent father as well as a loving husband.[90]

New Mexicans admired Grzelachowski for his integrity and superior education. His intellectual capacity stood out prominently in a frontier territory, where more than half of the population was illiterate in the period 1850-1900.[91] He impressed John Chisum as a very educated man, in addition to being genteel and polite.[92] Grzelachowski got along well with practically everyone. Although he liked people, he nonetheless became offended at those who tried to take advantage of his cooperative attitude, and he stubbornly sought redress when wronged. He lived by a strict code of

First court house of Guadalupe County, New Mexico, at Puerto de Luna, as it appeared in 1981. Of red cut stone, the court house was built on land donated by Alexander Grzelachowski. (Photo by the author).

honor and fair dealing. Many young men served their apprenticeship in his employ and later became prosperous merchants in the territory. They had been drilled in Grzelachowski's guiding precepts during their clerking days under him.[93]

Grzelachowski intuitively selected employees for their potential for development. He gave them responsibility, trusted them, and made them feel a part of his enterprise. Acting on behalf of the merchant, but proceeding on their own initiative, the clerks handled the orders for merchandise. One humorous letter to the Charles Ilfeld Company indicates the confidence that clerks felt while in Grzelachowski's employ. Answering an inquiry, E. T. Baca wrote: "Respecting your bill against Rafael Chavez dated Jan'y 1st/83, I would suggest that you give him perpetual credit, and charge same to eternity—as he died long ago, long ago."[94]

The padre's cowboys, too, were a capable lot. In 1881, G. M. Wilson was the foreman of Grzelachowski's ranch at Rincon del Alamo Gordo. He led the posse that captured the killer of Colonel Charles Potter. The editor of the *Las Vegas Daily Optic* was so impressed with Wilson that he wrote: "He would make a most excellent constable for that precinct. Run him."[95]

Grzelachowski's personal life revealed a strong belief in family ties. Although he had come to America to stay, he fostered a continuing relationship with his brothers in Poland. He wrote them and chided them when they failed to respond. The love for his Polish relatives was inculcated in his children. In particular, Amelia Sofia corresponded with her first cousin, Barbara Grzelachowski. The exchange lasted for more than forty years. With the outbreak of World War II on September 1, 1939, the communication ceased and contact was lost. Barbara, then an elderly woman in her seventies, undoubtedly perished in the war. Amelia's letters, unfortunately, were burned after her death in 1958.[96]

Another Polish tie survived — the surname. Interestingly, the spelling requires one-half of the English alphabet, and none of the thirteen letters is repeated. The pronunciation of the name confounded some Anglos and Hispanics. John Chisum referred to him as "Chowski." Yet, Grzelachowski never changed or even simplified the name. As a merchant, Padre Polaco advertised himself as "A. Grzelachowski, Dealer in General Merchandise." He did not succumb to the tendency of some professional people who Anglicize their names, with the excuse that it is necessary for the benefit of clients. Notwithstanding, Grzelachowski prospered, and he was widely respected for his integrity.[97]

One of Grzelachowski's civic contributions to New Mexico history was his successful effort to make Puerto de Luna the seat of the new County of Guadalupe. As New Mexico kept developing, the territorial government expanded the number of counties. The legislature passed the act that created Guadalupe County from the southern half of San Miguel County on February 26, 1891. Grzelachowski offered to donate a tract, one hundred yards square, to

Puerto de Luna, New Mexico, in 1982.
Church of Our Lady of Refuge (on right)
was erected in 1882. Pecos River flows
just beyond the village. (Photo courtesy
of the author).

the county. Located in the center of the town, the land would serve as the site for the county offices.[98]

Grzelachowski's gift to the Territory was indeed magnanimous. In 1892 he was deeply in debt, hounded by his creditors and by a depressed economy. He could have sold the land and used the proceeds to pay off, or scale down, a debt. Instead, he chose to make an outright donation. Perhaps, as the leading citizen of Puerto de Luna, he was expected to make a special effort for his community. He felt this responsibility. Indeed, he demonstrated a sense of history and responded to its challenge. His act was a grand gesture in the best romantic tradition.

The legislative committee chose Puerto de Luna for the county seat. In September 1892, the county began the construction of the courthouse and jail. The two-story building of red cut stone was divided into rooms for the offices of the county officials. The court room was on the upper floor. Grzelachowski occupied one of the offices when he became Probate Judge of Guadalupe County in 1893 and 1894. The county paid him $50 quarterly. Giving up the judgeship, he accepted the office of Justice of the Peace for Precinct 9 of the county on January 21, 1895.[99]

The following year Grzelachowski suffered a fatal injury while traveling in a wagon pulled by a team of frisky horses. Unexpectedly the horses stampeded and overturned the wagon. After a short illness, Padre Polaco died in Puerto de Luna on May 24, 1896, aged 72. A Catholic priest administered the last rites of the Church, and Grzelachowski's remains were buried in the local cemetery. Individuals who know the community remember the location of his grave, although there is no tombstone (1983).[100]

The obituary in the *Las Vegas Daily Optic* sketched his character as that of an upstanding citizen and concluded that "there can be no question, despite all creeds and dogmas, as to his future rewards." *The Las Vegas Examiner* likewise stressed his character: "He was a kind and loving husband and father, an upright citizen, and all his dealing were characterized by the strictest honesty and straightforwardness – a man like whom the world cannot have enough."[101]

Grzelachowski's dream of developing Puerto de Luna into an important city was not realized. In 1902 the railroad bypassed the county seat by eleven miles to the north, thus injecting life and political strength into a rival town, Santa Rosa. The legislature moved the seat of Guadalupe County to Santa Rosa in 1903, and Puerto de Luna faded to an obscure village.

Once prominent in the history of Territorial New Mexico, Puerto de Luna remains today a scene of pastoral beauty. Grzelachowski's store stands vacant and in disrepair. The old courthouse squats near a sandy street lined with sagebrush. Gone are the days when Don Alejandro's orchards bloomed, fine horses pranced in his corrals, bands of sheep grazed in the fields, herds of cattle carrying the A.G. brand dotted his lands, and Billy the Kid came to visit Padre Polaco.

The Battle of

Glorieta Pass

Was the Guide

Ortiz or Grzelachowski?

Introduction

I SEARCHED FOR DATA
about Alexander Grzelachowski in the five-volume *The Leading Facts of New Mexican History* by Ralph Emerson Twitchell and found nothing. I noted, however, that Twitchell managed to devote a full page biographical sketch to Frank Page, who clerked for Grzelachowski in his store in Puerto de Luna. Twitchell's omission was unfortunate because it may have prevented him from discovering the Pole's achievement at the Battle of Glorieta Pass. In that action on March 28, 1862, Chaplain Grzelachowski of the Second New Mexico Infantry Regiment saved Major John Chivington's command from likely capture by the Confederates. Not until 1987 was Grzelachowski credited with this singular deed.

The following essay, "The Battle of Glorieta Pass: Was the Guide Ortiz or Grzelachowski?" was published in *New Mexico Historical Review* 62, No. 1 (January 1987) and is republished herein with the permission of the Regents of the University of New Mexico, who hold the copyright.

Essay

A ROMAN CATHOLIC PRIEST, identified by historians only as Padre Ortiz, played a key role in the Battle of Glorieta Pass on March 28, 1862. It was Ortiz who led Major John Chivington's force, which earlier had destroyed the Confederate supply train, through the mountains in darkness to the safety of the Union lines.

On March 26, 1862, advance elements of the Union and Confederate forces clashed at Apache Canyon in Glorieta Pass, thirty miles southeast of Santa Fe. Chivington defeated the Confederates but broke off the engagement and retired to his camp at Kozlowski's Ranch. Here he was joined by the main Union command under Colonel John P. Slough. Slough planned a two-pronged attack on Brigadier General Henry Sibley's Confederate army, believed to be at Johnson's Ranch in Apache Canyon. Slough marched 900 men from Kozlowski's along the Santa Fe Trail toward the Confederate position. Meanwhile, Chivington with about 450 soldiers, and guided by Lieutenant Colonel Manuel Chavez, followed a mountain trail to the high ground overlooking Johnson's Ranch. Slough's plan called for both columns to converge on the enemy.

Becoming impatient, Lieutenant Colonel William Scurry, the senior Confederate officer at Johnson's, moved down the Glorieta Pass for about six miles near to Pigeon's Ranch where he collided with Slough. They battled each other to near exhaustion for six hours. Although the Confederates finally drove off the Union troops, their victory was only temporary, since Chivington struck a devastating blow to their rear. Arriving on the heights above Johnson's Ranch, he surprised the Confederate supply train, loaded with ammunition, clothing, commissary items, medical supplies, and forage. His soldiers attacked and destroyed the train of sixty to eighty wagons.[1] (See map on page 50.)

Leaving this scene of destruction, Chivington's raiders climbed back up to the mountain summit from where they had first attacked. They were met by Lieutenant Alfred S. Cobb, with orders from Colonel Slough to rejoin at once the main command at Kozlowski's Ranch. Cobb warned Chivington that the enemy held the trail he followed. Since it was almost dark, there seemed to be no way to get back safely, and Chavez knew only the trail along which they had come. He was unwilling to lead the strike force along any other path. William Clarke Whitford narrates what happened next:

> At this point in the deliberation, a Mexican Catholic priest on a milk white horse, and who is now known to have been Padre Ortiz, from a small hamlet near the Pecos ruin, rode into their midst and saluted the officers in Spanish. He offered to lead them to their camp over the mountain alongside the pass and by a shorter course, and warned them that if they returned by the old trail they would doubtless meet with some of Scurry's troops, and have trouble in the night. Chavis [sic] was acquainted with this priest, understood what he said, and advised Chivington to accept his service. In intense darkness, over steep ridges, through narrow defiles, and along a pathless route, he conducted the column in safety to the main road near the Pecos pueblo, where the troops had turned into the Galisteo trail in the morning.

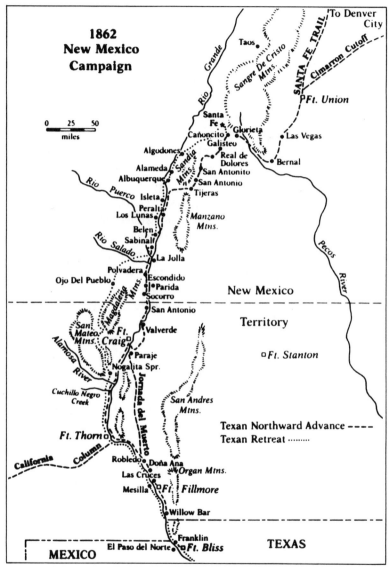

1862 Civil War Campaign in New Mexico, from Don E. Alberts, ed., Rebels on the Rio Grande: The Civil War Journal of A. B. Peticolas. (Courtesy of Don E. Alberts).

Shortly thereafter Chivington's exhausted command reached Kozlowski's Ranch. Their comrades "joyously welcomed the victors and eagerly listened to the account of their achievements."[2]

The destruction of the Confederate supply train turned the Battle of Glorieta Pass into the decisive action of the Civil War in New Mexico. Left without supplies, General Sibley became completely discouraged. His army retreated to Texas and never threatened New Mexico again.[3]

The crucial help of Padre Ortiz made the Union victory possible. Had Chivington's force been captured or destroyed, Sibley might have been encouraged to reach for his original goal of capturing Fort Union and its military stock. The outcome of his New Mexico campaign could have been much different.

Who was Padre Ortiz? Since this Hispanic surname is common, what was his given name? Martin Hardwick Hall writes that Ortiz came "from a small village near the Pecos ruins." Marc Simmons identifies him as "a priest from the village of Pecos." Reginald S. Craig, a biographer of Chivington, places Ortiz at the Pecos Pueblo. These historians, unfortunately, are not specific enough. They fail to provide not only the priest's given name but also his assignment to a parish or other religious duty.[4]

Given this uncertainty, this writer undertook to solve the mystery of Padre Ortiz. The archives of the Catholic Archdiocese of Santa Fe do not contain any such individual. Furthermore, Fray Angelico Chavez in *Archives of the Archdiocese of Santa Fe, 1678-1900*, lists four priests named Ortiz: Fernando, Jose Eulogio, Juan Felipe, and Rafael. But they all served prior to 1858. The national Catholic directory for 1855 shows the mission church at Pecos, *Nuestra Señora del Refugio*, as attended by the pastor at San Miguel del Vado, the Rev. Francisco Leyva. The 1855 directory also contains the name of the Rev. Fernando Ortiz at *San Juan de los Caballeros*. This Indian pueblo is located approximately forty miles north of Santa Fe, a considerable distance from Pecos.

The next available directory (1865) is devoid of the name Ortiz for the Diocese of Santa Fe. Priests from Santa Fe made visits to the mission church at Pecos, now called *Nuestra Señora de los Angeles*.[5]

Colonel John P. Slough commanded the 1st Colorado
Volunteer Regiment at the Battle of Glorieta Pass,
March 28, 1862. Courtesy of Colorado Historical Society.

Major John M. Chivington, 1st Colorado Volunteers,
commanded the attack force that destroyed the Confederate
supply train in Apache Canyon, March 28, 1862.
Courtesy of Colorado Historical Society.

The Rev. Philip Herndon, pastor of St. Anthony's Church in Pecos, told this writer that the parish was established on October 7, 1862 (six months after the Battle of Glorieta Pass). It was called initially *Nuestra Señora de los Angeles.* The first baptism took place on the same date. Father Herndon said the signature of the priest who recorded the baptism is fairly long but illegible. However, he was certain the signature bears no resemblance to "Ortiz." He opined that it is a name of French origin. Further entries in the church record book continue until November 30, 1863, when a gap occurs, to 1870. This break explains why the church reverted to the status of a mission, since the Catholic directory for 1865 shows that *Nuestra Señora de los Angeles* was attended by priests from Santa Fe.[6]

Could the name of Padre Ortiz be a mistaken identity? Historical evidence points strongly to Padre Polaco, the Rev. Alexander Grzelachowski and Chaplain of the Second New Mexico Infantry Regiment, as the priest who led Chivington's men over the pathless route to the safety of Kozlowski's Ranch.

The Las Vegas, New Mexico, *Daily Optic,* March 14, 1881, gave credit to Grzelachowski as the person who guided Chivington's men through the mountains to Johnson's Ranch. Noting the nineteenth anniversary of the Battle of Glorieta Pass, the *Optic* stated:

> With the assistance of A. Grzelachowski, a Polander and at the present day a prosperous merchant at Puerto de Luna, as a guide through a secret pass, Chivington started out on his dangerous errand...The Yankee sharpers reached the train, which was composed of thirty-six wagons at 2 o'clock in the afternoon...It was the work of a few minutes only to apply the torch, and the rations and ammunition of the Texans were soon sending up volumes of smoke.[7]

The *Optic* seems to have ignored the service of Manuel Chavez. However, a chance discovery of primary source data confirms and explains Grzelachowski's special role. These data are the facts contained in his letter to Captain Gurden Chapin, Acting

Assistant Adjutant General, Department of New Mexico. Writing to Chapin on August 4, 1862, Grzelachowski stated:
> In the engagement between our troops, and the so-called confederate forces, at Canon del Apache, while accompanying Col. Chivington's command, returning from the place where the enemy's train was by us destroyed, the horse I was riding, my private property, died. Will you please to inform me if I have a right to claim from the government an indemnification for my horse, and if so, what course must I pursue to receive such indemnification.[8]

That Grzelachowski's horse died from the ordeal of the march is not surprising. Even Chivington dismounted and led his horse on foot, as he stumbled behind the mounted priest. Grzelachowski undoubtedly had to ride his horse to be able to lead the soldiers through the trackless mountains.[9]

Additional evidence points to Grzelachowski as Chivington's guide. Whitford states that, when the priest rode up before Chivington and his officers, he greeted them in Spanish, a language in which Grzelachowski was fluent. Although he was a natural linguist and spoke several, Grzelachowski preferred Spanish. Even late in life, he continued to use that language in correspondence with his lawyer, Louis Sulzbacher, and his merchant friend, Charles Ilfeld.[10]

Whitford says that Manuel Chavez knew the priest. "Chavis [sic] was acquainted with this priest," Whitford wrote, "understood what he said and advised Chivington to accept his services." Indeed, Chavez and Grzelachowski knew each other well. Chavez was the lieutenant colonel, or second in command, of the Second New Mexico Volunteers and Grzelachowski was the chaplain of this regiment.[11]

Some historical accounts identify Chivington's guide as French. This view would rule out the name "Ortiz." Grzelachowski may have attended a French seminary, and he was in France at the time he was recruited for service in the Cleveland, Ohio, diocese. Grzelachowski, therefore, could have been referred to as a "French priest."[12]

In his official report of the fighting in 1862, Chivington mentioned an unnamed aide. In 1884, when he wrote his "Retrospective – The Prospective," he did not identify the nationality of the aide but stated that "a Roman Catholic priest had joined us at the top of the mountain...." In 1890, Chivington called the aide "a native Catholic priest" (probably because the priest spoke in Spanish). The Colonel wrote: "I wish to say of this priest – I wish I had his name – that he was the only native priest that I saw during the entire campaign and our stay afterward in New Mexico who was loyal to the Federal Government."[13]

No Catholic priest called Padre Ortiz can be identified in the region of Pecos, New Mexico, in 1862, when the Battle of Glorieta Pass was fought. On the other hand, primary and secondary historical sources prove that Grzelachowski took part in this decisive battle in the same role attributed to Ortiz. It was indeed Chaplain Alexander Grzelachowski, or Padre Polaco as he was affectionately known, who performed the fateful task that saved Chivington's command from possible capture and destruction.

Charles Radzimiński

The United States-Mexican

Boundary Survey

Introduction

AMERICAN SOURCES PROVIDE
little, if any, data about Charles Radzimiński's life in Poland, prior
to the Uprising of November 1830. The collapse of the rebellion
led to his deportation to the United States in 1834. The two essays
that follow document his contribution to American history. Information about Radzimiński's early years in Poland, however, has
been frustratingly unavailable. I tried to obtain some facts about
the family. Who were his mother and father? Did he have brothers
and sisters? In addition, was he actually born in 1805, as secondary
sources tell us? Radzimiński himself contradicts these sources. In
the War with Mexico, Radzimiński received a commission of second lieutenant and assignment to the Third U.S. Dragoons. Accepting the appointment in 1847, he wrote the Adjutant General
in Washington: "I beg leave to report my age to be 30." Three years
later, when he applied for a land bounty of 160 acres, he gave his
age as 33. Thus, Radzimiński claimed to be born in 1817.[1] Was he
lying? Perhaps he wished to take advantage of his good looks. The
Pole was handsome and gracious, manly and energetic. Having
begun a new life in America, he may have wanted to associate with
a younger set of people, to whom he was psychologically attuned.
Be that as it may, I attempted to resolve the questions of family
and age.

I sought data in Poland. The editor of the *Polish Biographical Dictionary* in Kraków informed me that an update of distinguished individuals (with surnames beginning with the letter "R") was in the process of publication. Having access to the draft for Charles Radzimiński, he replied that the biographical sketch does not answer any of my questions. Upon the publication of the addendum in 1986, my cousin Marzena Piasecka mailed me a reproduction of the Radzimiński entry. The writer, Florian Stasik, repeated "1805" as the year of birth, without a specific date, and said nothing about the family. Finally, I wrote to *Naczelna Dyrekcja Archiwów Państwowych* (Principal Directory of State Archives) in Warsaw. The reply was disappointing. The director stated that the Polish Archives have no information that could establish Radzimiński's specific date of birth or anything about his parents and family.[2]

I explored other leads to Radzimiński's Polish past. An opportunity emerged when I obtained copies of three letters from the Diplomatic Branch of the National Archives. The letters pertain to Radzimiński's death in Memphis, Tennessee, in August 1858. The Pole's former regimental commander and friend, Colonel Edward G. W. Butler, asked the Secretary of State, Lewis Cass, to attempt to make contact with Radzimiński's mother – to notify her and to send her son's effects. Butler knew the Secretary. In fact, Lewis Cass, Jr. served as major in Butler's Third U.S. Dragoons. In his letter, Butler said that Radzimiński often spoke of his mother, with whom he was unable to communicate. (The vengeful Russian government had prevented all contact between Radzimiński and the family). Since Radzimiński did not mention his father, I assumed that the father was deceased before 1831 when the rebellion failed and the son escaped to Austria. Replying to Butler on October 5, 1858, the Secretary wrote that he enclosed a copy of his letter in instructions to U.S. Minister Francis W. Pickens at St. Petersburg. The Secretary told Pickens to enlist the cooperation of Russian officials in locating the Radzimiński family.

The possibility of learning names and places from Pickens' reply excited me. I asked the archivist at the National Archives to make a search of diplomatic correspondence. He did, over a period of fifteen months, but he did not find any reply from Pickens. He suggested that I visit the Fort Worth, Texas, Branch of the National Archives, which has microfilm copies of State Department files. Accordingly, I conducted a search at Fort Worth in July 1988. I noted that the Minister to Russia periodically acknowledged the receipt of correspondence from the State Department. For a period of two and a half years, I reviewed "Dispatches from the U.S. Minister to Russia," Publication M35, from September 1858 to early 1861, when the Abraham Lincoln Administration took over the government. Pickens never acknowledged the Secretary's instructions of October 5, 1858, nor did he reply to them. I did find the three letters already in my possession – Butler's, Secretary Cass to Pickens, and to Butler, but nothing else.

Before giving up, I posed a scenario. Suppose, I thought, Minister Pickens considered the Secretary's instructions as a personal request and, therefore, did not acknowledge their receipt as official. Furthermore, suppose that he made the attempt to locate the Radzimiński family and reported his findings to Secretary Cass in a personal letter. Surely the Secretary would then inform Butler. Acting on this assumption, I examined the files of "Domestic Letters," M40, as well as "Miscellaneous Reports," M179, over the same two and a half years. Nothing!

I came to the disturbing conclusion that Secretary of State Cass may not have dispatched his letter of October 5, 1858 to St. Petersburg. The political reality was that the James Buchanan Administration was on friendly terms with Russia. Perhaps the Secretary felt that neither Butler nor Radzimiński was worth the risk of ruffling the feathers of the tsar's shako. Admittedly, the Secretary signed such a letter, and it is a matter of record. Nonetheless, if he, in fact, did not forward it to Francis Pickens, then Lewis Cass was guilty of hypocrisy and deceit.

In preparing my essay on Charles Radzimiński and the United States-Mexican Boundary Survey, I wanted to know the basis for his appointment as Principal Assistant Surveyor. The Treaty of Guadalupe-Hidalgo of 1848 called on each president to appoint a chief surveyor as well as a boundary commissioner. In addition, the treaty stipulated that any agreements between the commissioners required the approval of the chief surveyors. Thus, the chief surveyor held a very responsible position and exerted much power. To be appointed the principal assistant to the chief surveyor carried its own mark of honor and prestige.

I found the answer to Radzimiński's appointment in the "James D. Graham Papers" at the Beinecke Rare Book and Manuscript Library of Yale University. The Papers contain documents from the Northeast Boundary Commission, which Graham headed, as well as Graham's correspondence as Chief Astronomer of the U.S. Boundary Commission. The documents disclose that the War Department assigned Graham the task of performing a partial resurvey of the historic Mason-Dixon line. The project included the additional work of delineating the curved boundary between Pennsylvania and Delaware. Graham gave the project to Radzimiński, who worked for three months to complete it. Graham praised Radzimiński and his assistant, Henry C. Derrick, for surveying in bad weather, on the chance that it would clear. Often they returned from the field "drenched with rain, or covered with sleet, during the cold weather of December and January, never regarding their personal comfort, when the work could be forwarded by exposing themselves."[3]

Radzimiński narrowly escaped with his life on January 29, 1850. He was taking readings with a theodolite when a violent windstorm struck the area and toppled a heavy tripod station above him. As the structure fell crashing to the ground, a massive timber brushed past his head, without injuring him, but striking and demolishing the theodolite. By February 8, 1850, Radzimiński completed the field work, and Graham commended him for an excellent performance. The experience gained on the Mason-Dixon line led to Radzimiński's selection for the joint U.S.-Mexican boundary survey.[4]

When Radzimiński reached El Paso del Norte with Colonel Graham's party on June 24, 1851, he probably learned of the presence of a fellow Pole, Felix Michalowski, who was an employee of the Commission. Michalowski had served in the U.S. Army and was discharged at San Antonio, Texas. In 1850, the old soldier was hired as a servant by Lieutenant Colonel John McClellan, Chief Astronomer, and traveled with him to El Paso del Norte. While quartered at San Elizario, Texas, Michalowski and twenty-four other employees and members of the Commission, including J. Hamilton Prioleau, complained by letter to the Commissioner about the inadequate amount and poor quality of food from the commissary officer, George Bartlett, the Commissioner's brother. When Graham replaced McClellan, Michalowski stayed with the Commission to cook for Malcolm Seaton.[5]

I would like to comment on the personal relationship between Emory and Radzimiński. While doing research at the Beinecke Library, I sensed the friendly rapport that seemed to emerge from the correspondence between the two. I concluded that they were good friends. Indeed, their cooperative association over the years of the survey produced excellent results. When his work was completed, Radzimiński left the Commission in Washington to join the Second U.S. Cavalry, and Emory's farewell letter ended with the warm phrase, "I am very truly your friend." Notwithstanding, I was struck by Emory's scant mention of Radzimiński in his official report of the survey published the following year. It seems that Emory took pains to avoid mentioning Radzimiński. I have not tried to identify every occasion, but I can cite several examples in the report. First, Emory's appointment to the important post of Chief Surveyor. Radzimiński personally delivered the presidential letter to him at Samalayuca, Mexico, on January 30, 1852. Emory's boundary report reads simply that the letter of appointment was handed to him. Second, the drowning incident on the lower Rio Grande in 1853 when Radzimiński lost his assistant Thomas W. Jones. Emory reports this tragedy, but he never adds that his surveyor, Radzimiński, almost drowned, too, and that Jones was a member of Radzimiński's party. The third example occurs when the Commission landed at Indianola, Texas, for the survey of the

Gadsden Treaty line in September 1854. Commissioner Emory directed his Secretary and second-in-command, Radzimiński, to unload the equipment and supplies from the ships, organize the wagon train, and take charge of the movement of both men and train to San Antonio. Radzimiński faced a challenge that he carried out well, but with some difficulty. The violent storms that struck southern Texas just before the arrival of the Commission left a sea of mud and streams almost impassable. Radzimiński needed extra days to reach his destination. Despite Emory's documented instructions to Radzimiński, the Commissioner does not mention him. Instead, he writes that his "contractor" (Lucius Campbell) was delayed in delivering the equipment.[6]

Of all the omissions of Radzimiński's performance and activities, perhaps the most serious was Emory's failure to credit Radzimiński with the joint demarcation of the international boundary between Brownsville and the Gulf of Mexico. The government of Mexico had stressed the importance of the final segment along the Rio Grande. Having come down with yellow fever and forced to leave Texas, Emory turned the responsibility over to his Principal Assistant, who acted on behalf of the United States. But Emory failed to even mention the Charles Radzimiński- Francisco Jimenez Agreement of November 14, 1853 in his report. Because Emory included many routine activities of the Commission, I find his omission of the demarcation of the critical fifty miles between the two nations to be incomprehensible. Fortunately, the original agreement has been preserved in the Emory Papers.

The change in Emory's attitude towards Radzimiński apparently took place after the Pole departed the Commission in early February 1856. Emory's intense dislike of the former commissioner, John Russell Bartlett, was probably the cause. Radzimiński and Bartlett were friends. As Emory became progressively more bitter towards Bartlett, he engaged in sniping at Bartlett in the press under the pseudonym "Vindex." Emory even carried his vendetta into the official boundary report, in which he made disparaging remarks about Bartlett. Emory's behavior was unbecoming to a high-level official of the government.

The differences between Bartlett and Emory began at the end of 1851, when Emory arrived at Magoffinsville (El Paso) to replace James D. Graham as Chief Astronomer. At the time, Bartlett was absent, traveling in Mexico and California, and Emory did not know his whereabouts. Emory had no money; the Commissioner controlled the funds. Consequently, Emory could not pay his employees, nor members of the commission, nor the merchants for needed supplies. He persuaded the traders to continue to extend credit, and his personnel to work without pay. Emory stretched everyone's patience to the limit, while he inwardly fumed at Bartlett.

Emory also disagreed with the Commissioner over priorities. He advocated the drawing of the boundary line as the principal effort. On the other hand, Bartlett believed that exploring and recording the environment of the recently-acquired territory had as much priority as delineating the boundary. These conflicting viewpoints certainly led to misunderstanding.

Emory inadvertently released his resentment against Bartlett at a New Year's party that he hosted for members of the Commission at Magoffinsville on January 2, 1852. As the party grew more convivial and the alcohol flowed, Emory began to criticize the Commissioner openly. But, in the spirit of the occasion, no one gave Emory's remarks much thought, that is, not until the following May, when Lieutenant O. H. Tillinghast threw them in Emory's face. Tillinghast was reacting to court martial charges that Emory had preferred against him for allegedly failing to carry out the duties of quartermaster officer. In self-defense, the lieutenant preferred charges against his commanding officer, Emory, specifying conduct unbecoming an officer and a gentleman for publicly making disparaging remarks about the Commissioner. Emory was shocked and dismayed. At the height of this charged atmosphere, Radzimiński returned to headquarters, having completed the survey of the boundary from El Paso to Doña Ana. He mediated an amicable solution of the problem.

Emory did Radzimiński a disservice in yet another way when he glossed over the effect of yellow fever in the Rio Grande survey of 1853. This life-threatening sickness forced him to quit Texas, but he kept this fact out of the official boundary report. Emory acknowledged that "yellow fever made its appearance, and myself and several of the assistants were attacked." Notwithstanding, he downplayed the result. "No serious inconvenience was experienced, however, in the prosecution of the work, from this cause," he said, "and nothing happened to interrupt the harmonious and rapid execution of the field work."[7] In rebuttal, the unexpected and forced departure of the Chief Surveyor, before the completion of the Rio Grande survey, certainly was more than an "inconvenience." In fact, Emory had to delegate the responsibility and authority of the Chief Surveyor to his Principal Assistant. Fortunately, the experienced Radzimiński was fully competent to assume this position and carry out the international agreement with the Mexicans. But why did Emory not credit Radzimiński with the "harmonious and rapid execution of the field work"?

What are the facts about Emory's sickness that caused him to leave Texas more than two months before the end of the Rio Grande survey? He sailed from the mouth of the Rio Grande for Florida about September 1, 1853. By September 8 he was in Pensacola. Because he was ill, he proceeded first to Montgomery, Alabama, to seek medical help. He remained there at the home of a Dr. Hinckle, who treated the patient. Feeling better after about ten days, Emory continued to Washington, D.C., arriving on Saturday, September 24, 1853. Four days later, Emory thanked Dr. Hinckle and his wife for taking him into their home and restoring him to health. "I reached home on Saturday," Emory wrote, "completely restored to health and no apprehension of a relapse."[8]

Because he chose to omit the reason for his early departure from the Rio Grande Valley, he may inadvertently have caused some historians to make wrong judgments about the duration and scope of the boundary survey in 1853. For example, I was perplexed by the following statement of historian William H. Goetzmann:

By September 1853 the river survey was virtually concluded, and Major Emory, after leaving the usual skeleton crews to place the boundary markers, sailed for Washington.[9] Notwithstanding, the Rio Grande survey was not over by September 1853. Let me review the three tasks of the Commission in 1853. Lieutenant Nathaniel Michler did some work above Eagle Pass, left unfinished from 1852; Arthur Schott surveyed the river from Laredo to Ringgold Barracks (opposite Camargo); and Radzimiński surveyed the remaining distance to the Gulf of Mexico. Michler completed his work by late August; Schott wrote on October 5 that he was through; Schott then joined Radzimiński below Brownsville by October 26; and Radzimiński concluded his survey of 241 miles on November 3, 1853. Following the end of the field work, Radzimiński carried out the review and coordination of the American and Mexican surveys of the final fifty miles of the Rio Grande with Mexico's Chief Surveyor, Capitan Francisco Jimenez. The Pole then concluded the "United States-Mexico Agreement of November 14, 1853."[10]

The correspondence of The Emory Papers, primary source data, contradicts Goetzmann, who offers one letter in support of his statement, that of G. Clinton Gardner to Emory, September 20, 1853. Gardner, an assistant surveyor of the U.S. Boundary Commission, worked with the U.S. Coast and Geodetic Survey to extend the boundary from the mouth of the Rio Grande three leagues (nine nautical miles) out to sea, as prescribed by the Treaty of Guadalupe Hidalgo. This important but short task was completed early. On my second visit to the Beinecke Library in June 1986, I examined the letter of September 20, in which Gardner writes Emory that he is packing the survey instruments. (Gardner also reminded Emory that he did not pay his washer woman prior to departure, and that her oldest son died of yellow fever).

Obviously, if the instruments are being packed and the Chief Surveyor departs for Washington, the survey must virtually be over. But, it is a false conclusion. One must dig deeper by examining the geography and the conditions under which the survey teams operated. The three teams, and Gardner on the Gulf, were separated from each other by hundreds of miles. Consequently, Emory found it necessary to equip the teams for independent operation. When Gardner completed his work with the Coast and Geodetic Survey, he packed *his* instruments. The other teams continued their surveys and were unaffected by Gardner's packing.[11]

It seems that Goetzmann jumped to a conclusion lacking evidence. And this conclusion seems to cast the Rio Grande survey as routine. In part, he may have been misled by Emory's suppression of the impact of the yellow fever as it pertained to the Chief Surveyor. The net effect, I believe, tends to make Radzimiński's significant role merely perfunctory. Then, too, Emory's scant mention of Radzimiński in the boundary report, coupled with Emory's failure to include the Radzimiński-Jimenez Agreement, downgrades the overall importance of Radzimiński's engineering work. Radzimiński, as well as Bartlett, was a victim of Emory's spiteful whims.

Appreciation for Research Assistance

Marzena Piasecka, Sopot, Poland; Aleksander Miklaszewski, Poznań, Poland: Janina W. Hoskins, The Library of Congress; Brigadier General William A. Stofft and Lieutenant Colonel Charles R. Shrader, U.S. Army Center for Military History, Washington, D.C.; Joseph P. Frankoski, Newport News, Virginia; Robert L. Byrd, William R. Perkins Library, Duke University, Durham, North Carolina; Robert Ybarra and Maria Smith, International Boundary and Water Commission, El Paso, Texas; Susan Danforth, John Carter Brown Library, Providence, Rhode Island;

Paul Andrew Hutton and Charles E. Rankin, *New Mexico Historical Review*, Albuquerque, New Mexico; Michael E. Pilgrim, William J. Walsh, George C. Chalou, Michael Musick, Robert B. Matchette, Richard T. Gould, and Tod J. Butler, National Archives; Emanuel Rostworowski, *Polish Biographical Dictionary*, Kraków, Poland; George Miles, Beinecke Library, Yale University, New Haven, Connecticut; Alfred E. Lemmon and Patricia Brady, The Historic New Orleans Collection, New Orleans, Louisiana; John J. Slonaker, U.S. Army Military History Institute, Carlisle Barracks, Pennsylvania; Joel Wurl, Immigration History Research Center, University of Minnesota, St. Paul, Minnesota; Frances Fugate, Virginia Historical Society, Richmond, Virginia; Maria Kacprowicz, Polish Museum of America, Chicago, Illinois; Janie Hoff, Cameron University, Lawton, Oklahoma; and descendants of Colonel Edward G. W. Butler: Richard C. Plater, Jr. and David B. Plater of Thibodaux, Louisiana. Also, Inter-Library Loan Librarian, El Paso, Texas Public Library; cartographer George Shimshock, El Paso, Texas; John S. Salmon, Virginia State Library, Richmond; and Simeon H. (Bud) Newman, El Paso, Texas.

"Charles Radzimiński and the United States-Mexican Boundary Survey" was published in *New Mexico Historical Review* 63, No. 3 (July 1988) and is republished herein with the permission of the Regents of the University of New Mexico, who hold the copyright.

Essay

THE UNITED STATES-MEXICAN
boundary survey remains a unique experience for both countries.
It was extraordinarily long, some two thousand miles. But more
important, the survey had vast political consequence. For Mexico,
the established line finally stabilized the borderlands and undoubtedly dissuaded the Americans from seizing more territory.
To be sure, the Mexicans had witnessed the consequences of
"Manifest Destiny" as the United States asserted sovereignty over
Texas, New Mexico, Arizona, and California. For the United
States, the new boundary confirmed the huge acquisition of land
conquered during the war of 1846-1848.[12]

The two governments underscored the importance of the
survey by including it in the Treaty of Guadalupe Hidalgo and by
giving the Mexican and American boundary commissioners treaty-
making powers. Secretary of State James Buchanan told first U.S.
commissioner John B. Weller that the "action of the commission,
therefore, will be final and conclusive...." The treaty of February
2, 1848, directed the two commissioners to draw a boundary from
the Pacific to the Rio Grande, and along that river to the Gulf of
Mexico.[13]

Charles Radzimiński, a Polish émigré, played a significant role in the demarcation of the boundary. Appointed principal assistant surveyor in 1851, he joined the U.S. boundary commission, headed by John Russell Bartlett. Despite changes in commissioners, Radzimiński continued to serve in positions of increasing responsibility. When Major William H. Emory took charge following the Gadsden Purchase, he selected only those individuals who had proven themselves in past survey work. Emory not only chose Radzimiński but also gave him the next highest position, that of boundary commission secretary.

Radzimiński, like many of his compatriots who came to America, experienced a series of adventures. He was born into a patriotic family of Polish gentry in 1805. They lived in Warsaw in a part of the former Polish commonwealth called the Congress Kingdom of Poland, whose ruler was the Russian tsar. Although the Poles in the Congress Kingdom possessed some autonomy, they yearned for an independent country. Lieutenant Radzimiński took part in the uprising that erupted in November 1830. The year-long rebellion failed, however, and Radzimiński escaped to Austria. On March 28, 1834, he arrived in New York with a group of 234 exiles.[14]

Once in America, Radzimiński gravitated to the nation's capital, though what persuaded him to go there is not known. In 1840, he found employment as a civil engineer with the James River and Kanawha Company of Richmond, Virginia. With the outbreak of the war with Mexico in 1846, Radzimiński volunteered to serve his adopted country. Commissioned a second lieutenant, he joined the Third United States Dragoons as the quartermaster officer and later as adjutant. The regiment was divided and deployed in two zones, half joining General Zachary Taylor's army along the Rio Grande, and the other half being assigned with other reinforcements to General Winfield Scott in his campaign to capture Mexico City. Radzimiński served with the regimental headquarters in Matamoros and Mier and was honorably discharged at Jefferson Barracks, Missouri, on July 31, 1848.[15]

The former lieutenant returned to Washington, where he joined the Northeast Boundary Commission. Under the direction of Lieutenant Colonel James D. Graham of the Army Topographical Engineers, the Commission was busily reconstructing maps of the survey between Canada and Maine, which had been destroyed by fire in April 1848. The project received high priority when Great Britain asked for copies. Graham employed Radzimiński from September 1, 1848, at an annual salary of fifteen hundred dollars.[16]

Radzimiński's work impressed Graham, and he chose him and Lieutenant George Thom to re-survey a section of the Mason-Dixon line. The project involved the boundaries of Pennsylvania, Maryland, and Delaware. Beginning November 16, 1849, the field work was carried on for nearly three months. Thom worked the first and last weeks while Radzimiński ran the survey from beginning to end. The colonel's report acknowledged the valuable work of the two surveyors. Radzimiński's experience gained on the Mason-Dixon line led to his assignment with the joint U.S.-Mexican survey.[17]

Under Commissioner Weller, the demarcation between California and Mexico was made first. The incoming Whig administration of President Zachary Taylor replaced Weller with John Russell Bartlett of Rhode Island in June 1850 and made other changes as well. Graham became the principal astronomer and headed the commission's scientific corps. Radzimiński was appointed principal assistant to the surveyor, Andrew B. Gray, taking the place of Henry Clayton, who had resigned on August 6, 1850.[18]

Radzimiński linked up with Graham and his party at San Antonio on May 10, 1851. Traveling with an army supply train across west Texas, he reached present-day El Paso on June 24, 1851. He found the American side of the Rio Grande sparsely settled. In addition to Simeon Hart's flour mill and Hugh Stephenson's and Benjamin Coon's ranches, the main settlement was Magoffinsville, built by merchant James Wiley Magoffin. The village formed a large open square and included several stores and warehouses. The boundary commission made its headquarters there while surveying in the area. On the opposite bank of the river stood the Mexican town of El Paso del Norte (now Ciudad Juarez), which in 1851 had some five thousand inhabitants, with additional people on ranches and haciendas south of town.[19]

Prior to Radzimiński's arrival, Bartlett moved his headquarters to Santa Rita del Cobre (Copper Mines) near Silver City, New Mexico. While Graham remained in El Paso, Gray, Radzimiński, and Lieutenant Ambrose E. Burnside moved on to the Copper Mines. Soon the commissioner and Gray were in serious disagreement over the "initial point" on the Rio Grande. This critical point resulted from a compromise between Bartlett and the Mexican commissioner General Pedro Garcia Condé. As specified in the Treaty of Guadalupe Hidalgo, the initial point would be located where the river crossed the southern boundary of New Mexico (above El Paso del Norte). This boundary was defined by the J. Disturnell map, published in New York in 1847, which, unfortunately, contained grave errors. It mislocated El Paso del Norte more than one hundred miles east and thirty-four miles north of its actual position.[20]

Condé proposed a compromise: he would move westward (longitudinally) some one hundred miles, if Bartlett agreed to move north by thirty-four miles. The American accepted the proposal, which then established the initial point forty-two miles above El Paso del Norte and opposite the community of Doña Ana, and the joint commission began surveying the boundary westward along the compromise line. Gray objected to the agreement, however, and refused to sign it. At stake were more than six thousand square miles of land.[21] Moreover, Graham agreed with Gray. Both men thought the disputed land held the only suitable route for a railroad from Texas to the Pacific coast. In addition, Graham had his own quarrel with Bartlett. As head of the scientific corps, Graham, a colonel, believed he had the right to supervise Gray, the principal surveyor, as well as the other scientific personnel. Bartlett and Gray both disagreed with Graham. Petty differences also became magnified. Graham felt piqued because Bartlett had not introduced him to commission members by his full title, "Head of the Scientific Corps." Earlier, Graham bypassed the commissioner, Bartlett, and ordered Whipple to stop the survey along the

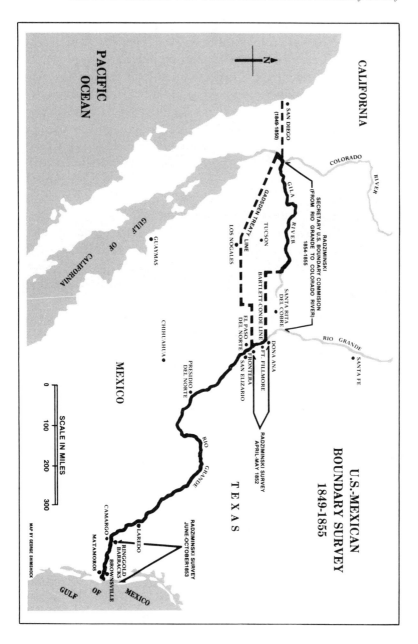

Radzimiński began the first portion of the survey he supervised on the Rio Grande near Frontera, Texas, shown here in a sketch from William H. Emory's Report. (Courtesy of El Paso Public Library).

Bartlett-Condé line, and to report to him in person at Frontera, just above El Paso. Graham's arbitrary action angered General Condé and the Mexican government. Clearly Graham had exceeded his authority.[22]

Greatly upset with Graham, Bartlett wrote: "Never, in the whole course of my life have I been placed in so trying a position." He strongly believed that as head of the commission he must maintain his position or, "in succumbing to the demands of Colonel Graham, make myself and the Chief Surveyor, Mr. Gray, subordinate to him, resign all power and control on the members of the Commission, and become a mere nullity." Bartlett decided to bring the problem to the attention of the Secretary of the Interior, and he believed the situation serious enough to send an emissary, Radzimiński.[23]

The presidio of Santa Rita del Cobre west of the Rio Grande in present-day New Mexico, as shown in a sketch from Bartlett's Personal Narrative. Radzimiński first joined the Boundary Commission at Santa Rita after John Russell Bartlett moved his headquarters there in the spring of 1851.

Why did Bartlett select Radzimiński? The commissioner offers no explanation in his *Personal Narrative*. Certainly he needed a responsible individual and experienced surveyor. Although several army engineers were present, they could be suspected of favoring Graham. As a civilian, however, Radzimiński could, perhaps, be considered neutral. No less important was Bartlett's personal evaluation of Radzimiński during their month-long association at Santa Rita. It soon became clear that Radzimiński's sympathies lay with the commissioner, and the two men joined forces.

Some historians maintain that Bartlett was not suited to be commissioner. Although he had his faults, Bartlett nevertheless possessed an astute, analytical mind, and he enjoyed considerable political support in Washington and Providence, where he sent Radzimiński to argue his case. Bartlett and Radzimiński apparently held several strategy sessions at the Copper Mines. On Sunday, August 10, 1851, Bartlett dined alone with Radzimiński. That afternoon, Bartlett visited with Gray, and later, Radzimiński and Gray joined Bartlett for tea. In the next few days, Radzimiński prepared himself for his trip east.[24]

Meanwhile, Graham got wind of the Radzimiński mission. Feeling threatened, he sought to protect himself with his military superiors and chose Burnside to carry letters to Washington. On August 15, Burnside informed Bartlett that he would leave for the nation's capital the following day at 10 a.m. Bartlett, who had been writing letters to officials and friends all day, redoubled his effort and sat up until 1 a.m. preparing dispatches. Several other members of the Commission helped him make copies. Finally, at the unusual hour of 1:30 a.m. on August 16, Radzimiński departed for Santa Fe. He rode Bartlett's horse and was accompanied by Edward Barry, who would return with the horses.[25]

Carrying letters of introduction to senators and officials in Washington, Radzimiński had confidential correspondence, some prized southwestern seeds for Secretary of the Interior Alexander H. H. Stuart, and a letter for Lieutenant Colonel W. W. S. Bliss, secretary to the late president, Zachary Taylor. He also carried letters for Bartlett's friends and wife, Eliza, in Providence, although to members of the commission, Bartlett tried to give the impression of having sent Radzimiński only with official correspondence for the Secretary of the Interior.[26]

Burnside also departed on August 16. Traveling with three companions, all mounted on mules, Burnside left at 3 p.m. with letters for Colonel John J. Abert, head of the Army Topographical Engineers. Burnside raced Radzimiński to Santa Fe and won. Henry Jacobs, assistant commissary officer, explained to Bartlett: "Your horse that went with mine to Santa Fe, Barry informs me, broke completely down, and he was obliged to sell him. Burnside got into Santa Fe 2 days ahead of Radzimiński. Burnside had changes every day, while Radzimiński could get no accommodations whatever from the officers of the Army and was obliged to ride my horse through to Santa Fe."[27]

Radzimiński arrived in the nation's capital about October 1 and delivered the Bartlett letters to Secretary of the Interior Stuart. Earlier, Stuart had received Bartlett's dispatches complaining of Graham's interference with the survey as well as General Condé's protest of Graham's decision. To Stuart, Graham's behavior was the last straw. Stuart already was dissatisfied with Graham because of Graham's "long, unnecessary delay in joining the commission in the field." On September 11, 1851, Stuart proposed to Secretary of War Charles M. Conrad that Graham be relieved and Emory appointed in his place. The change was made, and Emory, already present in the capital, was notified personally. Emory arrived in El Paso by November 26, 1851.[28]

While Stuart pondered Gray's future, Radzimiński traveled to Providence, where he spent a few days in the company of Henry B. Anthony, governor of Rhode Island and Bartlett's brother-in-law. They visited the country place of Senator John Hopkins Clarke, whose strong backing had secured Bartlett's appointment. Radzimiński gave the senator a detailed account of the quarrel between Bartlett and Graham. He also provided Clarke with useful background data should the problem come up for senate debate. Next day, Governor Anthony invited friends to a dinner party in Radzimiński's honor. "He made a favorable impression upon us all," Anthony wrote Bartlett, "and the women fell in love with him at sight, especially your wife and mine."[29]

The governor confirmed Radzimiński's loyalty to Bartlett. Anthony had been informed by one of Bartlett's protagonists in Washington that Radzimiński had given the impression while there of favoring Gray, who was then contacting friends about his dispute with Bartlett. "I did not see anything of this kind in him," Anthony wrote, "but judged from his conversation that he was wholly with you in this as well as in all other matters." Radzimiński assured the Providence circle that the Department of the Interior upheld Bartlett in his difficulties with Graham.[30]

Returning to Washington to pick up official correspondence for the commission, Radzimiński felt pleased with the success of his mission. "It was my good fortune to obtain all the points you asked at the hands of the Dept. of the Interior," he wrote to Bartlett. As for Gray, Secretary Stuart decided to keep the surveyor but ordered him to sign the Bartlett-Condé agreement in a letter dated October 31, 1851. At least that was Radzimiński's understanding of Stuart's decision on November 3, three days before he left Washington. The Secretary abruptly changed his mind, however, when the question of the initial point surfaced again. Conferring with Secretary of State Daniel Webster and President Millard Fillmore, Stuart decided to replace Gray with Emory. Stuart informed Emory of the appointment by letter of November 4, 1851, and entrusted it to Radzimiński. Although Radzimiński planned to meet Bartlett in San Diego, as the commissioner had instructed him, Stuart countermanded those instructions and directed him to Magoffinsville.[31]

When Radzimiński reached southern New Mexico, Bartlett was enroute to San Diego and Emory was out looking for him. At Doña Ana, on January 26, Radzimiński wrote Emory: "I have very important dispatches from the Department of the Interior for the heads of the commission – no small portion of them being for you." Radzimiński had learned from Henry Skillman, often employed as a courier for the commission, that Emory left El Paso the day before. Radzimiński advised Emory to return to headquarters, since Bartlett's trail would take him to San Diego. A messenger delivered the letter to Emory the next day at Samalayuca, Mexico, an oasis thirty-six miles south of El Paso. In reply, Emory asked Radzimiński to bring the correspondence to him before he would abandon his search for Bartlett. Emory instructed Lieutenant O. H. Tillinghast, the commission's quartermaster, to provide Radzimiński with three well-armed men and four of his best animals. Reaching Samalayuca, Radzimiński bore good tidings and handed Emory his presidential appointment as surveyor. Emory wrote the secretary: "I have the honor to acknowledge the receipt, by the hands of Mr. Radzimiński, of the Commission of Surveyor under the 5th Article of the Treaty of Guadalupe Hidalgo. I thank you and through you the President of this renewed mark of consideration." Emory returned to El Paso.[32]

The newly-appointed chief surveyor kept Radzimiński with him, turning over responsibility for delivering the letters for the commissioner to a specially hired courier, Ignatius Jenkins, who traveled nearly four months to accomplish the task. Prior to Jenkins' departure, Radzimiński gave him a letter for Bartlett, informing the commissioner of the results of his trip to Washington and Providence. Stressing confirmation of Bartlett's authority, he wrote and underlined, "you are the U.S. Commissioner in every sense of that term. I have fought the fight and we came off victorious."[33]

During Radzimiński's absence, Emory arrived at Magoffinsville and relieved Graham. With the commissioner gone, Emory could act only on the instructions given Graham, who explained that he had completed the survey of the Rio Grande from the initial point to El Paso del Norte and partially erected an observatory at Frontera (White's Rancho). After examining Graham's data, Emory rejected the survey, and this portion of the river became a problem. It began with J. Hamilton Prioleau, who did the work first, although he objected to the use of inadequate instruments. Another person repeated the survey, but it also was not suitable. A third attempt, by Charles Wright under Graham's direction, was not acceptable to Emory, who then assigned the task to Radzimiński.[34]

Field work began at the end of March 1852, when the required transportation, instruments, and technical personnel had been assembled. Directing Radzimiński to run the survey from Frontera to Doña Ana, in the opposite direction of Wright's survey, Emory cautioned: "The survey covers ground of much interest, and will therefore be done with all possible accuracy." At the same time he expressed confidence in Radzimiński, stating that previous instructions to surveyors and "your own knowledge and experience of surveying will render any detailed instructions here unnecessary." Accuracy was Radzimiński's motto, and he was determined not to allow anything to deter him. Nevertheless, there were difficulties, one of which was the weather. Spring windstorms filled the air with choking dust and sand, hampering the survey. Finally obtaining a clear day, he tested the Brithaupt theodolite and found it worn-out and unfit. He returned it to Emory, asking "whether the triangulation shall be prosecuted with the only instrument left in my hands." He progressed upriver less than two miles a day, paced by the axemen who cut down thickets along the river to clear the field of view. He could never hire enough axemen, and they were an unreliable lot. Some had to be discharged for various reasons; others ran away. Radzimiński pushed the survey from six o'clock in the morning until six in the evening, with a two-hour halt at noon. When one of the escort soldiers volunteered to be a flagman, the surveyor promptly hired him. But his sergeant objected on the grounds of a possible violation of army regulations. Radzimiński asked Emory to "smooth the matter with Col. Miles [commander of Fort Fillmore near Las Cruces] because the sergeant annoys me daily with his fears."[35]

Radzimiński continued a vigorous pace but with due regard for accuracy. He discovered that an assistant had employed a "field expedient" with an instrument whose movable parts could not be locked firmly. The assistant had applied grease to the screws to increase the friction, and the resulting accumulation of dirt rendered the measuring device unfit. Radzimiński returned it to Frontera by wagon and asked Emory to furnish a Young's goniometer.[36]

Emory, meanwhile, planned to go downriver about June 1 and looked for an escort. Since he had no soldiers at El Paso, Emory decided to employ Radzimiński's and therefore urged his surveyor to work as rapidly as he could. "Hire as many men as are necessary to keep the path before you cleared out," Emory wrote. By the third week of May, Radzimiński had surveyed sixty-three miles of the river. He took azimuth readings of all the peaks in sight, north and south, connecting the northern peaks to Whipple's observatory at the initial point (Doña Ana) and the southern peaks to Emory's observatory at Frontera.[37]

The desert sun began to burn hot by mid-May, prompting Radzimiński to remark that even the mornings were as "hot as that place intended for evil spirits." But, he added, "Nolens, volens, the survey goes on." One of his assistants, Charles A. Snowden, became ill and returned to Frontera. Notwithstanding, Radzimiński pressed on to meet his own target date of June 9. He reached Las Cruces by May 27. Emory kept exhorting him: "For God's sake, push your work to the utmost and get here as soon as possible." Emory told his surveyor that, should he not be able to finish on time, he would take the results of Wright's survey for the last six to eight miles. Radzimiński resisted these instructions, recommending instead that he be allowed to abandon a road survey (an added task), "which after all is of no importnce, and would save several days time." Emory agreed. Assuring Radzimiński of his confidence in his judgment, Emory left the decision to him, "only imposing the condition that you be here on or before the 9th." Radzimiński beat his own target date by three days. On June 6, 1852, he returned to Frontera, having completed the survey of the Rio Grande as directed by Emory. In addition, Radzimiński incorporated the towns of Las Cruces and Doña Ana into the survey.[38]

The grueling pace of the field work left the team exhausted, Radzimiński admitting, "I was quite willing to give up the ghost myself." But the job was done. He praised Snowden for his help in the last few days and also William White, Jr., who, "although of a phlegmatic temperament, worked like a Trojan." Commissioner Bartlett noted that Radzimiński's work "was executed in a highly satisfactory manner and accepted as the official Survey." Although the direct-line distance was thirty-four miles, Radzimiński measured the length of the river, following its curves (sinuosities), at a fraction less than ninety miles.[39]

Upon returning to El Paso, Radzimiński found Emory embroiled with Lieutenant Tillinghast in court martial charges. The feud began when Emory relieved Tillinghast of his duties as quartermaster because of allegedly disobeying orders. Emory placed Tillinghast under arrest and drew up charges and specifications. Not to be outdone, Tillinghast preferred court martial charges against his superior, believing the best defense an attack. Emory was shocked, calling the charges "scandalous and unfounded."

Radzimiński tried to patch things up, but Emory rejected the offer of mediation, adding, however, that he would drop the matter if Tillinghast withdrew "his offensive correspondence." Radzimiński slept on the issue. Early next morning he called on Tillinghast and mediated the problem. Tillinghast withdrew the countercharges and asked to be relieved from the commission. Emory then dropped all charges and advised the Secretary of the Interior to release Tillinghast to his regiment.[40]

By the first week of June 1852, Emory readied himself for a trip downriver to check on field work in progress. He also planned to meet with the Mexican commissioner, Jose Salazar y Larrequi, at Presidio del Norte on August 1. Expecting Bartlett to have unfinished work on the line west of El Paso, Emory instructed Radzimiński to await Bartlett's return. He regretted telling the commissioner that in the interim Radzimiński and his assistants would remain idle. Emory imposed some conditions on his principal assistant: "He cannot move west," Emory wrote, "without an escort of a company of troops and without money, five or ten thousand dollars." Meanwhile, Emory arranged with the commander of Fort Fillmore for Radzimiński to buy provisions there "at a much cheaper rate than can be transported from the States." Learning subsequently that Whipple would be returning to El Paso, Emory transferred the probable task to him, since Whipple had surveyed the greater portion of that line. Emory asked Radzimiński to join him at the first opportunity. Awaiting Bartlett, Radzimiński moved to San Elizario to take charge of the commission's supply depot.[41]

Bartlett reached El Paso on August 17, 1852, and prepared to meet with Emory on the Rio Grande at Fort Duncan (Eagle Pass). He intended to travel some six hundred miles through west Texas, but he could not obtain American soldiers for protection. Whereupon the Mexican commander at El Paso del Norte, Colonel Emilio Langberg, offered Bartlett an escort of Mexican soldiers if he would travel through Mexico via Chihuahua. Bartlett accepted the offer and advised Emory to meet him at Camargo, a lower point on the river. Bartlett's reliance on Mexican troops surprised Radzimiński. He wrote Emory: "Now, is it not a pretty state of affairs that U.S. Agents should be compelled to seek foreign protection in transacting U.S. business and in pursuance of their orders?"[42]

Bartlett's including Radzimiński in his travel plans upset Emory. On October 30, 1852, Emory replied to Bartlett: "I regret to learn by your letter that you have taken Mr. Radzimiński and assistants with you, as two opportunities presented themselves since your arrival…at El Paso, by either of which he and his party could have joined us with ease and safety." Earlier, Emory wrote Radzimiński that he needed his survey data and maps for the meeting with the Mexican commissioner. In the absence of these data, Emory was forced to rely on Mexican maps. Meanwhile, he waited for Bartlett.[43]

The commissioner's wagon train left El Paso on October 7, 1852. Some ten days later, a band of thirty to forty Indians attacked the Americans, who repulsed the Indians but not before a Mexican herdsman and an Indian were killed. The attack was the first and only such incident in two years, and everyone became more cautious. When Bartlett received word that Comanches were in the area, he ordered an inspection of firearms, passed out extra ammunition, and "placed the party under the orders of Mr. Radzimiński, chief engineer, who had had experience as a military officer."[44]

In Chihuahua, Bartlett's party rested while the wagons were refitted. Calling on Governor Jose Cordero, the commissioner found a large map of the state of Chihuahua in the governor's office. He noted that the northern boundary of the Mexican state lay well to the north of the Bartlett-Condé line of 32°22′. Radzimiński drew the map for the U.S. commission, and Cordero certified the copy as authentic. Bartlett used the map in defense of the Bartlett-Condé agreement.[45]

Almost eleven weeks after departing El Paso, the American party approached Camargo. Taking Radzimiński with him, Bartlett rode ahead to the town and, crossing the Rio Grande in a scow, continued to nearby Ringgold Barracks where the two men were greeted by Emory and his party. Bartlett had come in the expectation of completing the survey of the river. But there was no

APACHE INDIANS ATTACKING THE TRAIN AND PARTY.—p. 412.

Indians attacked Bartlett's wagon train in October 1852, as it wound its way from El Paso through Mexico to Camargo. An Indian and a Mexican herder were killed in the attack. Sketch from Bartlett's Personal Narrative.

more money, and further work depended on new appropriations. Rejecting the Bartlett-Condé line, Congress stipulated that an additional $120,000 voted for the survey could not be spent until New Mexico's southern boundary was established just north of El Paso del Norte. Interpreting this condition as an attempt to break up the survey, Bartlett disbanded the commission and returned to his home in Providence. Radzimiński, Emory, and the others traveled to the nation's capital.[46]

Congress soon lifted the restriction, and President Franklin Pierce appointed Robert B. Campbell as the new U.S. commissioner, in charge of completing the survey of the Rio Grande. Continuing as chief astronomer and surveyor, Emory assigned specific portions of the river to Radzimiński, Lieutenant Nathaniel Michler,

Surveyor's camp near Brownsville, Texas, as shown in a sketch from Emory's Report. Swarms of mosquitoes in Radzimiński's camp cost the survey many days of work as the men lay wracked with yellow fever. (Courtesy of El Paso Public Library).

and Arthur Schott. Michler was to complete the unfinished work above Eagle Pass, and Schott, the stretch of river from Laredo to Ringgold Barracks. Radzimiński was to survey from Ringgold Barracks to the mouth of the Rio Grande, a distance of 241 miles.[47]

Radzimiński had two principal assistants, Thomas W. Jones and James H. Houston, both of whom had been with the commission since August 1850. Jones, the son of General Walter Jones of Washington City, had been recommended by Senator Clarke. The survey proceeded steadily but not without difficulty. Both the American and Mexican teams were exposed to yellow fever, especially at the Gulf of Mexico. Among those who came down with the sickness were Emory and Radzimiński. Don Felipe de Iturbide, secretary of the Mexican commission, died of it. By the

149

end of August 1853, Emory felt so threatened by the epidemic that he was forced to leave Texas. Arriving in Washington, he wrote Dr. John Torrey, a botanist with the commision: "I have just returned home convalescent from an attack of yellow fever." The mosquito-spread disease never abated during the course of the field work. Upon completing his survey, Radzimiński reported that "yellow fever is raging here with violence" and that it was bad at Brownsville as well.[48]

The epidemic was spread by swarms of mosquitoes that bred in pools of water from persistent rains. Radzimiński experienced "a continuous wet season and sickness among my best men." The mosquitoes were both obnoxious and dangerous, "the size of Buffalo Bulls, and there are hives or herds of them in every square foot of ground." He lost days of work as he lay wracked with fever in his tent.[49]

Full working days also held unexpected danger, like that of July 23, 1853, which ended in tragedy when Radzimiński lost Jones in a drowning accident. After a day of surveying, Radzimiński and Jones were returning to camp below Reynosa. A squall struck the area and buffeted them in their small boat, which began shipping water rapidly. Handing the survey instrument to Radzimiński, Jones began bailing desperately, but to no avail. The skiff sank and overturned in deep water. Radzimiński could not swim, but he kept his presence of mind. Upon touching the river bottom, he sprang up and came to the surface. Nearby he saw his Mexican laborer straddling the capsized boat. In a desperate effort, Radzimiński reached the outstretched hand of the Mexican, who pulled him to safety. Meanwhile, Jones swam for the shore, burdened by his clothes and a Colt pistol strapped to his waist. He failed. Halfway, he sank from view and never reappeared. Darkness prevented immediate search.

Reaching camp, a distraught Radzimiński wrote Emory a short letter. "I am at present not equal to the task," he said, "of giving you a more detailed account...." Next day, Radzimiński described the circumstances surrounding the tragedy. He and the search party found Jones's body a few miles downriver. Leading the mourners with a reading of prayers for the dead, Radzimiński buried Jones on the banks of the Rio Grande at the ranch of a Dr. Merryman.[50] Prioleau took Jones's place, joining Radzimiński at Rancho Blanca on August 4, 1853. Two months later Radzimiński sent him to the mouth of the river, where Prioleau measured the tide every hour from sunrise to sunset for two weeks. While performing this task, Prioleau used Commissioner Campbell's ambulance as a living quarters.[51]

Although the survey was a joint venture, the American and Mexican parties operated separately and compared results periodically. The curving river caused the parties to cross from one side to the other. On one occasion Mexican troops confronted Radzimiński when he found himself on the neighbor's territory. Captain Francisco Carillo, military commander at Reynosa, rode into Radzimiński's camp on the evening of July 12, 1853. Two officers and six lancers, all mounted and armed, escorted Carillo. After Radzimiński introduced himself, the mounted Carillo looked down on him with a haughty, penetrating look Radzimiński described as: "A look calculated to drive my soul to my very heels." But he stood his ground, while answering the Mexican captain's sharp questions. Surprised that Carillo and the Alcalde of Reynosa were unaware of the terms of the Treaty of Guadalupe Hidalgo, Radzimiński objected to the Mexican's behavior and tone of voice. "I should sooner reckon on your protection than on this conduct," he told the *commandante*. The meeting ended in a standoff. Radzimiński immediately wrote Emory, who had informed the Mexican authorities previously of the presence of American surveying parties along the Rio Grande. Emory reminded Major Crispin del Poso, commander at Camargo, that American teams had the right to survey on the Mexican side. There were no further incidents.[52]

Of the entire river line, the Mexicans seemed to be most concerned about the mouth of the Rio Grande. Even before the field work began in June 1853, Mexico's commissioner pronounced surveying the final miles of the river jointly as a priority. Having already organized his teams and planned their activities, Emory was reluctant to make changes. He wrote Captain Francisco Jimenez, chief surveyor of the Mexican commission: "As soon as either commission reaches Matamoros with the survey [and it was quite apparent the American survey would reach Matamoros first], I would name the Engineer to cooperate with you in the joint survey from Matamoros to the mouth." Two months later Emory told Jimenez that he would name "Charles Radziminski, Esq. to survey the River as far down as Barita [between Matamoros and the Gulf] and authorize him to agree with you on the line which is to constitute the Boundary from Brownsville to that place, subject to the confirmation of the joint Commission." Emory also informed the captain that Radzimiński was at work about thirty miles below Reynosa and could be expected to reach Fort Brown about September 1.[53]

Plagued with yellow fever, Emory decided apparently in mid-August 1853 to leave Texas. He gave Radzimiński full responsibility and informed Jimenez that his principal assistant had complete charge of the survey. To Radzimiński he wrote, "I have named you as the Ass't Surveyor on the American side to agree with Capt. Jimenez upon the principal channel of the River from Brownsville to the mouth." Radzimiński's assigned responsibility meant that he had the authority not only to act for the U.S. commission but also to commit the United States to an international boundary.[54]

Because Radzimiński had run into unavoidable delays, Emory decided to have Arthur Schott help him with the last leg of the survey, should Schott reach Ringgold Barracks before Radzimiński finished his survey. On October 26, Schott and his party came down the river to join Radzimiński, who then was about midway between Brownsville and the Gulf. He assigned Schott to surveying half the remaining distance (about twelve miles) from Rancho Lomida to the sea. Radzimiński wrote to Emory in Washington that he gave Schott the easier portion, "where there is no cutting [of thickets] and where the ranchos are fewest." He had no control over yellow fever, however, and Schott immediately lost three men, one a day. Fortunately, not too much work remained. On November 3, 1853, Radzimiński notifed Emory that he was through. Commissioner Campbell confirmed the end of the field work, informing Emory that all of Radzimiński's laborers had been discharged and that Schott's laborers would be discharged as well on his return to camp.[55]

Having surveyed the Rio Grande from Ringgold Barracks to the Gulf of Mexico, Radzimiński conferred with Jimenez on that last leg, from Brownsville to the sea, a distance of 49.81 miles. Upon comparison of maps, the American found his data and that of the Mexican to be in agreement. The American proposed a joint statement, dated November 14, 1853, one copy in English and the other in Spanish, which reads as follows:

> We, the undersigned, duly empowered to agree upon the principal channel of that portion of the Rio Grande which is embraced between the town of Brownsville, Cameron County, State of Texas, and its mouth, do decide, and hereby jointly agree that the deepest section of the Rio Grande, as lately surveyed by orders of our respective Governments, and embraced as aforesaid, is its principal channel.

The two surveyors signed the document, Radzimiński as "Assistant Surveyor on the part of the United States." Having invoked the power of his delegated authority, Radzimiński established the international boundary of the United States for a distance of fifty critical miles.[56]

The three survey teams had done the job, and Emory reported: "All the field-work was completed within the time and for a less amount than had been estimated." By the end of 1853, the U.S.-Mexican boundary along the Rio Grande had been surveyed from Doña Ana, New Mexico, to its mouth on the Gulf of Mexico, a distance of some 1,400 miles. But much administrative work remained. Survey data had to be plotted, maps drawn, reports written, and other matters carried out. Radzimiński was engaged in such work at the boundary commission's office in Washington.[57]

On the national level, President Franklin Pierce determined to end the controversy over the southern boundary of New Mexico. He sent James Gadsden to Mexico City to negotiate purchase of enough territory to include the disputed area and be sufficient and suitable for the construction of a transcontinental railroad. Gadsden concluded a treaty with Mexican President Antonio López de Santa Anna on December 30, 1853. During ratification, the U.S. Senate reduced the area of purchase somewhat and lowered the price from $15 million to $10 million. After the Senate approved the revised treaty and Santa Anna agreed to the changes, Pierce proclaimed the treaty in effect on June 29, 1854. It called for a joint survey of the east-west boundary, from the Rio Grande to the Colorado River, a distance of some 530 miles across desert terrain.[58]

Anticipating the requirement, Campbell asked several key members of the commission to submit estimates of the cost of the new survey. Assuming he would survey one-third of the distance, Radzimiński gave an estimate of $35,220 for his portion of the field work. Others made varying estimates, and Congress voted $168,130 for running and marking the Gadsden line. Campbell, however, did not continue in his post. On August 4, 1854, the president appointed Emory U.S. commissioner.[59]

Perhaps remembering the dissension that plagued Bartlett, Emory kept the positions of astronomer and surveyor for himself, becoming a trinity of three officials in one person. He selected seventeen technical personnel, who were organized into two survey teams. For secretary of the commission and second-in-command, Emory chose Radzimiński. As chief astronomer and surveyor, Emory planned to run the technical work, and he required a strong executive for administration and logistics. In this respect, Emory behaved as a military commander. Soon Radzimiński was immersed in a multitude of activities relating to organizing and equipping the commission. He traveled to the army quartermaster office in Philadelphia to purchase twelve army wagons Emory had required from the War Department. Radzimiński also bought arms from the Samuel Colt Company of Hartford, Connecticut, then journeyed to Baltimore and other points around the capital, while Emory obtained survey instruments. Laborers were hired and horses and mules procured in

United States-Mexico Agreement by Charles Radzimiński
and Francisco Jimenez on the Rio Grande boundary between
Brownsville and the Gulf of Mexico. (Courtesy of Beinecke
Rare Book and Manuscript Library, Yale University).

Texas, which the commission reached on September 23, 1854. Upon debarking at Indianola, Emory told Radzimiński to organize the wagon train and lead it with the equipment to San Antonio.[60]

The weather remained hot in October 1854, and Radzimiński showed discretion in handling a group of rough western men. He did not "push our schooner hands for fear of getting them all sick." Some of the laborers turned out to be misfits. Others were good and a few, first rate. He told Emory: "If you had seen me load the wagons, you would have given them a gallon of wine apiece, not having the same authority I only gave them a little of my own whiskey." At the same time, however, Radzimiński could be unyielding, forcing some members of the commission to walk because of a shortage of healthy animals. A number of mules were lame and sickly, and they followed the train. Reaching Goliad on October 12, he wrote the commissioner: "Some of the young gentlemen that have no animals to ride look daggers at me, but I cannot help it."[61]

Leading the train to San Antonio, Radzimiński became increasingly concerned over the adverse conditions the commission was meeting in Texas. Violent storms in the Gulf of Mexico brought heavy rains that soaked the ground between Indianola and San Antonio, causing delays in gathering the equipment and transporting it to San Antonio. Property of the commission, previously stored in Texas, decayed, became unsuitable, and had to be replaced. Additional animals were bought to make up for the sick and unfit, and members of the commission grew sick. With expenditures running more than anticipated, Radzimiński recommended that Emory apply for additional money from the Congress rather than face a possible suspension of the survey. Emory accepted the advice. At Fort Clark, he asked the Secretary of the Interior to seek another appropriation of $71,450. Secretary Robert McClelland reacted with surprise, since he believed the survey could be made within the time and means as planned. Nonetheless, he informed Emory that the administration would make the request, although he still hoped Emory would not exceed the original appropriation.[62]

View of the Initial Point, on Rio Bravo.

*This view of the initial point on the Rio Grande,
according to the Gadsden Treaty, is taken from
Emory's Report. From this point, the boundary
would be surveyed westward to the Colorado River.*

At San Antonio Emory prepared for the long trek to El Paso.
Radzimiński joined him with the wagon loads of equipment on
October 18. Emory hired sixty-eight support personnel—teamsters, herders, cooks, guards, ambulance drivers, and servants. Brevet Captain Edmund Kirby Smith and a company of the Seventh
Infantry provided initial security. On October 26, 1854, the march
began, slowly at first, because the rains left the ground soggy and
difficult for the heavily-laden wagons. Later the roads were better,
grass and water plentiful, and the train reached El Paso.[63]

On December 2, 1854, Emory held his first meeting with the
Mexican commissioner, his old friend Jose Salazar y Larrequi. The
first order of business called for determining the initial point, that
is, the location where parallel 31°47' strikes the Rio Grande.
Astronomical observations gave them this point on the ground.

157

*International Boundary Marker No. 1 on the Rio Grande.
Charles Radzimiński and key members of the Joint
U.S.-Mexican Boundary Commission laid the foundation
in a ceremony on January 31, 1855. (Courtesy International
Boundary and Water Commission).*

On January 31, 1855, senior members of the joint commission and prominent local individuals met at a ceremony – the laying of the foundation for the monument at the initial point. Among those present were Lieutenant Colonel Edmund B. Alexander, commanding officer at Fort Bliss, and officers and ladies of the post. A brief document, one copy in English and the other in Spanish, was signed by Emory, Salazar y Larrequi, Radzimiński, four Americans, and a like number of Mexicans. The paper read:

> We, the undersigned, have this day assembled to witness the laying of the foundation of the monument which is to mark the initial point of the boundary between the United States and the Republic of Mexico, agreed upon, under the treaty of Mexico, on the part of

the United States by William Helmsley Emory, and on the part of the Republic of Mexico by Jose Salazar y Larrequi, latitude 31°47'.

The signed paper was placed in a glass bottle and deposited five feet under the center of the monument.[64]

With the initial point marked and publicly proclaimed, Emory was eager to start surveying the boundary line westward. His technical team consisted of himself, Radzimiński, and twelve astronomers, surveyors, and assistants. While in Washington, he had organized the Pacific party under Lieutenant Michler for the eastward survey from the Colorado River to the intersection of 31°20' north latitude with the 111th meridian of longitude. Emory planned to have the two parties meet at this junction near Nogales, Arizona.[65]

In accordance with terms of the Gadsden Treaty, Emory ran the survey along latitude 31°47' for 100 miles, then due south for about 30 miles to latitude 31°20', and westward again along 31°20' for about 170 miles to the 111th meridian, which he reached the first week of May 1855. Radzimiński, at Emory's side during the survey, may or may not have taken part in the technical operations. Meanwhile, Michler surveyed the Colorado River from the California border south for the specified 28 miles. He was then to move on a direct line for some 240 miles to the planned junction.[66]

Emory arrived at Nogales and waited for Michler. Not hearing from his subordinate, Emory sent out scouts, who found the Michler group on the Gila River. Michler had concluded that running the survey across the desert of Arizona was impossible at the time, since the water holes were dry. For a large group of four officers, twenty men, and sixty soldiers, the problem of water loomed as an insurmountable obstacle. The Mexican surveyor, Francisco Jimenez, and Michler agreed to suspend the survey and travel via the Gila River to Nogales. There they would run the line westward, hoping rainfall would refill the water holes in the interim.[67]

Responding to Emory's urgent call to meet with him, Michler rode ahead with a small party to report to Emory, who was angry over his subordinate's failure to complete the survey. What upset

Emory was the thought of spending money for work he believed should have been done. Worried that he might be forced to resort to the emergency fund of $71,450, which the Secretary of the Interior had cautioned him about, he reacted drastically. He decided to disband Michler's team and conduct the remaining survey with his own group. Lieutenant Francis Patterson, commanding the escort for Michler, shocked Emory, however, by denying him the escort. Patterson maintained that he and his soldiers were assigned by military orders specifically to Michler's party, which was nonsense because the War Department had provided the security to the commission. Assigning Patterson to Michler was simply a matter of administrative arrangement. Clearly Patterson was insubordinate to the commissioner and superior officer of the army. Emory communicated his frustration over Patterson's behavior to the Secretary of the Interior. "The course pursued by him," Emory wrote, "has defeated my plans to repair the disaster of Lt. Michler, and I am forced as the least [sic] of two evils to keep that expensively organized party in the field to complete the unfinished work between the 111° and the Colorado." Nevertheless, Emory showed good sense. His mission was overriding, that is, to run the survey in the shortest time with the utmost economy. Bowing to the inevitable, he instructed Michler to complete the survey under the protection of Patterson's soldiers.[68]

Discharging the larger component of the commission, Emory divided his team into two divisions and instructed Radzimiński to lead the first division to San Antonio, where the Secretary would

Exacting and difficult to get along with, William H. Emory, shown here in an engraving many years after the boundary survey, nevertheless found Charles Radzimiński a valuable and dependable associate. Emory expressed his satisfaction in a letter of farewell to Radzimiński in early 1856. Photo courtesy of The Library of Congress.

pay and release the men. Emory followed with the second division after refitting and restarting Michler's party. Radzimiński departed Los Nogales on June 21, 1855. Several officers traveled in his division, including Lieutenant Charles Turnbull, Marine T. W. Chandler, Frank Wheaton, John G. O'Donoghue, Winder Emory, and James Houston. Upon arriving at Franklin (El Paso) on July 19, Radzimiński rested the train and repaired the wagons for the remaining journey to San Antonio. He felt a sense of discourtesy in not returning the farewell calls of the officers at Los Nogales. In a letter to Emory he added a postscript: "You will please defend me before the officers and others, if you hear them complaining of my want of politeness in not returning their visits, but I was so busy and so occupied that I had not time."[69]

At San Antonio, Radzimiński accepted a commission of First Lieutenant, U.S. Army, from Secretary of War Jefferson Davis on September 24, 1855. Reluctant to part with his long-time assistant, Emory asked Secretary of Interior McClelland to request the War Department to allow Radzimiński to serve to the end of the year. Subsequently, the commissioner applied for an additional month. In approving the second stay, Adjutant General Samuel Cooper asked that as soon as Emory could dispense with Radzimiński's services to direct him to the adjutant general's office for orders.[70]

When the two parted, Emory wrote Radzimiński a letter of farewell in which he stressed his associate's fidelity and ability with the commission. Expressing his sincere wishes for happiness and success in a military career, Emory closed with "I am very truly your friend." And well might Emory be pleased with Radzimiński. Their smooth relationship insured the success of the boundary survey. In contrast to the dissension and frequent personnel changes of the Bartlett commission, Emory's commission performed as a coordinated team. As Emory stated in his report: "This organization was continued with scarcely a change until the successful conclusion of the field-work in the fall of 1855."[71]

Undoubtedly Radzimiński's tact, spirit of cooperation, and sense of humor formed the basis of an amicable relationship, since Emory was not easy to get along with. Exacting and demanding,

Emory had had differences with surveyor Gray during the California survey in 1849 while he was chief astronomer. He also had trouble with junior officers. Although lieutenants Tillinghast, F. W. Smith, and Michler were excellent officers and hand-picked for the commission, Emory became dissatisfied with them, angry over their performance, and tried to punish them. Then, too, Lieutenant Whipple came to dislike Emory. He told Colonel Graham frankly: "I have ever said that I would not again serve under the command of Major Emory, if I could avoid it." Radzimiński, however, seemed to understand Emory and won his confidence. Without doubt, Emory made an exceptional choice in Radzimiński, whose service as surveyor and secretary of the boundary commission reflected his engineering ability, leadership, and sterling character.[72] Notwithstanding, Emory gave Radzimiński scant credit in his published report of the survey, and historians have tended to overlook him. Fortunately, the archives have preserved the record of Charles Radzimiński's substantial role in drawing the long boundary between Mexico and the United States.[73]

Charles Radzimiński

in the

Military Service

of America

Introduction

CHARLES RADZIMIŃSKI SOLDIERED
in the War with Mexico with the Third United States Dragoons,
1847-1848, and on the Texas western frontier with the Second
United States Cavalry, 1856-1858. He may have played a distinguished role in the Civil War had he not died prematurely.

In gathering data on Radzimiński in the Mexican War, I
searched for a published history of the Third Dragoons. Much to
my dismay, I found none – not even a memoir by one of its members. I faced the task of reconstructing the history of the unit, a
Regular Army regiment authorized by the Congress for the duration of the war. I had to learn something about the unit in order to
understand what Radzimiński did. Whatever favorably or unfavor-
ably impacted on the regiment also influenced his service. This
relationship led me to include a considerable amount of information about the regiment and, perhaps, to suffer some loss of focus
on Radzimiński.

Radzimiński performed a modest role in the Mexican War. As
a regimental staff officer, he carried out his responsibilities well.
However, he had no opportunity for distinguished combat action
because the staff and half the regiment (five companies) were
assigned to General Zachary Taylor's Army of Occupation along
the Rio Grande. The War Department committed the remaining
five companies to General Winfield Scott's Army for the capture of
the Mexican capital.

General Robert E. Lee,
CSA. (Courtesy Library
of Congress).

The split deployment of the Third Dragoons, an unfortunate Presidential decision that the regimental commander deplored, may have caused some historians to make wrong interpretations of Radzimiński's service. He was assigned to Company D, commanded by Captain Alphonse Duperu, and the monthly company returns list Radzimiński as a second lieutenant of that company. But, he never served with the company. In trying to determine Radzimiński's role, these historians may have followed the fortunes of Company D and, consequently, have credited Radzimiński with taking part in the battles around Mexico City in August and September of 1847. In actuality, Radzimiński at the time performed the duties of regimental quartermaster in Matamoros on the Rio Grande.

In 1855, Radzimiński was appointed a first lieutenant in the Regular Army and assigned to the Second United States Cavalry in Texas. It was his good fortune to serve under one of America's most distinguished military men, Robert E. Lee. Their relationship was more than casual, and Radzimiński made a very favorable impression on Lee and members of his family in Virginia. My essay brings out this relationship.

Essay

DURING THE AMERICAN CIVIL WAR, some sixty Union officers met at Fort Lyon, Virginia, on November 29, 1861, to commemorate the Polish Uprising of 1830 against the Russian tsar. Colonel Wladimir Krzyzanowski, commanding the Fifty-Eighth New York Infantry Regiment ("Polish Legion"), played host to Polish officers of the Army of the Potomac and the German officers of his regiment. The guests included Lieutenant Colonel Joseph Kargé, commanding the First New Jersey Cavalry Regiment. For the Poles, the failed uprising remained a rallying point in an unending quest for Polish independence.[1]

The observance at Fort Lyon was also a tribute to the Poles who dared to rebel against Russia, one of whom was the young Lieutenant Charles Radzimiński. Born of gentry stock in Warsaw in 1805, Radzimiński lived in a land that had been dismembered by Prussia, Austria, and Russia in the late eighteenth century. The tsar gave the area around Warsaw some autonomy by establishing the Congress Kingdom of Poland, with himself as ruler. The ploy, however, did not satisfy the Poles' deep yearning for independence. In November 1830, they rebelled, and Radzimiński joined the Corps of General Józef Dwernicki. The Poles fought for one year until superior Russian might defeated them. Rather than surrender, many units crossed the borders into Prussia and Austria where they were disarmed and interned. Radzimiński escaped to Austria. When Tsar Nicholas I demanded the return of his subjects, Austria forced the enlisted men to go back but demurred with respect to the officers, knowing that death or other harsh punishment awaited them. Meanwhile, looking for a country that would accept the exiles, the Austrian government found the United States willing to do so.[2]

On November 22, 1833, one group of 235 Poles sailed from the Adriatic seaport of Trieste aboard the Austrian frigates *Hebe* and *Guerriera*. Radzimiński was among them. The warships reached Gibraltar and anchored there for two weeks for the repair of damage caused by violent storms in the Mediterranean. The ships continued across the Atlantic to New York, arriving on March 28, 1834. On first contact the exiles found New Yorkers to be indifferent. Those in the Castle Garden area, where the ships had anchored, showed more curiosity than sympathy. Many came out to look the immigrants over. The variety of their dress, and especially their mustaches, fascinated the natives. A number of prominent Americans sought to aid the Poles. In particular, Albert Gallatin, former Secretary of the Treasury in the Administrations of Thomas Jefferson and James Madison, organized the American Relief Committee and asked for money. He also encouraged the formation of similar committees in other cities and the sponsorship of groups of Poles for resettlement.[3]

Radzimiński gravitated to the nation's capital, and in 1840 he found employment as assistant engineer with James River and Kanawha Company of Richmond, Virginia. The company operated and maintained a canal for 147 miles from Richmond to Lynchburg. At the time, the company was also extending the canal westward to Buchanan.[4]

Upon the outbreak of the War with Mexico in 1846, Radzimiński volunteered to serve his adopted country. He received a commission of Second Lieutenant in the Army of the United States and took his oath of office in Washington, D.C. on March 15, 1847. The War Department assigned him on April 9, 1847 to the Third United States Dragoons, one of the ten new regiments

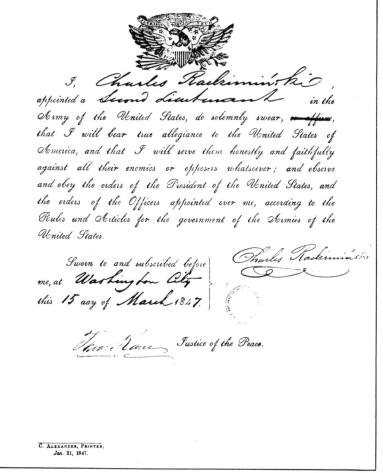

Oath of Office, 2d Lt., March 15, 1847.

organized for and during the war by Act of Congress of February 11, 1847. Colonel Edward G. W. Butler commanded the regiment, which was authorized a strength of 851 personnel, including forty-seven officers. A West Pointer of the Class of 1820, Butler had resigned his commission in 1831 to become a Southern sugar planter. His estate, "Dunboyne," lay on the Mississippi River at

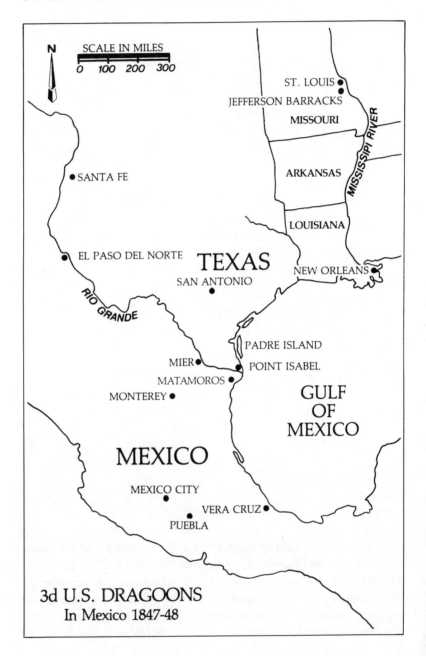

3d U.S. DRAGOONS
In Mexico 1847-48

Bayou Goula, Louisiana. When the United States declared war on Mexico, Butler returned to active duty in the grade of colonel.[5]

During a two-month period of recruiting, Colonel Butler located his headquarters in New Orleans. Meanwhile, each of the ten company captains set up enlistment stations in one of the following states: Michigan, Indiana, New York, Pennsylvania, North Carolina, South Carolina, Alabama, Louisiana, Maryland, and Kentucky. Perhaps not coincidentally, the manpower represented a balance of political sentiment from four free, four slave, and two border states.[6]

Although Radzimiński was assigned to Company G, commanded by Captain Alphonse Duperu of Virginia, he served as a staff officer. Colonel Butler appointed him the regimental quartermaster in official orders of April 23, 1847. It was a new staff position. The War Department authorized each regimental commander to fill the position from among his most qualified subalterns. With thirty lieutenants in the Third Dragoons to choose from, Butler's selection of Radzimiński indicated the colonel's high regard for him. In fact, Butler made the appointment immediately, without waiting for the complete organization of the regiment. Because the order had to be confirmed by the Secretary of War, the colonel forwarded a copy to him. In response, the Adjutant General told Butler that the quartermaster post could not be filled until the regiment was fully recruited and organized. Thereupon, Butler suspended Radzimiński's appointment until June 14, 1847, after the colonel and staff reached Matamoros, Mexico. As regimental quartermaster, Radzimiński received ten dollars in additional pay per month (a 30 percent boost) and forage for two horses. He was responsible for keeping the companies supplied with uniforms, arms, ammunition, and other military items.[7]

Prior to the movement of the Third Dragoons to the war zone, President James K. Polk split the regiment between the armies of General Zachary Taylor located along the Rio Grande and General Winfield Scott in the interior of Mexico. Butler was devastated. He complained to Brigadier General Roger Jones, the Adjutant General: "I cannot express to you the regret and mortification,

which the President's determination to separate the two wings of my Regiment has caused me; as I look upon its efficiency and opportunities of distinction as thereby measurably destroyed."[8]

Companies of the Third Dragoons landed at Point Isabel, Texas and at Vera Cruz, Mexico in May, June, and July of 1847. Colonel Butler sailed from New Orleans for Point Isabel on June 3, 1847, and his headquarters began to function there five days later. Facing the southern tip of Padre Island, Point Isabel served as the base of operations for General Taylor. The five companies landing here marched to Matamoros, where Butler set up his headquarters. The town lay in the region seized the year before by Taylor. But now Taylor had to mark time, as his army was stripped to reinforce General Scott in the bold campaign to capture Mexico City. Taylor's depleted force became an army of occupation, with the headquarters at Monterey.[9]

At Vera Cruz, the five companies of the Third Dragoons landed separately and marched inland to Puebla to join Scott. As Company G with other units departed the port city, the Americans were stopped by manned barricades at the National Bridge. Captain Duperu's dragoons joined the spirited attack upon the Mexicans who were dispersed handily. By July 10, 1847, three companies of the Third Dragoons had arrived in Puebla, and Scott assigned them to the Cavalry Brigade of Colonel William S. Harney. Organizing the brigade into two battalions of six companies each, Harney gave the command of the second battalion to Lieutenant Colonel Thomas P. Moore of the Third Dragoons. Moore's battalion consisted of his three companies and one company each of the First Dragoons, Mounted Rifles, and Mounted Volunteers.[10]

Colonel Harney was not pleased with the Third Dragoons. "The officers and men," Harney wrote to General Scott's adjutant,"

Colonel Edward G. W. Butler commanded the 3d U.S. Dragoons in the Mexican War, and Lieutenant Charles Radzimiński served as his regimental quartermaster and adjutant. (Courtesy of the Historic New Orleans Collection, Louisiana).

[were] all perfectly ignorant of everything like military instruction and discipline." He complained that the officers lacked the desire to learn their duties and appeared to have neither professional self-esteem nor pride in their companies. Yet the dragoons fought well. At Churubusco near Mexico City, the companies of Duperu and Captain Andrew T. McReynolds (K) took part in the battle, August 20, 1847. Both captains were wounded, and Reynolds received a promotion to brevet major for gallant behavior. At El Molino del Rey, September 8, 1847, Lieutenant James C. D. William's detachment fought as part of Major Edwin V. Sumner's cavalry command. Williams was wounded. Lieutenant Hermann Thorn also fought at Churubusco and El Molino del Rey, being wounded in the second battle and brevetted a captain for gallant behavior.[11]

While the southern wing of the Third Dragoons was marching and fighting, the northern wing was immobilized for lack of horses. Butler complained to Washington, telling the Adjutant General that the companies have not received their horses for four months. Consequently, he added, drill on horseback could not be carried on. More serious was the loss of morale. "The long delay in furnishing our horses," Butler wrote the Assistant Quartermaster in New Orleans, "created great dissatisfaction amongst the officers and men of the Regiment." When a shipment of horses from New Orleans and Texas arrived, Butler became upset with their poor quality, and he rejected the animals as unfit for service. The colonel continued to spar verbally over horses with the Quartermaster Department for the remainder of the year.[12]

In September 1847, General Taylor promoted Colonel Butler to the command of the District of Upper Rio Grande head-quartered at Mier, Mexico. The district was a geographical sub-division of Taylor's Army of Occupation and encompassed the military posts along the Rio Grande, including Reynosa, Camargo, Mier, Laredo, and Cerralvo. Butler marched his Third Dragoons to Mier and officially assumed command on September 23, 1847. He promptly appointed Radzimiński the adjutant, who gained the long title, "Assistant Adjutant General of the District of Upper

Rio Grande." In this capacity, Radzimiński wrote a continuous flow of correspondence and orders to military elements in the District. Being a junior officer and staff member, he issued orders in the name of the commander, always stating that "Colonel Butler directs me to say...." Radzimiński, however, did not sign the letters to the commanding general at Monterey. Protocol and military courtesy required that Butler do so, even though most of the correspondence was addressed to the Assistant Adjutant General, whether Lieutenant Colonel W. W. S. Bliss with General Taylor or Captain Irvin McDowell with Brigadier General John E. Wool, who succeeded Taylor.[13]

Often instructions to subordinate units were quite precise so as to avoid ambiguity and misinterpretation and to insure the success of a mission. For the Third Dragoons, which entered the war zone directly from recruiting areas, Butler insisted that instructions be detailed, and his adjutant carried them out. On October 20, 1847, Radzimiński directed Captain John Butler (the colonel's kinsman) to take charge of an escort for a supply train from Mier to Monterey since guerrillas and bandits dared to attack military shipments and the civilian merchants who availed themselves of the convoy. Captain Butler's force consisted of his Company B and Captain James Hagan's Company I, Third Dragoons, one piece of artillery, and two companies of the Tenth Infantry. Butler was advised to take at least six days for the march (to keep from exhausting the animals). Radzimiński specified an exact disposition of Butler's escort. He told the Captain:

> Your order of march will be as follows: – a company of Dragoons in front and one in rear of the train; the two companies of Infantry in the center, with the artillery between them; and an advanced guard and flankers. The companies of Infantry will be relieved by two others of the 10th at Cerralvo, and will remain on duty at that Post till the return of the train.

Radzimiński placed the responsibility for the convoy squarely on Captain Butler. "You will be the Commander of everybody and everything pertaining to the train and escort," Radzimiński wrote,

Lieutenant Charles Radzimiński is appointed Assistant
Adjutant General of the District of Upper Rio Grande at
Mier, Mexico, October 13, 1847, by Colonel Edward G. W.
Butler, commanding the District. (Courtesy National Archives).

"and you will hold the waggon [sic] masters strictly responsible for
the conduct of the teamsters and the condition of their waggons
and teams."[14]

Escort duty never became routine. On March 4, 1848, unknown persons stole two very valuable bars of silver from a train
commanded by Lieutenant Alfred Pleasonton, Second U.S. Dragoons. The theft occurred near Mier where the train encamped for
the night. An intensive search and public offers of pardon to the
thieves led to the recovery of the silver. Nonetheless, the incident
reflected on Pleasonton's competence. Before the commanding

general took disciplinary action, Radzimiński interceded on the young officer's behalf. Butler accepted Radzimiński's counsel and wrote to Captain McDowell at army headquarters:

> I am inclined to think, from the statement of Lieut. Radzimiński, that no blame should attach to Lieut. Pleasonton, the commander of the escort, as Lieut. Pleasonton declined his invitation to pass the very inclement night of the 4th with him, on account of the silver which had been entrusted to his keeping.[15]

Radzimiński's intercession may have kept Pleasonton's military record untarnished. A West Pointer of the Class of 1844, Pleasonton received a brevet promotion for Mexican War service. In the Civil War, he was advanced to major general of volunteers and the command of the Cavalry Corps of the Army of the Potomac.

One unexpected enemy of the Third Dragoons proved to be the unhealthful environment of the Rio Grande Valley. With the advent of cold weather in the fall of 1847, much sickness resulted in Dragoon Camp. In particular, three captains – John Butler, John Sitgraves, and Richard Merrick – became so ill that they were moved into the town of Mier. Greatly concerned, Colonel Butler informed General Jones that "I shall recommend a leave of absence in the case of Captains Butler and Merrick, to enable them to recover their health at my plantation in Louisiana, where they will have the benefit of Mrs. Butler's attention." Before the colonel's recommendation could be carried out, however, Captain Butler died, December 23, 1847, after a confinement of three weeks. The colonel was away with Radzimiński on an inspection of the posts of the District, but he rushed back to Mier. He buried the captain on the evening of December 24 at Dragoon Camp "with the honours of war." Colonel Butler was now all the more determined to insure the recovery of his other two sick captains. He told McDowell that he would transfer Captain Merrick to the Brazos on the Gulf of Mexico and thence to his plantation in the care of Captain Sitgraves.[16]

The New Year ushered in an outbreak of smallpox in Dragoon Camp. Although Butler did his best to stamp out the disease, he had some 100 cases in a month. By the end of February 1848, the smallpox began to abate, but it attacked the Arkansas Cavalry. In May, scurvy followed on the heels of the smallpox. As late as mid-June 1848, when the Americans were leaving Mexico, some fifty dragoons were sick. Radzimiński asked Major Ebenezer S. Sibley, Assistant Quartermaster at Camargo, to provide wagons for evacuating the sick to the river where they would board a steamer for the trip to the Gulf.[17]

Chronic sickness was just one of a series of problems that plagued Colonel Butler, not the least of which was dueling among officers. In mid-19th Century America, men still resorted to dueling as a way of settling differences. Two officers of Lieutenant Colonel J. J. Fay's Tenth Infantry at Camargo engaged in a duel in which one was killed. Fay reported the incident in a "somewhat routine fashion" to the District Commander, who became greatly upset over the loss of the officer. Radzimiński conveyed Butler's strong disapproval of the duel, an act contrary to army regulations. Radzimiński instructed Fay that "the man who shot Capt. [Thomas] Postley will be put in irons and confined till further orders."[18]

Colonel Butler undoubtedly became embarrassed when two of his lieutenants fought a duel. On the morning of March 16, 1848, Lieutenant Joseph H. Maddox shot and killed the Regimental Adjutant, Edward McPherson. Maddox commanded Company H in the absence of Captain Merrick on sick leave. Butler placed Maddox in arrest at once and asked General Wool to convene a general court for the lieutenant's trial. To replace McPherson, Butler chose Radzimiński, who now performed the dual duties of adjutant of the District of Upper Rio Grande and of the Third Dragoons.[19]

Colonel Butler had come to value Radzimiński's conscientious performance of duty. The Louisiana patrician mentioned him in letters to family members. When answering, wife Frances and daughter Isabel included greetings for Radzimiński. The daily association of the commander and his adjutant at District Headquarters gave both the opportunity to become well acquainted. Radzimiński sometimes spoke of his life in Poland and the 1830

Uprising. He had not heard from his mother for many years, not since he became an exile. His letters were intercepted and confiscated by Russian authorities as punishment for rebelling against the tsar.[20]

With the ratification of the Treaty of Guadalupe Hidalgo by Mexico and the United States on May 30, 1848, the American occupation forces began to depart Mexico. Colonel Butler issued Orders No. 15 for the troops in his District on June 15, 1848. In well-coordinated and orderly movements, the Third Dragoons and other units displaced downriver to Palo Alto and Matamoros. Radzimiński's last official act as Assistant Adjutant General was a letter of instructions on June 30, 1848 to Major Sibley, calling on him to provide transportation for two detachments of the Virginia and North Carolina regiments that were assigned the task of rear echelon troops.[21]

On June 30 Radzimiński likewise performed his last known duty in the war zone as adjutant of the Third Dragoons. At Palo Alto, Texas, he signed and issued Regimental Orders No. 14, in which Colonel Butler expressed his appreciation and farewell to his dragoons. The commander singled out their hardships and suffering, especially by disease that decimated the regiment. He praised them for the prompt discharge of the many tasks, and their discipline and subordination in the pursuit of a common goal. His parting hope was that his prayers and best wishes would accompany them "wheresoever their lots may cast them, and whatsoever fortunes may attend them."[22]

Companies of the Third Dragoons sailed from Brazos Island and Vera Cruz for New Orleans and continued to Jefferson Barracks, Missouri, where the regiment was mustered out of the service on July 31, 1848. Captain Albert G. Brackett, military historian, summed up the service of the northern wing of the Third U.S. Dragoons: "This battalion had no opportunity to distinguish itself particularly, though it was a fine body of men and was well disciplined." Brackett confirmed Colonel Butler's regret and prediction that the split and deployment of his regiment in widely separated areas would severely limit the favorable chances for distinction.[23]

Having served his adopted country in war, Radzimiński returned to Washington, D.C. He found employment with the Northeast Boundary Commission as a civilian assistant to Lieutenant Colonel James D. Graham of the Topographical Engineers. The commision was completing the survey of the disputed boundary between New Brunswick, Canada, and Maine, in accordance with the provisions of the Webster-Ashburton Treaty of 1842. Although he was gainfully employed, Radzimiński longed to return to military service. He followed closely the various proposals in the Congress for additional cavalry regiments to protect the Southwestern frontier, and he asked Colonel Butler to intercede for him with "our old Chief [President Zachary Taylor] and obtain for me a commission for whatever rank you may think me most fit." Radzimiński, however, was not interested in becoming a soldier of fortune. He turned down an offer of a cavalry command from a filibustering force that was being organized in the United States for the purpose of freeing Cuba from Spain. He wrote Butler: "Some of the 'leaders' of the 'Cuban expedition' tempted me strongly to join the invading force with a command of cavalry, which I had, thank Heavens, moral courage to decline."[24]

At the Northeast Boundary Commission, Graham assigned Radzimiński the task of a partial re-survey of the historic Mason-Dixon Line, a project handed Graham by the War Department after a tri-state commission requested technical help from the military. Graham was pleased with Radzimiński's survey work. When the colonel was appointed Chief Astronomer of the U.S. Boundary Commission, Radzimiński got the post of Principal Assistant to the Surveyor, Andrew B. Gray.[25]

Radzimiński served under three commissioners. In 1851, when John Russell Bartlett headed the Commission, Radzimiński surveyed the Rio Grande line from El Paso to Doña Ana, New Mexico, for a distance of ninety miles along the river. In 1853, under Commissioner Robert Campbell, he surveyed the lower Rio Grande for 241 miles, from Camargo, Mexico, to the Gulf. Following the Gadsden Purchase, President Franklin Pierce appointed Major William H. Emory the U.S. Commissioner. Emory kept the posts of Chief Astronomer and Surveyor for himself and gave Radzimiński the next ranking position in the U.S. Commission, that of Secretary. While he was still with the Commission in 1855, Radzimiński received the appointment of First Lieutenant, United States Army. Having come to rely on his Secretary, Emory deferred Radzimiński's departure twice.[26]

In March 1856, First Lieutenant Charles Radzimiński met Lieutenant Colonel Robert E. Lee in San Antonio, Texas. The Polish and Virginia patricians arrived there to join their regiment, the Second United States Cavalry ("Jeff Davis's Own"). Recently organized and now stationed in Texas, the unit protected the western settlements against marauding Indians. Both officers possessed and demonstrated the high, professional qualities of the small Antebellum Regular Army. But they proved improbable fates, too, and herein lies the tragedy of Radzimiński. While Lee became the great Confederate wartime commander, Radzimiński suffered an untimely and unheralded, lonely death. Meanwhile fate brought them together in Texas.[27]

In 1856, San Antonio was the largest city in Texas. Its multiethnic population was estimated at 10,500. "Of these," Frederick Law Olmsted wrote, "about 4,000 are Mexicans, 3,000 German, and 3,500 Americans." The renowned traveler observed that "the money-capital is in the hands of Americans, as well as the officers, and the Government." The town had become a military headquarters, beginning with the War with Mexico, 1846-1848, when the U.S. Army built an arsenal and quartered troops on the Military Plaza.[28]

Lee and Radzimiński prepared to travel together to Fort Mason, near the Llano River, and report there to Colonel Albert Sidney Johnston, commanding the Second Cavalry. On March 20, 1856, the day before departure, Lee wrote his wife: "I have left it with Mr. Radiminski [sic] (a native of Poland and a lieutenant in the Second Cavalry) to make provisions for the journey, and have merely indicated that I should be content with a boiled ham, hard bread, a bottle of molasses, and one of extract of coffee — all of which have been provided."[29]

No 67.	War Department,

Sir:

You are hereby informed that the President of the United States, by and with the advice and consent of the Senate, has appointed you First Lieutenant in the Second Regiment of "Cavalry." (Authorized by the Act approved March 3, 1855. Section 5.)

in the service of the United States, to rank as such from the thirtieth _____ day of June, _____, one thousand eight hundred and fifty five (A. de witteler, letter)

You will, immediately on receipt hereof, please to communicate to this Department, through the Adjutant General's Office, your acceptance or non-acceptance of said appointment; and in case of accepting you will report, by letter, to your Colonel, commanding, by whom you will be assigned to a company, and from whom you will receive further orders.

(signed) Jeff. Davis
Secretary of War

First Lieutenant Charles
Second Regiment of Cavalry
Care of May. W. W. Bmay.
Fort Bliss, N. San Antonio, Texas.

Accept'd, Sept. 24, 1855.
Age 36 years.
Born in Poland.

NOTE.—Fill up, subscribe, and return to the Adjutant General of the Army, with your letter of acceptance, the oath herewith enclosed, reporting at the same time your age, residence when appointed, and the State in which you were born.

Radzyminski
a
Maj. Wd. 2d. Army
" " C. O. 2d Cavalry

The two officers reached Fort Mason four days later and were welcomed by the tall, personable Johnston. The colonel was well known and respected in Texas, having served the Republic in the army and as Secretary of War. Johnston gave Lee the command of Camp Cooper with its complement of four companies of the regiment. He assigned Radzimiński to Company K, commanded by Captain Charles J. Whiting and located at Camp Cooper. Lee and Radzimiński continued their journey north for another 165 miles. Enroute they were greeted by a journalist who wrote that he met the two officers "on their way to their post at Comanche Reservation." Located on the Clear Fork of the Brazos River, Camp Cooper was a lonely, primitive outpost and infested with rattlesnakes.[30]

Living in tents at Camp Cooper, the soldiers experienced a difficult life, especially during the winter months. Lee replaced many of the tents with rough buildings built of mud and shingle roofs. Nevertheless, tents continued to serve as troop shelter for the five-year period of the camp. Storehouses were simply wooden frames covered with tarpaulin. Despite its primitive condition, Camp Cooper supported an important role in an army experiment to domesticate the Indian. Located a mile to the north of the camp was the Comanche Indian Reserve (Upper), where some 500 Comanches under Chief Katumse were trying to plant crops and raise cattle. The experiment failed when drought and grasshoppers combined to defeat the effort.[31]

At Camp Cooper, Radzimiński joined an outstanding group of officers. Captain Earl Van Dorn, the senior captain in the regiment, commanded Company A. This dashing Mississipian from Port Gibson was an excellent horseman. Handsome and possessed of unquestionable courage, he had been brevetted a major for his service in the War with Mexico. Captain George Stoneman, Jr. led

Jefferson Davis, Secretary of War, notifies
Charles Radzimiński of his appointment as
First Lieutenant in the United States Army
and assignment to the 2d U.S. Cavalry, June
30, 1855. (Courtesy of National Archives).

Company E, and Captain Theodore O'Hara, Company F. Van Dorn, Stoneman, and Radzimiński's superior, Charles J. Whiting, were West Pointers. O'Hara, a veteran of the War with Mexico, was appointed to the Second Cavalry from civilian life. The Massachusetts-born Whiting took part in the survey of the southern California boundary in 1849 as a member of the U.S. Boundary Commission. At the time, he was a civil engineer like Radzimiński. He had resigned his officer's commission one year after graduating from the United States Military Academy in 1835. Whiting re-entered the service in the grade of captain upon the activation of the Second Cavalry in 1855.[32]

Although most of the regiment was armed with the Springfield rifle-carbine, one squadron (two companies) had carbines with a movable stock and a barrel from ten to twelve inches long. Another squadron carried the breach-loading Perry carbine. Additional arms for all included the Colt Navy revolver and dragoon saber. Horses of distinctive color identified the companies. Thus, as a member of Company K, Radzimiński rode a roan bought by the government.[33]

In early June 1856, Lee led an expedition to punish the marauding Comanches. Company K and Radzimiński did not participate, since Lee chose Companies A and F from Camp Cooper and Companies B and G from Fort Mason. The colonel's two squadrons of 160 men rode over 1,100 miles of drought-stricken land during a forty-day period. The cavalry met no Indians, except for Captain Van Dorn's brief attack on a camp of four Indians.[34]

The presence of the cavalry in 1856 sharply changed the dangerous environment on the Texas frontier. The previous year had been one of disaster. The Indians murdered and pillaged as far south as the Blanco River, within twenty-five miles of Austin. But, the killing and plundering had stopped. As Colonel Johnston reported on August 21, 1856: "Our troops have driven them far into the interior, and I hope they will not venture in again." The regiment carried out patrols along the entire line of the Texas frontier and conducted some thirty minor expeditions during the year of 1856. The operations served to train the troopers for field duty and to make them thoroughly familiar with the terrain. These acquired capabilities were indispensable to survival. Whenever the cavalry engaged the Indians in a firefight, it took place usually after a relentless pursuit for days and even weeks – a pursuit under a tormenting sun during the day and plagued frequently by a lack of water. At night, the soldiers shivered from the cold that often descended on their campsites. The cavalryman's safety depended on his scoring continual victories and maintaining the upper hand. Captain George Price, historian of the Fifth Cavalry, explained: "If troops are defeated in Indian warfare, there is no surrender. If they cannot successfully retreat, those of the number not fortunate enough to be killed outright in the combat will be subjected to cruel tortures for the amusement of the women and children of the warriors."[35]

In the summer of 1856, Colonel Johnston ordered several companies to new locations. The re-deployment followed the departure of the Regiment of Mounted Rifles for New Mexico Territory. Johnston placed Company K at Fort Inge, and Captain Whiting took command of this post on the Rio Leona (near present-day Uvalde). Fort Inge was named after Lieutenant Zebulon Inge, Second U.S. Dragoons, who was killed at the Battle of Resaca de la Palma in 1846. It was not much of a post, having been started in 1849, abandoned twice, and then reoccupied. Consequently, the few buildings, constructed of upright poles and thatched roofs, were in a dilapidated condition. Some of the men had to live in tents. Undoubtedly, Radzimiński found the primitive environment of Fort Inge not much different from that at Camp Cooper. The drab life taxed the ingenuity of the officers to keep the men occupied. Some desertions and frequent absences occurred; Company K recorded forty-six absences without official leave (AWOL) during 1856.[36]

Radzimiński saw Lee again on September 16, 1856, when the colonel and Major George Thomas stopped at Fort Inge on their way to Ringgold Barracks where they were to sit on a court martial. Company K gave the two travelers a hearty welcome. As Lee noted, the post consisted of about a dozen small buildings: officers' quarters, barracks, bakery, hospital, commissary, quartermaster, guard house – all located loosely around a central parade ground. Although these temporary buildings were of a rough construction, they were whitewashed and neatly kept. Their appearance indicated the pride and discipline of the company.[37]

With Company K the sole occupant of Fort Inge, Captain Whiting commanded the post. Radzimiński was the second-in-command and also performed the duties of quartermaster and subsistence officer. Second Lieutenant William W. Lowe (USMA, 1853) served as post adjutant. Whenever Whiting was away on detached service (usually for court martial duty), Radzimiński assumed command of Fort Inge. In February 1857, both Whiting and Lowe were absent, and therefore Radzimiński carried out all the officer duties, including those of post adjutant. He prepared the Post Return for February 1857. Writing in his usual clear hand, Radzimiński reported himself and fifty-four enlisted men present for duty. Whiting and Lowe, with twenty-six men, were away on a scouting mission.[38]

In May 1857, the War Department relieved Colonel Johnston of the command of the Second Cavalry and of the Department of Texas. The army ordered him to Washington to take charge of an expedition to Utah. Brigadier General David E. Twiggs assumed command of the Department, and Lee took over the regiment in July. Lee kept it continually engaged, patrolling and skirmishing on a long line, from the Red River in the north to Fort McIntosh (near Laredo) on the Rio Grande. Company K, too, rode hard in these actions, having displaced westward some forty miles to Fort Clark in March 1857. Captain James Oaks commanded the post and the garrison, consisting of his own Company C and Company K. Radzimiński knew the post, having paused there with the wagon train of the U.S. Boundary Commission in 1854. The fort lay on the road between San Antonio and El Paso and became a stop of the San Antonio-El Paso Mail Line. Although Fort Clark offered a more pleasant environment than Fort Inge, Radzimiński was forced by poor health to take sick leave for nearly seven months. Upon

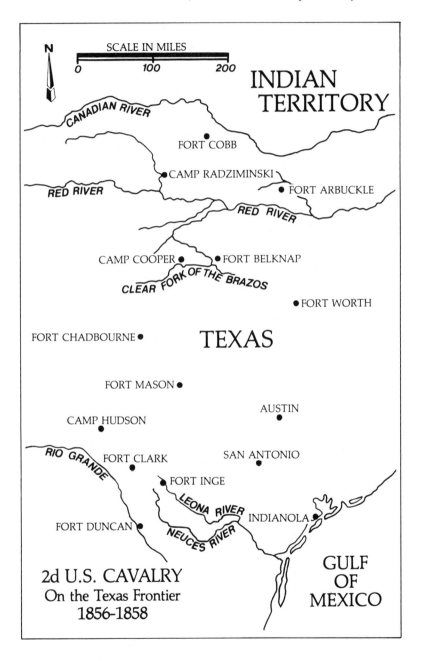

SCALE IN MILES

0   100   200

INDIAN
TERRITORY

CANADIAN RIVER

●FORT COBB

●CAMP RADZIMINSKI

RED RIVER

●FORT ARBUCKLE

RED RIVER

CAMP COOPER ●   ●FORT BELKNAP

CLEAR FORK OF THE BRAZOS

●FORT WORTH

FORT CHADBOURNE ●

TEXAS

FORT MASON ●

AUSTIN
●

CAMP HUDSON
●

RIO GRANDE   FORT CLARK
●

SAN ANTONIO
●

●FORT INGE

LEONA RIVER

FORT DUNCAN ●   NEUCES RIVER   INDIANOLA ●

2d U.S. CAVALRY
On the Texas Frontier
1856-1858

GULF
OF
MEXICO

189

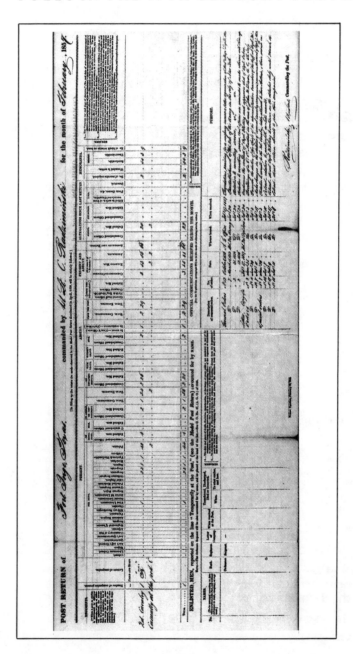

Post Return of Fort Inge, Texas, commanded by First Lieutenant Charles Radzimiński, for the month of February 1857. (Courtesy of National Archives).

his return in November, Company K again had its normal complement of three officers. Among its eighty-two enlisted men, un-
authorized absences dropped significantly during 1857. Only seven
AWOLs occurred, and two of these were apprehended.[39]

In April 1858, the War Department instructed General Twiggs
to prepare the Second Cavalry for a march to Fort Leavenworth,
Kansas, where it would link up with Colonel Johnston's Utah Expedition. Accordingly, Twiggs relieved the regiment of duty in
Texas and placed it under the command of Major Thomas (Lee
was absent). The companies began to assemble in the vicinity of
Fort Belknap, camping along the Clear Fork of the Brazos and
other streams. Thus, Company K rode to Fort Mason in April,
and at the end of June it set up camp along Perch Creek.[40]

The Second Cavalry did not leave Texas because its marching
orders were revoked. Radzimiński, however, could not have made
the long journey to Fort Leavenworth and Utah. His rapidly failing health again caused him to apply for leave. The regimental
surgeon issued a certificate of disability, and on July 17, 1858, four
days before Company K left the Brazos River for Camp Hudson,
Major Thomas placed him on leave for seven days. The commander's considerate action gave Radzimiński relief from arduous duties,
while the regimental adjutant gained some time to refer the matter
to the Department of Texas in San Antonio. On August 4, 1858,
in Special Orders No. 29, the commanding general granted Radzimiński a leave of absence of two months, effective from July 17.[41]

Radzimiński left the Brazos River on July 24, 1858, and traveled to Memphis, Tennessee. While registering at the historic
Gayoso House, he asked about Colonel J. Knox Walker, a prominent citizen whom he apparently intended to visit. Walker, unfortunately, was away from the city. That evening Radzimiński dined
at the hotel; but feeling sick, he requested a doctor. Upon examina-
tion of the patient, the physician diagnosed the illness as tuberculosis. The following morning, August 18, Radzimiński was
found in his room, sitting on the side of his bed, dead. Although
he had been gravely ill, neither he nor his physician anticipated an

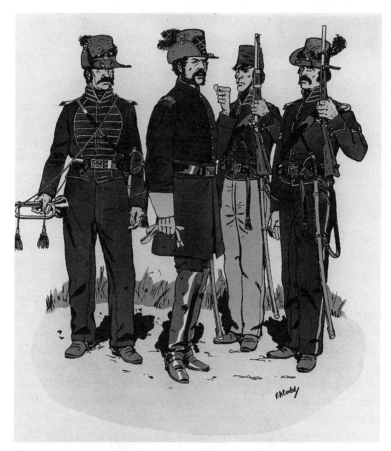

First Lieutenant Charles Radzimiński wore the company officer's uniform in the photograph (second from left). (Photo courtesy of the Company of Military Historians).

early death. Radzimiński, therefore, left no instructions as to the disposition of the remains and effects. The Pole died alone, without the benefit or comfort of family and friends.[42]

Some details of Radzimiński's demise are contained in a letter to John B. Floyd, Secretary of War, from Thomas P. Shallcross, Special Agent of the Post Office Department at Wheeling, Virginia.

Site of Camp Radziminski in Kiowa County, Oklahoma.
Mount Radziminski and Wichita Mountains in background.
(Photo by Stanley F. Radzyminski, 1957).

Shallcross did not know Radzimiński and happened to be in Memphis. From a feeling of civic duty, however, he took the initiative to inform the War Department of the lieutenant's death. He wrote that Radzimiński had in his possession about $145 in cash and a draft on the U.S. Treasury for $837.00. The deceased also left an extensive wardrobe. His remains were placed in a metalic coffin and deposited in a private vault temporarily. The hotel manager delayed the burial for only four days. Shallcross explained: "Col. Walker failing to arrive and doubting the propriety of keeping the body in the vault longer, Mr. Knowlton of the Gayoso House had it deposited in the Cemetery yesterday morning [August 22]."[43]

Radzimiński's friends were saddened by his untimely death. The news reached Colonel Lee at Arlington, Virginia, where he had taken leave to settle family matters in the fall of 1857. Lee told the family of the death of his lieutenant, and daughter Agnes wrote her brother, Lieutenant Fitzhugh Lee in California, that Radzimiński died while on his return home [presumably Washington, D.C.]. Her cousin Ella Calvert was especially affected. "Poor Ella is of course much distressed," Agnes wrote, "has put on mourning for him."[44]

193

Radzimiński's regimental commander in the War with Mexico, Edward Butler, was also deeply moved, and he sought to make contact with the lieutenant's mother in Poland. He wrote the Secretary of State, General Lewis Cass, urging him to attempt through the U.S. Minister to Russia to locate the mother, so that the son's effects could be sent to her. On October 5, 1858, the Secretary asked Minister Francis W. Pickins "to set on foot an enquiry in the proper quarters concerning the whereabouts of the family." He enclosed a copy of Butler's letter and instructed Pickins to "report the result to this Department." Apparently Cass never received a report.[45]

Radzimiński's gravesite in Memphis soon disappeared from memory, but the officers of the Second Cavalry did not forget him. In September 1858, Captain Van Dorn led four companies of the regiment (A, F, H, K) and a detachment of the First Infantry Regiment into Indian Territory where he set up a supply station on Otter Creek, in the shadows of the Wichita Mountains. Van Dorn named the base "Camp Radziminski," and the War Department recognized the designation. As an added tribute, the cavalrymen called a prominent, nearby peak "Mount Radziminski." Van Dorn's thrust into Indian Territory signaled the army's change to offensive tactics. While the infantry manned the camp, the cavalry mounted expeditions in search of hostile Indians. Camp Radziminski remained an active base of operations until December 1859, at which time it was abandoned.[46]

Earl Van Dorn, with whom Charles Radzimiński served in the 2d U.S. Cavalry Regiment in Texas. After Radzimiński's untimely death in 1858, Captain Van Dorn established a base of operations in Indian Territory (Oklahoma) and named it Camp Radziminski. During the Civil War Van Dorn was a major general of cavalry in the Confederate Army. (Photo courtesy of The Library of Congress).

During its brief history, Camp Radziminski was the scene of much horseracing, a favorite pastime of the officers. They owned the sleek race horses, whereas the sturdy animals they rode in the field were bought by the government. At Camp Radziminski, Lieutenants William B. Royall and Fitzhugh Lee wagered and raced their favorite mounts in the presence of the entire garrison. Lee on Bumble-Bee won. In the regiment, Van Dorn's horse won more money than any other. Radzimiński, too, had owned a race horse named Minnehaha. This beautiful mare, trained in the Baucher system, was capable of great endurance. Minnehaha became the property of Colonel Lee. However, she was left behind in Texas when the regiment departed for the North, upon the outbreak of the Civil War in 1861.[47]

What would have been Radzimiński's role in the Civil War had fate not intervened to strike him down? He served with a group of superb officers, the best to be found in the Regular Army and in civilian life. Twenty of the thirty-four officers appointed initially were West Pointers; the remaining fourteen came from civilian pursuits. Nearly all of them fought in the War with Mexico. The Secretary of War, Jefferson Davis, selected the officers for the Second U.S. Cavalry with great care. Thus, they demonstrated their quality not only in Indian fighting but also in the War of the Rebellion, when this regiment alone produced eighteen generals for the Union and Confederate armies. Radzimiński, too, served with professional skill and devotion, and he rode in the company of great commanders, none greater than General Robert E. Lee. Would Radzimiński have followed Lee into the Confederacy? Perhaps one should not speculate on the service that might have been. As a soldier of the Southwest frontier, Charles Radzimiński made his mark, albeit modest, on America's past.[48]

Camp Radziminski historical marker on U.S. Highway 183, one mile north of Mountain Park, Oklahoma. (Courtesy of Stanley F. Radzyminski).

Napoleon Kościalowski

and the

Santa Fe Trace

Battalion

Introduction

NAPOLEON KOŚCIALOWSKI'S LIFE in America ended on a tragic note. In Poland, he was consumed with a fighting passion for regaining his country's independence. Virtually the entire Polish gentry joined him in this great crusade. They rebelled against Russia in November 1830, but the failure of the uprising and the deportation of the leaders to the United States left them bitter and disillusioned. Many adjusted in time and began a new life. Charles Radzimiński is a prime example. Others included Florian Liskowacki, who became a banker in Memphis, Tennessee, and later in San Antonio, Texas. Paul Sobolewski and Eustachy Wyszynski turned to writing and publishing. In 1842, they began the publication of the first Polish magazine in the English language: *Poland, Historical, Literary, Monumental, and Picturesque.* Kazimierz Gzowski departed for Canada, where he excelled as an engineer and bridge builder. Queen Victoria knighted him for his achievements. Hipolit Oladowski rose to be a Confederate colonel in the Civil War, serving as General Braxton Bragg's ordnance officer in the Army of Tennessee. Wladyslaw Sokalski settled in Troy, New York, from where his son George Oscar entered the United States Military Academy. George Sokalski is the first Polish American graduate of West Point, Class of 1861, and classmate of prominent Civil War generals Emory Upton and Judson Kilpatrick.

Napoleon Kościalowski seemed to adjust well at first. He married, raised a family, and engaged in engineering in St. Louis, Missouri. He served in the War with Mexico and retained a strong desire to continue military life. Despite high level political backing, he did not gain a Regular Army appointment as an officer. It is evident that he failed to make his marriage work, and he left the family in Jacksonville, Illinois, for military service, which seemed to give him comfort. Nevertheless, he and his fellow exiles carried their anguish over a subjugated homeland to their dying days. One of them expressed the sadness in verse:

Oh! Poland, my Poland, the fond heart will break
Of him who hath loved thee, and bled for thy sake,
Oh! why have I lived the dark moment to see
When thou hast no longer a shelter for me![1]

Appreciation for Research Assistance

Napoleon Kościalowski's great granddaughter, Marilyn Williams Thomas of Ingram, Texas; Michael E. Pilgrim, Tod J. Butler, William E. Lind, Rebecca Livingston, National Archives, Washington, D.C.; Jacek M. Nowakowski, Polish Museum of America, Chicago, Illinois, Rev. Ladislas Siekaniec, St. Louis, Missouri; Wayne C. Temple, State Archives, Springfield, Illinois; Barbara Stole, Missouri Historical Society, St. Louis, Missouri; Thomas F. Schwartz, Illinois State Historical Library, Springfield; Charles Brown, St. Louis Mercantile Library, St. Louis, Missouri; Carol M. Antoniewicz, Washington University Libraries, St. Louis, Missouri; Naval History Division, Washington, D.C. Navy Yard; Mary Beck, State Archives, Jefferson City, Missouri; Inter-Library Loan Department, El Paso Public Library; and cartographer George Shimshock, El Paso, Texas.

Essay

CAPTAIN NAPOLEON KOŚCIALOWSKI'S
company of Missouri volunteers, "The Kosciuszko Guards," boarded
the steamer *Archer* at St. Louis and sailed up the Missouri River to
Fort Leavenworth on September 1, 1846. The 113 civilian-soldiers
formed one of nine companies of the Third Missouri Regiment. As
volunteers in the regiment, the soldiers elected John Dougherty of
Liberty, Missouri, their colonel.[2]

The Third Regiment and several other Missouri units were
recruited for service in the War with Mexico. The Third Regiment,
however, never saw action. In less than three months after President James K. Polk made his call for troops, July 16, 1846, the War
Department disbanded the regiment. Between September 29 and
October 2, 1846, the nine companies were mustered out of the service and left for home, greatly dissatisfied. Thus, Kościalowski's
rush to the colors ended in disillusion.[3]

The discharge of the Third Missouri Regiment upset the citizens of Missouri. The St. Louis *New Era* called attention to the
wasted money and effort: "The regt. of Vols. now at Leavenworth
and ordered to be disbanded will, at the time of discharge, have
cost the Government upward of *fifty thousand dollars*. But the expense, trouble, and loss of time of the officers and privates will

amount to a much larger sum." The editor of *The Weekly Tribune* of Liberty showed less restraint. He charged the President and the Secretary of War with bungling the war effort, and he urged the President to dismiss the Secretary and then to resign himself.[4]

The emotion of the newspaper editors was understandable. Nevertheless, the unfolding military situation in New Mexico made the anticipated opposition less formidable. It is true that General Stephen W. Kearny had asked for 1,000 footmen to augment his small army of 2,700 soldiers against an estimated force of some 5,000 Mexicans, and Missouri Governor John Edwards responded with nine companies of the Third Regiment. Reaching Bent's Fort in Colorado, Kearny felt confident enough to accomplish his mission with the forces under his command. In a letter to the War Department on August 1, 1846, he predicted the capture of Santa Fe by August 20, and he proved to be a prophet. The favorable turn of events caused the War Department to disband the Third Regiment. Governor Edwards agreed with the decision, although he regretted disappointing "many good and brave men and gallant officers."[5]

To native Missourians the name Kościalowski undoubtedly sounded strange. In mid-19th Century America, however, Westerners valued a person's ability more than his background. Kościalowski, nonetheless, had experienced a challenging life. Born into a gentry family in Warsaw on May 16, 1812, he lived in the Congress Kingdom of Poland, whose ruler was Russian Tsar Alexander I. When the Poles rose up against Russian domination in November 1830, young Napoleon joined the uprising. Russian might, however, crushed the rebellion after one year of fighting. With many others, Kościalowski escaped to Austria, where the Hapsburg monarchy, wishing to rid itself of the Polish freedom fighters, obtained the consent of the United States government to deport the exiles to America. The 22-year-old Kościalowski was one of 235 exiles who arrived in New York on March 28, 1834.[6]

Most of the exiles had trouble adjusting to the American environment, even with the modest help of an American Relief Committee that sought to resettle the Poles. Kościalowski left for

Napoleon Kościalowski, Polish aristocrat and exile, had blue eyes, brown hair, was fair-complexioned, and stood five feet, eight inches tall (ca. 1850). (Photo courtesy of Marilyn Williams Moore, great granddaughter of Ingram, Texas).

Albany, New York, with a group of about twenty-five compatriots. Being an accomplished artist, he found employment in Albany, but soon moved to the Northampton Female Seminary in Massachusetts and joined the teaching staff. Later he traveled to Illinois, where a number of other Poles had gone, in anticipation of receiving a land grant from the Andrew Jackson Administration. Thus, by 1839, Kościalowski was in Jacksonville, where he courted 18-year-old Mary Ann D. Chenoweth of Kentucky and married her on November 12, 1839. They bought land and engaged in farming, but not successfully. Kościalowski's life was further marked by two deep tragedies. His close friend and fellow-exile, 30-year-old Edward Mlodzianowski, died at his side in 1842. The following year he lost his second child, Clara Polonia, who had just passed her first birthday. Kościalowski decided to change his environment and his fortunes. He moved with Mary Ann and son Paul Casimir to St. Louis where Sophia Carah was born on July 13, 1844. In St. Louis, Kościalowski formed a surveying and engineering partnership with H. W. Leffingwell, located at 42 North Fourth Street. He was thus engaged when the war with Mexico occurred.[7]

Kościalowski's first attempt to serve the nation ended with the quick dismissal of the Third Missouri Regiment. Before gaining a new opportunity, however, he had the honor to greet the return of Colonel William Doniphan and his First Regiment of Missouri Mounted Volunteers. St. Louis Mayor Bryan Mullanphy appointed Kościalowski to a Committee of Arrangements composed of twenty-one distinguished citizens. On July 2, 1847, some 7,000 residents gave Doniphan's veterans a rousing welcome. The ceremonies included a parade and speeches by James B. Bowlin and Thomas Hart Benton.[8]

Shortly after Doniphan's soldiers left for their homes, President Polk called on Governor Edwards for a new military effort. On July 20, 1847, the President asked the Governor to organize a special battalion of volunteers for the protection of the Santa Fe Trail, that vital link between "the States" and the conquered territory of the Southwest. Scores of supply trains, mostly military, were being attacked by Indians. These depredations had to be stopped, and the battalion would be the counter force. Edwards first asked Colonel Doniphan to take command of the unit. But, having just returned from a successful year-long campaign, Doniphan declined the offer. The Governor turned to William Gilpin, who accepted the responsibility. The 32-year-old Gilpin likewise had come home from the war, having served as a major under Doniphan. The 3,000-mile march and the fighting of the regiment had left Gilpin physically weak and sick. Nonetheless, he answered the challenge to serve the nation once again.[9]

Gilpin took command of some 500 volunteers who confirmed the Governor's choice by electing Gilpin lieutenant colonel of the battalion. Companies A and B were mounted. Company C was a foot artillery battery. Companies D and E were infantry. Kościalowski recruited and commanded Company E, which was mustered into federal service for the duration of the war as "Captain Koscialowski's Company, Gilpin's Battalion, Missouri Infantry." Later, the designation was changed to "Company E." The 35-year-old Kościalowski raised the company of eighty-six officers and men from the St. Louis area. On September 3, 1847, the *St. Louis Daily Reveille* reported: "We understand that the company of the Koskiusko [*sic*] Guards is full and that the members will meet at their rendezvous at 8 o'clock on Monday morning, preparatory to their departure for Fort Leavenworth on board the steamer *Amelia*."[10]

All five companies were mustered into the service at Fort Leavenworth by Lieutenant Colonel Clifton Wharton, who commanded the frontier post. The War Department tasked him with supplying Gilpin's Battalion for the field. Unfortunately, the two lieutenant colonels harbored mutual feelings of antagonism, and Wharton's support proved minimal. Gilpin stated bluntly: "That officer displayed towards the companies of the battalion and myself the most unrelenting malice." Gilpin charged that Wharton supplied the battalion with old and defective arms, worn and decayed camp equipment, insufficient transportation, and no medical supplies. Furthermore, he reported: "Time to furnish themselves with clothing was denied. The soldiers and the whole rushed upon the wilderness in a raw and crippled condition."[11]

Despite the poor condition of his battalion and the expected severity of the weather, Gilpin began his mission at once. By October 6, 1847, all companies had departed Fort Leavenworth, preceded by the two cavalry companies, which rode out two weeks in advance of the others. Marching along the Trail for some 200 miles, the battalion reached Walnut Creek on November 1. Here Gilpin paused while he learned of Indian attacks from passing trains and travelers from New Mexico. Accordingly, he made his plans for the winter, resulting in a further march to Fort Mann. He garrisoned the post with the three dismounted companies, under the command of the senior officer, Captain William Pelzer. With the two mounted units, Gilpin rode into Eastern Colorado near Bent's Fort and camped in the wintering areas of the Cheyenne and Arapahoe Indians. His purpose was to intimidate the Indians from attempting raids on the Santa Fe Trail in the spring.[12]

Before leaving Fort Mann, Gilpin ordered Pelzer to repair and enlarge the small stockade. Located just east of Cimarron Crossing, it was built by the Quartermaster Department as a wagon repair station in the spring of 1847. The army never intended that Fort Mann be a post for soldiers. Gilpin's adjutant, Lieutenant Henry L. Routt, condemned the post. "Fort Mann is certainly the most desolate and uninteresting place upon the face of the earth," he wrote. "I never want to see such another, and never will, if I should be fortunate to see Missouri again." The bleak, depressing environment of Fort Mann probably was not so damaging to discipline and morale as the strained relationship between Company E, recruited with "native" Americans, and the all-German companies, C and D. Few of the officers and men of the latter units spoke English, so that hostility towards them had grown quickly, not only in Company E but also in the two cavalry companies. Thomas L. Karnes, Gilpin's biographer, wrote that "a hostile nativism immediately developed in the other three companies, and the immigrants concluded that the 'Americans' would as soon attack them as they would the Indians."[13]

Under the circumstances, Fort Mann needed a strong and experienced commander. But Pelzer possessed little, if any, leadership. He was a habitual drunk who demoralized the men by his sodden appearance among them. No sooner had Gilpin left the fort than Pelzer demonstrated gross lack of judgment. He met with a group of Pawnee Indians outside the stockade and shook hands

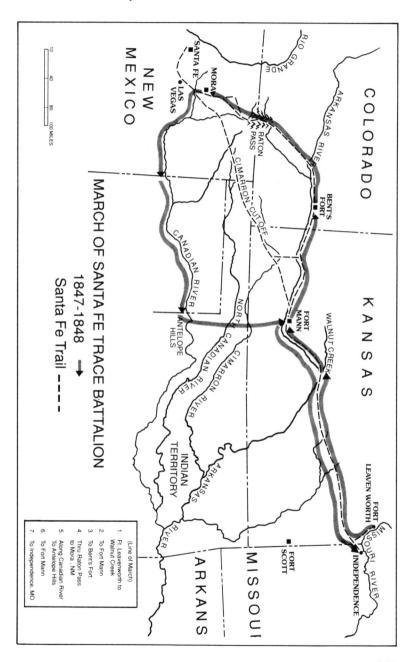

MARCH OF SANTA FE TRACE BATTALION
1847-1848
Santa Fe Trail ----►

(Line of March)
1. Ft. Leavenworth to Walnut Creek
2. To Fort Mann
3. To Bent's Fort
4. Thru Raton Pass to Mora, NM
5. Along Canadian River To Antelope Hills
6. To Fort Mann
7. To Independence, MO

with their chiefs in friendship. He invited the Indians into the fort but betrayed them when he attempted to take them prisoner. Suspecting Pelzer's motive, the Pawnees dashed for the gate, and Pelzer ordered his men to fire. In the bedlam that followed, four Indians were killed and two, taken prisoner. The rest got away, including some wounded. Calling the incident "a small skirmish," Pelzer reported the circumstances to Gilpin, adding that "i understood that Capt. Koscialioski [sic] had forbitten his men to load after i hat given the Command, he could not see any necessity of it." The St. Louis *New Era* placed the blame squarely on Pelzer. "We have reason to believe," the editor said, "that he was strongly advised to refuse the Indians admission to the fort, but he utterly disregarded such counsel."[14]

Kościalowski's "disobedience" of the order to fire demonstrated his outrage of Pelzer's conduct. But Pelzer was not the only odd character in the command. First Lieutenant Amandus Schnabel secretly recruited a female to serve as his concubine. Caroline Newcome posed as Private Bill Newcome, and she traveled with the troops to Fort Mann. Other members of Company D may have known of this fraud. Nonetheless, Bill Newcome was totally unmasked when she became pregnant and deserted. Earlier, Schnabel had been reprimanded for spreading a rumor that Company E planned an attack on the two German companies. Other incidents at Fort Mann involved hunting accidents in which some soldiers shot at one another.[15]

The insufferable conditions at Fort Mann drove Kościalowski to desperate action. He fired off a letter of resignation directly to the Adjutant General in Washington, thereby bypassing his commanding officer, Colonel Gilpin. Perhaps he did not intend to resign but merely wanted to gain the attention of the War Department to the circus of events at Fort Mann. In Washington, Brigadier General Roger Jones, the Adjutant General, did not take the time to refer the matter to Gilpin for his recommendation. Instead, Jones quickly accepted the resignation. In reply, Jones wrote Kościalowski that his letter of resignation has been submitted to the Secretary of War and in a contradictory breath added that "you are hereby discharged from the Service of the United States." Before the Adjutant General's response reached Kościalowski, Gilpin rescued the captain from the purgatory of Fort Mann.[16]

In organizing his battalion for the spring campaign, Gilpin ordered Kościalowski's Company E and an artillery detachment (one six-pounder) under Lieutenant Phillip Stremmel from Company C to join him at Bent's Fort. Although Kościalowski had submitted his resignation, he nevertheless loyally carried out Gilpin's order. He set out with the augmented force on January 21, 1848, travelling up the Arkansas River. After a weary march of thirty-five days, during which he lost half the oxen to starvation, Kościalowski reached Gilpin's camp on February 24. Meanwhile, Gilpin had been rounding up fresh animals for his command. He mounted some 300 soldiers on mules, and in early March he rode south across the Raton Mountains to Mora, New Mexico. Here he bought supplies and transportation before commencing a campaign against the Apaches and Comanches camped along the Canadian River. He planned to attack them before they began their annual northward migration. Tactically, the more damage and casualties he inflicted on the tribes, the better. But, strategically, he sought to disorganize the tribes and keep them away from the waters of the Arkansas River and the Santa Fe Trail. The latter objective was the more important. The battalion marched down the Canadian River to Texas and across the Panhandle during March and April, reaching the Antelope Hills in Indian Territory by May 18. Gilpin met few Indians. Warned of the advance of the soldiers, the Apaches and Comanches hastily abandoned their campsites and fled, meanwhile setting the plains on fire for hundreds of miles. At Antelope Hills, Gilpin turned due north and arrived near Fort Mann by the end of May. He believed he had pacified the western half of the Santa Fe Trail, and so he concentrated his entire command at Fort Mann for the protection of the eastern half.[17]

Having marched long and hard against the Indians, Kościalowski felt a sense of accomplishment. Gilpin's call to join him at Bent's Fort for the spring campaign proved the colonel's need for his service, and now the captain sought to withdraw his resignation.

With the help of his business partner, Leffingwell, he got the support of prominent individuals in St. Louis: Mayor John M. Krum, Brigadier General William Millburn of the Missouri Militia, and Thomas T. Gantt, U.S. District Attorney. The trio penned a letter to the Secretary of War in which they asked that Kościalowski's resignation be laid aside since the letter had not gone through Gilpin. They said that Gilpin had persuaded Kościalowski to continue in the service and that Gilpin assumed the letter of resignation would not be acted upon by the War Department. "Under this impression," they said, "the Captain has continued in duty ever since, and has given great satisfaction to Major Gilpin."[18]

If Kościalowski had realized at the time that his tender of resignation would lead to a financial crisis for the family, he assuredly would not have submitted it. Prior to campaigning with Gilpin in the wilderness, Kościalowski forwarded his pay accounts to his wife in St. Louis. The resignation issue, however, caused the army paymaster to stop Kościalowski's payments, thus depriving the family of its only source of income. Mayor Krum underscored this problem: "In as much as his duties were *not* suspended (nor does he now wish them suspended), it is the object of this [letter] to have his resignation set aside, and the captain to be considered as on continued duty, entitled to continued pay."[19]

Kościalowski also gained the support of Ceran St. Vrain and William Bent, two famous Westerners who were partners in the firm of Bent, St. Vrain & Company, Indian Traders. Before a justice of the peace in St. Louis, June 3, 1848, St. Vrain and Bent testified that Captain Kościalowski and Company E reached Bent's Fort and joined Gilpin about February 20, 1848, and that Gilpin had ordered him up from Fort Mann. Furthermore, they said that Kościalowski's Company E formed a part of Gilpin's command when it departed Bent's Fort for the Mora settlements of New Mexico. They stressed that at Bent's Fort Kościalowski "was constantly performing duty as a captain with energy and efficiency; that...from their own observations as well as from conversation with Lt. Col. Gilpin, said Capt. Koscialowski is an excellent officer and is so regarded by all who know him." Leffingwell forwarded the two letters to Missouri Congressman in Washington James B. Bowlin, who delivered the correspondence to the Secretary of War on June 17, 1848. The last-minute appeal did some good. Although Secretary of War William L. Marcy accepted Kościalowski's original tender of resignation, the Secretary delayed the effective date to July 1, 1848, thus validating the captain's service during Gilpin's successful spring campaign along the Canadian River. Lieutenant Caleb S. Tuttle was promoted to captain and the command of Company E. Three months later, on September 30, 1848, the company was mustered out of the service.[20]

Upon its discharge at Independence, Missouri, Kościalowski's company of volunteers had marched more than 3,000 miles across an untamed landscape and mostly during the severe months of winter. As a unit of the Santa Fe Trace Battalion, Company E surpassed the heralded march of Colonel William Doniphan's First Regiment of Missouri Mounted Volunteers. In 1847, William Cullen Bryant, senior editor of the *New York Evening Post*, hailed Doniphan as the modern Xenophon by a comparison to the ancient Xenophon who had successfully led a force of 500 Greeks some 3,500 miles in retreat from the Persians. Gilpin, who also made the earlier march with Doniphan, described the conditions surrounding the longer march of the Santa Fe Trace Battalion: "The field of operations having been in the middle of the wilderness, the sufferings, privations, and hardships, cheerfully borne by the soldiers of my command, have been greater than those of any other battalion in the public service."[21]

Having served his country, Kościalowski returned to Jacksonville with his family. He worked as an architect, but he longed for a military career. The time was right since the Congress was debating proposals for several additional Regular Army regiments for the defense of the Southwest frontier. In support of his application for a commission, he marshaled the political leadership of Illinois, thus displaying a remarkable degree of persuasion. On February 20, 1850, twenty-two prominent citizens addressed a recommendation to the Secretary of War, George W. Crawford, for an appointment for Kościalowski in the grade of major. They stressed his

Springfield Illinois, Feb. 20 1850

Hon: Secretary of War.
Sir:

Capt. Kozialowski who will present you this letter, is an applicant for an appointment of Major in the new Regiments proposed to be raised by Congress. I have always placed my name among others, to a general recommendation of him for their appointment, but I now desire to say, a little more specifically, that I shall be much gratified if he shall be successful in his application. He is very anxious — a gentleman of great favour with his acquaintance has, and can sustain himself with any capacity for arduous (voyage) has a military connection, fitting him peculiarly for the position he seeks —

Your Obt Servt
Lincoln

military service in Poland and in America. They called him an accomplished civil engineer. The signers included Governor Augus-
tus C. French, Secretary of State David L. Gregg, State Treasurer
John Moore, future Civil War Governor Richard Yates, and Abraham Lincoln. The future president showed his enthusiastic support of Kościalowski by adding a personal letter to Crawford. "He
is in every way a gentleman," Lincoln wrote, "a great favorite with
his acquaintances here, and (as I understand, without any capacity
for deciding myself), has a military education, fitting him peculiarly for the position." Kościalowski delivered the two letters in person to the Secretary, with Lincoln's letter serving as an introduction. Unfortunately, the effort did not bring any result.[22]

In Jacksonville, Kościalowski was the architect for the design
and construction of the Illinois Institution for the Blind. He produced a well-designed building. Next, the State House Board of
Commissioners, with Governor French as President, engaged him
as architect for construction work around the base of the State
Capitol. While Kościalowski superintended the project in Springfield, the family resided in Jacksonville. Upon completion of the
work, Kościalowski abruptly departed Illinois, without the family.
He evidently had developed a serious marital problem. In fact, he
did not wait for his final pay. Son Paul Casimir collected the
money due his father.[23]

At age forty-one, Kościalowski reached a low point in his life.
Unhappy and groping for an environment where he could feel
secure and needed, he turned once again to soldiering. He enlisted
in the U.S. Marine Corps at New York on December 22, 1853.
Because of his military experience and capability, Kościalowski
was quickly promoted to corporal (in six months) and to sergeant a

*Abraham Lincoln recommends Captain
Napoleon Kościalowski to the Secretary of War
for an appointment to Major, United States
Army, February 20, 1850. (Courtesy of Illinois
State Historical Library, Springfield).*

year later. His duties included assignment to the navy training ship, *U.S.S. John Adams*. Notwithstanding rapid promotions, his service became erratic. After one year in grade, he was demoted. Again, the Corps promoted him to sergeant, but reduced him three weeks later. Finally, he was discharged at Gosport, Virginia, on May 5, 1858. Broken in spirit and health, he drifted to Washington, D.C., and, following a long illness, he died there on May 30, 1859. He was remembered and supported in death by members of the Masonic Order, which he first joined in St. Louis in 1845. The Washington *Daily National Intelligencer* reported the death, mentioning his service as a captain in the U.S. Infantry during the Mexican War and being a Polish exile of 1830. The *Intelligencer* said: "Friends and brother Masons are respectfully requested to attend his funeral this day, May 31st, at four o'clock, at the Washington Infirmary." The cemetery and gravesite, if they survived, are unknown.[24]

Kościalowski's life reflected the tragic experiences in America of many Polish exiles, who arrived with him in 1834. They came from the best families of Poland, from the educated and cultured gentry class, but who lived on the labor of serfs. They pledged their lives and fortunes in the struggle for an independent Poland. These patriots looked at the failure of the Uprising of 1830 as a temporary setback, and they were determined to remain in Europe where they could assemble quickly for the next try for freedom. Their deportation to the United States, therefore, placed them effectively out of reach of any future action (and this distancing had been the whole purpose of the Austrian government). In America, they found a strange culture and a tongue difficult for most Slavs to master. One freedom here hit them hard—the right to work. Many were able to adjust when they applied their linguistic, artistic, and engineering skills. But for others, the need simply to survive forced them into menial, dirty work that debased their dignity and pride.[25]

Nobel Laureate Henryk Sienkiewicz described the difficulties for a European to adjust to social democracy in America. Based on his astute impressions from his travels in 1876-1878, he writes:

In our country [Russian-occupied Poland] a person of society who is compelled by circumstances to engage in manual labor as the only means of earning a living becomes degraded both in his own and in popular opinion — despite everything we say and write to the contrary. To be frank, he loses caste, severs all ties which united him with his previous estate, and sinks into the so-called lower classes of society.[26]

Kościalowski, too, shared the problem of adjustment, and he personally was aware of the humiliation and suffering of fellow exiles. Undoubtedly this knowledge weighed heavily on his soul. But Kościalowski also demonstrated a noble Polish characteristic — an intensely patriotic duty to defend one's country against its enemies. This attribute surely prompted him twice during the War with Mexico to volunteer to serve his adopted country and to recruit a company of fellow-citizens for the war. As a captain in the indomitable Santa Fe Trace Battalion, Napoleon Kościalowski soldiered under the most difficult conditions. And, with William Gilpin and his battalion, he contributed a proud page to American history.

Notes

Analysis and Comparison

1. A clue to Grzelachowski's birthplace of Gracina lying in Eastern Poland (now a part of the Soviet Union) could be the stationing of Major Tomasz Grzelachowski and his battalion at Brześć Litewski (Brest-Litovsk) in 1883. Military men have a strong desire in peacetime to serve in their home areas.
2. Mrs. Isaac D. Rawlings, "Polish Exiles in Illinois," *Transactions of* *Illinois State Historical Society*, Vol. 13 (1927), 95.
3. Great granddaughter Marilyn W. Thomas to author, October 17, 1986, author's files.
4. *Report: James River and Kanawha Company, 1840/41-1844/45*, (Richmond, Virginia: Shepherd and Colin Printers, 1846), 70-72, 423, Virginia State Library, Richmond.

Louis William Geck
Soldier, Merchant, and Patriarch
of Territorial New Mexico

1. *Las Animas* (Colorado) *Leader*, July 31, 1874, p. 3, provided by historian Stanley L. Cuba of Denver, Colorado. In the 19th Century, the press employed the term "Polander" for a native of that country.
2. "Captain Nathan Boone's Journal," *Chronicles of Oklahoma*, Vol. VII (Oklahoma City: The Oklahoma Historical Society, 1929), 58-105.
3. Geck's Pension Records, Records Group 15, Veterans Administration, National Archives.
4. The author theorizes that young William Geck came to America with a group of Polish emigres from the Uprising of 1830. Some 300 Polish leaders fled to Austria, following the collapse of the rebellion. Although the tsar demanded their return, the Austrian government got the United States to agree to take them. On March 28, 1834, two Austrian warships landed 235 exiles in New York. Smaller groups followed. As a minor and subject of the tsar, William could not be listed on the ship's manifest. But he undoubtedly had the tacit approval of the captain. For an account of the Polish exiles, see Jerzy Jan Lerski's *A Polish Chapter in Jacksonian America* (Madi-

son: The University of Wisconsin Press, 1958).

5. Interview of granddaughter Albina Geck Provencio, Anthony, New Mexico, February 15, 1977.

6. Clifford Dowdey, *Lee* (Little, Brown and Company, 1965), 64-66.

7. Geck's Enlistment Papers, Records Group 94, Adjutant General's Office, National Archives.

8. Albert G. Brackett, *History of the United States Cavalry* (New York: Harper & Brothers, 1865; reprint ed., New York: Greenwood Press, Publishers, 1968), 35, 37.

9. Theo. F. Rodenbough and William L. Haskin, *The Army of the United States* (New York: Maynard, Merrill & Co., 1896), 156.

10. "John Fynn Memoirs," U.S. Army Military History Institute, Carlisle Barracks, Pennsylvania, 2. Fynn served in Company H, 1839-1844.

11. Brackett, *History of U.S. Cavalry*, 5.

12. Rodenbough, *Army of the U.S.*, 155.

13. Geck's Military Records, RG 94, AGO, National Archives.

14. Rodenbough, *Army of the U.S.*, 156; and Geck's Service Records.

15. Report from the Adjutant General's Office, War Department, December 13, 1887, in Geck's Pension Records, National Archives. The War with Mexico officially ended on February 2, 1848, with the signing of the Treaty of Guadalupe Hidalgo.

16. Aurora Hunt, *Major General James Henry Carleton* (Glendale, California: The Arthur H. Clark Company, 1958), 46-47, 97.

17. Interview of Albina Geck Provencio, February 15, 1977.

18. Affidavit of Charles H. Coleman in favor of Sarah A. Geck's pension claim, 1894, Louis William Geck Papers, New Mexico State Records Center and Archives (NMSRCA), Santa Fe.

19. *Rio Grande Republican* (Las Cruces, New Mexico), June 14, 1890.

20. In the Civil War, Buford commanded a division of cavalry in the corps of General Nathan Bedford Forrest.

21. Geck's Pension Records; George W. Cullum, *Biographical Register of the Officers and Graduates of the U.S. Military Academy* (Boston: Houghton, Mifflin and Co., 1891), II:37; Francis B. Heitman, *Historical Register and Dictionary of the United States Army* (Washington: Government Printing Office, 1903), I:919.

22. Brackett, *History of U.S. Cavalry*, 82-83, 127-28; and Heitman, *Historical Register*, II:400.

23. Geck's Service Records, National Archives.

24. James E. Heath, Commissioner of Pensions, to William Geck, June 7, 1851, Louis William Geck Papers, NMSRCA.

25. Interview of Albina Geck Provencio, February 15, 1977.

26. Interview of Geck's granddaughter Lillian Weir Dukeminier, El Paso, Texas, October 2, 1978.

27. John Trevitt to Don L. Geck, August 24, 1852, Louis William Geck Papers. John Trevitt was a graduate of West Point, Class of 1844.

28. The *vara* varied from 32.808 inches (Mexican) to 39.90544

inches (Alicante), according to J. Villasana Haggard, *Handbook for Translators of Spanish Historical Documents* (Austin: The University of Texas, 1941).

29. Louis William Geck Papers. The disputed land is believed to be Geck's bounty from the Federal government.

30. Documents of Third Judicial District, County of Doña Ana, Territory of New Mexico, November 18, 1852 and November 1854, Louis William Geck Papers.

31. Entry in Geck family Bible, Louis William Geck Papers.

32. Interview of great grandson Fletcher Newman, El Paso, Texas, February 11, 1977.

33. Leon C. Metz, *The Shooters* (El Paso: Mangan Books, 1976), 93.

34. Interview of Caroline Geck Weir, May 23, 1937. Writers Program of Work Progress Administration (WPA), NMSRCA.

35. The birth was premature, and the death of Beatriz may have been influenced by a prior accident. Twelve men broke into the Geck home one night in search of money. They knocked Geck unconscious and assaulted his wife. A posse caught four of the desperadoes and hanged them, Interview of Caroline Geck Weir, May 23, 1937, WPA Writers Program.

36. Entry in prayer book given to W.C.P. Geck, in remembrance of his First Holy Communion. Interview of daughter Albina Geck Provencio, March 24, 1977.

37. *Anthony* (New Mexico) *Times*, July 4, 1976. The *Times* identified the school as "St. Michael's Brothers College," in St. Charles, Missouri. The name is believed to be in error, according to the Archives of the Catholic Archdiocese of St. Louis. (Telephone interview of Rev. A.M. Rieckus, archivist, May 4, 1981). Catholic Directories for the years 1860-70 show that in St. Charles the Jesuit Priests and Brothers conducted the St. Stanislaus Novitiate (Julie Colombo, secretary, Archdiocese of St. Louis to author, April 24, 1981, author's files).

38. *Anthony Times*, July 4, 1976. Interview of Albina Geck Provencio, February 5, 1977.

39. William Geck's Pension Records. Sarah Aguirre was born April 25, 1847.

40. S. H. Newman III, "The Las Cruces Thirty-Four Answers the School Question," *Password*, Vol. 14, No. 1 (Spring 1969), 13 (a publication of the El Paso County Historical Society). On December 22, 1863, Geck was allowed to proceed from Fort Craig to Doña Ana by the Provost Marshal, First Lieutenant Thomas A. Young, 5th Infantry, California Volunteers (Pass No. 129, Provost Marshal's Office, Fort Craig, New Mexico December 22, 1863, from the National Archives). Young authorized the travel for Geck, his wife, one child, and four teamsters with one carriage and a train of three wagons loaded with groceries and whiskey. Perhaps Geck had gone to St. Louis to buy merchandise as well as to bring Sarah and daughter Jesusita home for the holidays.

41. Interview of Lillian Weir Duke-minier, April 5, 1979; and *Las Cruces* (New Mexico) *Citizen*, March 6, 1958. Children's dates of birth are recorded in the family Bible; Sarah's year of birth comes from the 1880 Federal Census of Doña Ana County.

42. Interview of Lillian Weir Duke-minier, April 5, 1979: and *Las Cruces Sun-News*, August 3, 1977.

43. *The Mesilla* (Arizona) *Times*, July 27, 1861.

44. Proclamation of August 1, 1861, *War of the Rebellion: A Compilation of the Official Records of the Union and Confederate Armies*, 128 vols. (Washington: Government Printing Office, 1880-1901), IV:20; and Warren A. Beck and Ynez D. Haase, *Historical Atlas of New Mexico* (Norman: University of Oklahoma Press, 1969), 31.

45. *Official Records*, IV:22. Geck's name is listed as "L.W. Greek." George Grigg shows the name as "L.W. Greke," in *History of the Old West* (Las Cruces: Bronson Printing Co., 1930), 71.

46. A number of invoices have survived. One of $65 for 130 pounds of soap was signed by Captain J.H. Beck on May 30, 1862, and approved by Colonel Thomas Green, commanding the 5th Regiment of Texas Mounted Volunteers, Louis William Geck Papers; and War Department Collection of Confederate Records, Citizen File (Louis William Geck), Records Group 109, National Archives.

47. Louis William Geck Papers, NMSRCA.

48. Louis William Geck Papers.

49. Luis W. Geck to General J.H. Carleton, Albuquerque, New Mexico, December 25, 1862, RG 109, War Department Collection of Confederate Records.

50. Certification by C.P. Hall, Clerk of Second Judicial District Court, February 21, 1863, Louis William Geck Papers.

51. Abraham Cutler to Francisco Fanio, February 26, 1863, Louis William Geck Papers.

52. Frank Higgins to Colonel George W. Bowie, April 13, 1863, Louis William Geck Papers.

53. Special Orders No. 22, Headquarters, District of Arizona, Franklin, Texas, April 28, 1864; Major John C. McFerran to Lieutenant Cyrus H. DeForrest, Aide-de-Camp and Acting Assistant Adjutant General, Department of New Mexico, Santa Fe, June 6, 1864, Louis William Geck Papers.

54. General Orders No. 65, Headquarters, District of Arizona, Franklin, Texas, December 3, 1864, Louis William Geck Papers.

55. Frank Higgins to Major Joseph Smith, December 12, 1864, Louis William Geck Papers. There appears to be no record of a reply from Smith.

56. Special Orders No. 46, Headquarters, Department of New Mexico, December 8, 1864, *Official Records*, Vol. 41, Part 4, 803.

57. A search of the military records of the Department of New Mexico at the National Archives failed to identify any documents related to the board's action, in Charles A. Shaughnessy, Military Archives Division, to author, June 5, 1981, author's files.

58. Bills of Lading, Louis William Geck Papers.

59. *Daily New Mexican* (Santa Fe), November 4, 1955.
60. Interview of Charles C. Geck, grandson of Beatriz Aguirre Geck, May 17, 1937, WPA Writers Program, NMSRCA.
61. Interview of Lillian Weir Dukeminier, November 21, 1978. Caroline Geck Weir said in 1937 that the melodion was manufactured in 1850 (WPA Writers Program).
62. *Las Cruces* (New Mexico) *Citizen*, March 6, 1958.
63. Interview of Jess D. (Jay) Weir, Jr., Geck's great grandson, January 17, 1977. An artist of Las Cruces painted the house shortly before it was demolished. Mr. Weir owns the painting.
64. Pension claim of Louis William Geck, No. 15,582, Mexican War, May 10, 1888, National Archives.
65. Wm. E. McLean, Acting Commissioner, Pension Office, Department of the Interior, to S.H. Newman, El Paso, Texas, October 3, 1888, Louis William Geck Papers; and Mexican War Pension, Survivor's Brief (Wm. Geck), National Archives.
66. *Rio Grande Republican* (Las Cruces), June 14, 1890, p. 3; *Esquela* (printed funeral announcement), original in the possession of Albina Geck Provencio, interview of February 15, 1977; and Record Proof of Marriages, Births, and Deaths, in support of Widow's Brief (Sarah Geck), Mexican War Pension, August 16, 1891, National Archives.
67. Interview of Jess D. (Jay) Weir, Jr. and author's visit to the cemetery, January 17, 1977.
68. Widow's Brief (Sarah A. Geck), Mexican War Pension, October 16, 1891, National Archives.
69. S.H. Newman to Isaac D. Laferty, December 11, 1893, Pension Records, National Archives.
70. Wm. Lochren to S.H. Newman, December 8, 1893, Louis William Geck Papers.
71. *Esquela*, Louis William Geck Papers.
72. Interview of Lillian Dukeminier, March 12, 1982.
73. Interview of Lillian Dukeminier, October 2, 1978.
74. *Esquela* prepared by Bagues Mortuary, Los Angeles, California, Louis William Geck Papers.
75. In one instance in 1857, Geck preferred charges against his former post commander at Doña Ana, Major Oliver L. Shepherd, Louis William Geck Papers.
76. The term "Anglo" is used herein as a matter of convenience, to differentiate those of non-Hispanic origin. The term, however, is misleading, since it implies a person of Anglo-Saxon ancestry.
77. If the author's theory should prove correct that young William came to America with the Polish exiles from the Uprising of 1830, Geck would have spent more than two years with them in Austria.
78. Interview of Albina Geck Provencio, February 15, 1977.
79. Interview of Caroline Geck Weir, May 23, 1937, WPA Writers Program. Mrs. Weir's daughter Lillian Dukeminier told the author that Geck's original surname was *Guykoski*, although no documentation has been found. Pronounced the same in Polish, the name would be *Gaykowski* or *Gajkowski*.
80. Pension Records of William Geck, National Archives.

Martin Kozlowski
Role in New Mexico History

1. *El Paso Times*, December 2, 1987, January 14 and July 3, 1990.
2. William Clarke Whitford, *Colorado Volunteers in the Civil War* (Denver: The State Historical and Natural History Society, 1906), 84.
3. Myra Ellen Jenkins and Albert H. Schroeder, *A Brief History of New Mexico* (Albuquerque: The University of New Mexico Press, 1974), 50-51.
4. Whitford, *Colorado Volunteers*, 84.
5. Martin Hardwick Hall, *Sibley's New Mexico Campaign* (Austin: University of Texas Press, 1960), 138-40: and Whitford, *Colorado Volunteers*, 97.
6. Hall, *Sibley's Campaign*, 140-60; Jenkins, *History of New Mexico*, 51; and Colonel John M. Chivington, "Retrospective – The Prospective," Microfilm No. P-L 12, Bancroft Library, University of California – Berkeley, 35.
7. Whitford, *Colorado Volunteers*, 84.
8. Ovando J. Hollister, *Boldly They Rode: A History of the First Colorado Regiment of Volunteers* (Lakewood, Colorado: The Golden Press, Publishers, 1949) (reprint ed. of original published in 1863), preface.
9. Whitford, *Colorado Volunteers*, 84; Kozlowski's Pension Records, Records Group 15, National Archives; and Piotr Wandycz, *The Lands of Partitioned Poland, 1795-1918* (Seattle: University of Washington Press, 1974), 137-41. Elena Kozlowski could neither read nor write. She retained only the phonetic pronunciation of her maiden surname. The spelling "Celenan" appears in several official documents. It is the Spanish phonetic equivalent of Elena's name. According to family tradition, Kozlowski traveled to America with a younger brother, Charles, who wanted to become a priest. While on board ship, Elena gave birth to a son. Undoubtedly this child died prematurely because the 1860 Federal Census does not list him. Interview of great grandson Joseph M. Kozlowski, Albuquerque, New Mexico, October 27, 1983.
10. Kozlowski's enlistment papers, Records Group 94, Records of the Adjutant General's Office, 1780-1917, National Archives.
11. Report of Adjutant General's Office to Commissioner of Pensions, Kozlowski's Pension Records, National Archives. Kozlowski's son Joseph was born in Missouri in 1854. Wife Elena may have been living near Fort Leavenworth, but on the Missouri side of the river. Kozlowski's second son Thomas was born at Los Lunas, New Mexico, in January 1857, Federal Census of 1860, New Mexico, Vol. 2, San Miguel County, M-653, Roll 713.

12. Albert G. Brackett, *History of the United States Cavalry* (New York: Harper & Brothers, 1865), 137-38; Aurora Hunt, *Major General James Henry Carleton* (Glendale, Calif.: The Arthur H. Clark Company, 1958), 141-42; and House Executive Document No. 1, Part II, 34th Congress, 1st Session, Annual Report for 1855 of the Secretary of War, 59-61.
13. Herbert M. Hart, *Old Forts of the Far West* (New York: Bonanza Books, 1965), 36.
14. Brackett, *History of Cavalry*, 172-73; Adjutant General to Commissioner of Pensions, December 4, 1902 (listing Kozlowski's part in Indian fighting), Kozlowski Pension Records; and House Executive Document No. 2, Part II, 35th Congress, 1st session, Annual Report for 1857 of Secretary of War, 135-41.
15. James H. Tevis, *Arizona in the '50's* (Albuquerque: The University of New Mexico Press, 1959), 61-64.
16. Hart, *Old Forts*, 36.
17. Kozlowski's Pension Records; and Deed Book No. 4, 243, San Miguel County Court House, Las Vegas, New Mexico. Three of the boundaries were based on natural terrain features and remain identifiable, but the western boundary (fence) has no meaning today.
18. Acting Commissioner of General Land Office to Commissioner of Pensions, May 14, 1903, Kozlowski's Pension Records. The land warrant was No. 80728. The final assignee was John C. Julian who used it

to obtain land at Little Rock, Arkansas.
19. Deed Book No. 4, 243, San Miguel County Court House; and Colonel J.M. Chivington, "The First Colorado Regiment," Microfilm No. P-L 11, Bancroft Library, University of California-Berkeley, 6.
20. "Trouncing the Texans," *The Daily Optic* (Las Vegas, New Mexico, March 14, 1881: Chaplain Alexander Grzelachowski, 2d New Mexico Volunteers, to Captain Gurden Chapin, Acting Assistant Adjutant General, Department of New Mexico, August 4, 1862, Register of Letters Received, Headquarters, Department of New Mexico, 1854-1865, microfilm F801R42 1980, Reel 16, Frame 0436, Library of the University of New Mexico, Albuquerque. Major John Chivington's report, March 28, 1862, *Official Records*, IX, 539, speaks of an unnamed volunteer aide, guide, and interpreter.
21. Morris F. Taylor, *First Mail West: Stagecoach Lines on the Santa Fe Trail* (Albuquerque: University of New Mexico Press, 1971), 1,3,20; Colonel Henry Inman, *The Old Santa Fe Trail* (New York: The Macmillan Company, 1898), 147-49; and *New Mexico: A Guide to the Colorful State*, WPA Writers' Program (New York: Hastings House, Publishers, 1940), 238.
22. Federal Census of 1870, Town of Pecos, San Miguel County, Territory of New Mexico, 9, New Mexico State Archives and Records Center (NMSRCA), Santa Fe; interview of great

grandson Joseph M. Kozlowski, Albuquerque, NM, October 27, 1983.

23. James F. Meline, *Two Thousand Miles on Horseback: Santa Fe and Back* (London: Sampson Low, and Son, and Marston, 1868), 110, 113-14.

24. Inman, *Old Santa Fe Trail*, 148-49, 490.

25. Testimony in Spanish recorded by Manuel Varela, Justice of the Peace, 8th Precinct, County of San Miguel, January 28, 1878, Criminal Case No. 921, NMSRCA, Santa Fe.

26. *Las Vegas* (New Mexico) *Gazette*, February 2, 1878; and Santa Fe *Weekly New Mexican*, February 9 and July 20, 1878, and March 22, 1879.

27. Criminal Case No. 898, Territory of New Mexico vs. Martin Kozlowski, March 1879 Term, San Miguel County District Court, NMSRCA, Santa Fe.

28. "Court Proceedings of San Miguel County," Santa Fe *Weekly New Mexican*, March 22, 1879.

29. Criminal Case No. 898, Commitment and Execution, U.S. vs. Martin Kozlowski, NMSRCA; and Federal Census of the Territory of 1880, Las Vegas Precinct 5026, San Miguel County, NMSRCA. The laws of the Territory of New Mexico defined Murder in the Fourth Degree (applicable to Kozlowski's case) as follows: "The killing of another in the heat of passion, without a design to effect death, by a dangerous weapon, in any case except such wherein the killing of another is herein declared to be justifiable or excusable, shall be deemed murder in the fourth degree," in Hon. L. Bradford Prince, comp., *The General Laws of New Mexico* (Albany, New York: W.C. Little & Company, Law Publishers, 1882), 260.

30. Writ of Sheriff Hilario Romero, March 11, 1881, Criminal Case No. 898, San Miguel County District Court Records, NMSRCA; and Santa Fe *Daily New Mexican*, March 15, 1881. This newspaper's story on Kozlowski's release from jail contains gross errors. It identifies him as Joseph Kasloski. That Martin had taken wood and other materials from the old Pecos Mission is true, but he had the permission of Bishop Jean B. Lamy. No son was struck and killed by lightning, nor was Kozlowski imprisoned for killing his only son and committing the alleged crime while in an insane condition. Kozlowski was not insane. With reference to the Pecos Ruins (Mission of Nuestra Señora de Los Angeles de Pecos), see John L. Kessell, *Kiva, Cross, and Crown: The Pecos Indians and New Mexico, 1540-1840* (Washington, D.C.: National Park Service, Department of the Interior, 1979), 474-75.

31. Las Vegas, New Mexico *Daily Optic*, March 8, 1881; and Francis C. Kajencki, "Alexander Grzelachoswki: Pioneer Merchant of Puerto de Luna, New Mexico," *Arizona and the West*, Vol. 26, No. 3 (Autumn 1984), 243-60.

32. Interview of Jennie (Mrs. Patrick) Kozlowski, Albuquerque, NM, October 27, 1983; and Federal

Census of 1900, Bernalillo County. Precinct No. 26, NMSRCA.

33. Kozlowski's Pension Records; and Federal Census of 1880, Pecos, San Miguel County, NMSRCA.

34. Albuquerque City Directory for 1901, University of New Mexico Library, Albuquerque; Federal Census of 1900, Bernalillo County, Precinct No. 26, NMSRCA. For many years family members lived at 462 West Santa Fe, S.W. Sacred Heart Church is located at 412 West Stover Avenue, S.W.

35. Kozlowski's Pension Records: Certificate of Death of Martin Kozlowski, Sacred Heart Church, Albuquerque, issued to author October 18, 1982; author's visit to Santa Barbara and San Jose Cemeteries, Albuquerque, October 27, 1983.

36. Hollister, *Boldly We Rode*, 59; Inman, *Santa Fe Trail*, 148; and *Official Records*, IX, 533.

37. Parish Register of Baptisms, I:113, 143: II:16, 75, 127: Parish Marriage Register, 1904-1939, 59, St. Anthony's Church, Pecos, New Mexico.

38. Interview of Isabel Gutierrez, Albuquerque, NM, July 1, 1984. She worked at Tex Austin's guest ranch for several summers; interview of Mike Disimone, manager of E. E. Fogelson Enterprises, Dallas, Texas, July 3, 1984. Disimone said that, after Fogelson married Hollywood actress Greer Garson, some people mistakenly refer to the Forked Lightning spread as the "Greer Garson Ranch." A new, or restored, structure occupies the original site of the Kozlowski tavern; Thomas Kozlowski died of a heart attack in 1939 at age 82. At the time, he was enroute to son Raymond's ranch at Pajarito, a small community south of Albuquerque, Interview of Thomas's granddaughter, Josie K. Woodlief, San Leandro, Calif., June 26, 1984.

39. Inman, *Old Santa Fe Trail*, 149; *Who Was Who in America* (Chicago: A.N. Marquis Co., 1943), 1888; *The Denver* (Colorado) *Republican*, September 2, 1906; and Whitford, *Colorado Volunteers*, "Introductory."

40. Whitford, *Colorado Volunteers*, 84. The author's research visits to New Mexico are believed to have occurred before the turn of the century. He died in 1902, having drafted his manuscript that was published four years later. Kozlowski left the ranch in 1898. The ranch house in Whitford's photograph appears deserted.

Alexander Grzelachowski New Mexico's "Padre Polaco" and Pioneer Merchant

1. *New Mexico Historical Review*, Vol. 18, No. 4 (October 1943): 398, 402.

2. William J. Parish, *The Charles Ilfeld Company* (Cambridge: Harvard University Press, 1961), 316.

3. Telephonic interview of grandson Alexander Grzelachowski of Albuquerque, New Mexico, August 20, 1984, author's files.

4. Frazier Hunt, *The Tragic Days of Billy the Kid* (New York: Hastings House Publishers, 1956), 131.

5. Telephonic interview of grandson Charles C. Grzelachowski, Fort Worth, Texas, May 10, 1983. The name "Gracina" could possibly be "Kracina," since the grandson said he remembers only the phonetic pronunciation from his father Adolph. The author believes that Grzelachowski was born in eastern Poland, in the area seized by the Soviet Union in World War II (1939).

6. Hrabia (Count) Seweryn Uruski, et al, eds., *Rodzina: Herbarz Szlachty Polskiej [Family: Heraldry of Polish Gentry]*, 15 vols. (Warszawa: Bookstore of Gebethner and Wolff, 1908), V:38, National Library, Warsaw, Poland.

7. Józef Grzelachowski to brother Alexander, March 24, 1883. Original in possession of granddaughter Oma Gallegos, Las Vegas, New Mexico. Today *Carskie Siolo* is the city of Pushkin, Russia.

8. Paul Horgan, *Lamy of Santa Fe: His Life and Times* (New York: Farrar, Strauss, and Giroux, 1975), 62.

9. Rev. W. J. Howlett, *Life of the Right Reverend Joseph P. Machebeuf, D.D.* (Pueblo, Colorado: N.P., 1908), 150-51.

10. Christine L. Kroesel, Director of Archives, Diocese of Cleveland, Ohio, to author, October 5, 1982, author's files.

11. Horgan, *Lamy of Santa Fe*, 74.

12. Horgan, *Lamy of Santa Fe*, 70, 73.

13. Howlett, *Joseph Machebeuf*, 159; and *El Palacio* (The Museum of New Mexico, Santa Fe), Vol. 65, No. 1 (February 1958): 27, 29.

14. Howlett, *Joseph Machebeuf*, 157-165; Horgan, *Lamy of Santa Fe*, 108; and *El Palacio*, 29.

15. Fray Angelico Chavez, OFM, *Archives of the Archdiocese of Santa Fe. 1678-1900* (Washington, D.C.: Academy of American Franciscan History, 1957), 259.

16. Warren A. Beck and Ynez D. Haase, *Historical Atlas of New Mexico* (Norman: University of Oklahoma Press, 1969), 27; and author's visits to San Miguel del Vado, New Mexico, May 10, 1978 and March 18, 1990.

17. Microfilm, "Records of Baptisms, 1852," San Miguel del Vado, New Mexico, New Mexico State Records Center and Archives (NMSRCA), Santa Fe.

18. In 1864 the congregation of Our Lady of Sorrows Church outgrew its small building and moved to another location, one block west of the plaza. The former church was torn down in 1870 to make way for a two-story mercantile store owned by Charles Emil Wesche, in Milton W. Callon, *Las Vegas, New Mexico: The Town That Wouldn't Gamble* (Las Vegas, New Mexico: Las Vegas Daily Optic, 1962), 45.

19. Ovando J. Hollister, *Boldly They Rode: A History of the First Colorado Regiment of Volunteers,*

1863; Reprint ed., Lakewood, Colorado: The Golden Press, Publishers, 1949), 57.
20. Beck and Haase, *Atlas of New Mexico*, 27.
21. *Lamy Memorial: Centenary of the Archdiocese of Santa Fe, 1850-1950* (Santa Fe: Schifani Brothers Printing Co., Inc., 1950), 64; Parish, *Ilfeld Company*, 94, 316; and *El Palacio*, Vol. 65, No. 2 (April 1958): 74.
22. Chavez, *Archives of Santa Fe*, 259.
23. Louis H. Warner, *Archbishop Lamy: An Epoch Maker* (Santa Fe: Santa Fe New Mexican Publishing Corporation, 1936), 177.
24. "District Court Records, 1847-1856," Santa Ana County, Territory of New Mexico, 80-90, NMSRCA. In 1876 the original Santa Ana County was annexed to Bernalillo County and thus disappeared from the map of New Mexico, in Beck and Haase, *Atlas of New Mexico*, 45.
25. *Lamy Memorial*, 67.
26. *Index to Real Property*, Book 3, page 29, San Miguel County Courthouse, Las Vegas, New Mexico.
27. "List of Commissioned Officers," *Description Book of Military Units*, NMSRCA. The National Archives has no record of Grzelachowski's service in the Civil War.
28. *The War of the Rebellion: A Compilation of the Official Records of the Union and Confederate Armies*, 128 vols. (Washington: Government Printing Office, 1880-1901), IX:487-93.
29. *Official Records*, IX: 535, 538-39, 553.

30. Martin Hardwick Hall, *Sibley's New Mexico Campaign* (Austin: University of Texas Press, 1960), 155-60. Hall makes no mention of Grzelachowski.
31. "Trouncing the Texans," *The Daily Optic* (Las Vegas, New Mexico), March 14, 1881, 4.
32. *Description Book of Military Units*, NMSRCA.
33. F. Stanley, *The Puerto de Luna New Mexico Story* (Privately printed, 1969), 9.
34. Stanley, *Puerto de Luna Story*, 9.
35. Ralph Emerson Twitchell, *The Leading Facts of New Mexican History*, 5 vols. (Cedar Rapids, Iowa: The Torch Press, 1917), V:252, 265; and Stanley, *Puerto de Luna Story*, 9. Henry Göke came to Sapello in 1867. He prospered as a merchant. Later he became the president of the Las Vegas Savings Bank.
36. Deed Book No. 5, San Miguel County Court Records; and Parish, *Ilfeld Company*, 38. Grzelachowski's lot measured 120 feet by 42 feet, and it held improvements.
37. Report of the Quartermaster General, October 20, 1869, *House Executive Document* (HED) 1, 41st Congress, 2d Session (Serial 1412), II, part 2, 213; and Report of the Quartermaster General, October 20, 1868, HED 1, 40th Congress, 3d Session (Serial 1367), III, part 1, 830. Charles C. Grzelachowski had his grandfather's army contract in his possession for many years, interview of May 10, 1983.
38. Bill of Lading, A. Grzelachowski to Juan Antonio Sarracino, Las Vegas, New Mexico, Janu-

ary 3, 1873, Bernalillo County Civil Case No. 522, NMSRCA.

39. Printed Sales Invoice of A. Grzelachowski; and Parish, *Ilfeld Company*, 22.

40. Case of Alexander Grzelachowski vs. Louis Badreaud, March 1876, District Court Records of San Miguel County, NMSRCA.

41. Federal Census of 1870 for Las Vegas, San Miguel County, Territory of New Mexico, 18.

42. Printed Invoice of A. Grzelachowski, Dealer in General Merchandise, Las Vegas, New Mexico.

43. Parish, *Ilfeld Company*, 21-22, 29, 316.

44. Grzelachowski's obituary in *Las Vegas* (New Mexico) *Daily Optic*, May 28, 1896; and A. Grove Day, *Coronado's Quest* (Berkeley: University of California Press. 1964), 227, 356n3.

45. Stanley, *Puerto de Luna Story*, 9.

46. Hunt, *Tragic Days of Billy The Kid*, 131; and Notice of Possession of A. Grzelachowski (320 acres of land at Rincon del Alamo Gordo), December 7, 1880, San Miguel County Court House, Deed Book 15, 172.

47. Application of Jack D. Rittenhouse of Albuquerque, New Mexico, for the registration of the Alexander Grzelachowski store, warehouse, and home with the New Mexico State Register of Cultural Properties, April 23, 1970. The structure stands today (1990) in a badly damaged condition.

48. State Register Index, Guadalupe County, Form A, Register Date, "7-4-70," NMSRCA.

49. Parish, *Ilfeld Company*, 59, 99, 370n60, 376n50, 377n5 and n10.

50. William J. Parish, "The German Jew and the Commercial Revolution in Territorial New Mexico, 1850-1900," *New Mexico Historical Review* (NMHR) 35 (April 1960):137.

51. Parish, *Ilfeld Company*, 316-17.

52. Parish, *Ilfeld Company*, 203.

53. William A. Keleher, *The Fabulous Frontier* (Albuquerque: University of New Mexico Press, 1962), 58; *Las Vegas* (New Mexico) *Gazette*, November 25, 1875; and Harwood P. Hinton, "John Simpson Chisum, 1877-84," NMHR 31 (July 1956):190.

54. Co-signer Peter Maxwell was the son of the fabulous Lucien Bonaparte Maxwell, former owner of the Maxwell Land Grant, which covered 2,680 square miles of north-eastern New Mexico and southern Colorado. Peter Maxwell witnessed the killing of Billy The Kid by Sheriff Pat Garrett at Fort Sumner, New Mexico on July 14, 1881, in William A. Keleher, *Maxwell Land Grant* (New York: Argosy-Antiquarian Ltd., 1964), 30.

55. William A. Keleher, *Violence in Lincoln County, 1869-1881* (Albuquerque: University of New Mexico Press, 1957), 44; Assumpsit (an action to recover damages for breach of a simple contract), *Alexander Grzelachowski vs. John S. Chisum*, District Court, San Miguel County, New Mexico Territory, March 3, 1876, NMSRCA; and Lilly Klasner, *My Girlhood among Outlaws* (Tucson: The University of Arizona Press; 1972), 282. At the time of Grzelachowski's suit against Chisum, William

Breeden was the attorney general of the territory, in W.G. Ritch (compiler), *New Mexico Blue Book*, 1882; (new edition, Albuquerque: University of New Mexico Press, 1968), 120.

56. Grzelachowski's agent, Captain Ford, is believed to be Captain James H. Ford, who commanded a company of Colorado volunteers in the Civil War and took part in the Battle of Glorieta Pass, 1862, under Major John M. Chivington.

57. Keleher, *Violence in Lincoln County*, 48; Klasner, *My Girlhood among Outlaws*, 260, 279-81; and *Book of Brand Records*, Guadalupe County, 134, NMSRCA.

58. Klasner, *My Girlhood among Outlaws*, 296; Injunction Bond of January 3, 1878, *Alexander Grzelachowski et al. vs. John S. Chisum*, District Court, San Miguel County, NMSRCA; and Keleher, *Violence in Lincoln County*, 50-51. Grzelachowski's lawyer, Thomas B. Catron, became one of the first two United States senators from New Mexico in 1912.

59. Stanley, *Puerto de Luna Story*, 9. Stanley's data are based in large part on personal interviews in recent times. The stories about Billy the Kid are likely to have been embellished, but the details are not significant. What is important is that Grzelachowski and Billy the Kid knew each other well from personal contact. Biographers of Billy corroborate this relationship.

60. Keleher, *Violence in Lincoln County*, 58; and Stanley, *Puerto de Luna Story*, 9-10.

61. Carrie L. Hodges, "Puerto de Luna," submitted July 10, 1936 to WPA Writers' Project, Museum of New Mexico, Santa Fe; and Keleher, *Violence in Lincoln County*, 58.

62. Hunt, *Tragic Days of Billy The Kid*, 250-51; and Pat F. Garrett, *Authentic Life of Billy The Kid*, edited by Maurice Garland Fulton (New York: Macmillan Company, 1927), 183.

63. Keleher, *Maxwell Land Grant*, 30.

64. Telephonic interview of granddaughter Florentina Flores, Santa Rosa, New Mexico, October 19, 1982.

65. Our Lady of Refuge Church in Puerto de Luna is an attractive edifice. The dome is quasi-Byzantine and the windows are Moorish-shaped. In 1982, the parish issued a historical brochure in observance of its centennial.

66. *La Voz del Pueblo* [The Voice of the People], Las Vegas, New Mexico, "Mencion Personal," December 24, 1892.

67. Parish, *Ilfeld Company*, 190. The name of the firm was changed to the Pastura Trading Company in 1910.

68. Stanley, *Puerto de Luna Story*, 10.

69. Keleher, *Fabulous Frontier*, 63.

70. "Mencion Personal," *La Voz del Pueblo*, March 19, 1892.

71. Richard W. Helbock, *Post Offices of New Mexico* (Las Cruces, New Mexico: Published by the author, 1981), copy at NMSRCA.

72. Keleher, *Violence in Lincoln County*, 58. In 1881 the General Land Office of the Federal gov-

ernment named Alexander Grzelachowski as one of many individuals suspected of land fraud, that is, the purchase of land through intermediaries for the purpose of gaining access to water for the grazing of cattle. The General Land Office investigated and brought a number of individuals and parties, mostly cattle companies, to trial. Few were found guilty. One difficulty in prosecuting the cases was the absence of defendants who simply skipped out of the territory. Grzelachowski was never prosecuted or even indicted. He was well known throughout east-central New Mexico, and his whereabouts were no secret. The allegation of land fraud against Grzelachowski remains unconvincing in view of his reputation for honesty and integrity. Victor Westphal explains that the Federal land laws were not applicable to most of the arid land of New Mexico. "Cattle grazers," he adds, "persistently violated the land laws of the United States, many of them did so knowingly and with the firm conviction that they had a strong moral, if not legal, case in doing so." As a matter of interest, Charles Ilfeld was one of those indicted for land fraud, in Victor Westphal, "The Public Domain in New Mexico, 1854-1891," NMHR 33 (April 1958): 128-43.

73. Index to Real Property, Books 26, 27, 30, San Miguel County Court Records, Las Vegas, New Mexico; and Indenture, Alexander Grzelachowski and Secun-

dina Grzelachowski, his wife, San Miguel County, and Robert H. Longwill, Santa Fe County, September 15, 1886, NMSRCA.

74. Indenture, September 15, 1886.

75. Subpoena issued by Thomas Smith, Chief Justice of the Supreme Court of the Territory of New Mexico and Judge of the Fourth Judicial District Court, January 15, 1894, Charles Ilfeld Collection, Letters Received, Library of the University of New Mexico (NMUL). Albuquerque.

76. Parish, *Ilfeld Company*, 200.

77. Louis Sulzbacher to Alexander Grzelachowski (in Spanish), December 8, 1893, Folder 14, Box 4, Charles Ilfeld Collection, NMUL.

78. Twitchell, *Leading Facts of New Mexican History*, III:291.

79. Max Nordhaus to Charles Ilfeld, December 19, 1983. Folder 13, Box 4, Ilfeld Collection.

80. Parish, *Ilfeld Company*, 121.

81. Louis Sulzbacher to Charles Ilfeld, December 22, 1893, Folder 14, Box 4, Ilfeld Collection.

82. Louis Sulzbacher to Charles Ilfeld, December 26, 1893, Folder 13, Box 4, Ilfeld Collection.

83. Subpoena to the Grzelachowskis, January 15, 1894, Box 6, Ilfeld Collection.

84. Cause No. 8, Fourth Judicial District Court, County of Guadalupe, *Longwill vs. Grzelachowskis*, April 2, 1894, NMSRCA. In 1891 the New Mexico Territorial Legislature established the County of Guadalupe from the southern half of San Miguel County. Therefore, part of Grzelachowski's mortgaged property remained in San Miguel County, where Longwill also

brought suit against the Grzela-chowskis. The court there made a prior decree for the sale of the mortgaged land. Judge Smith ordered the sale of property in San Miguel County, followed by that in Guadalupe County.

85. The author reviewed the *Las Vegas Daily Optic* for the months of July, August, and September of 1894 and found no announcements of a public auction of Grzelachowski's property.

86. Donald R. Lavash, Historian at New Mexico State Records Center and Archives, to author, December 7, 1983, author's files.

87. Frank N. Page to Max Nordhaus, December 29, 1894, Box 6, Ilfeld Collection.

88. Page to Charles Ilfeld (or Max Nordhaus), February 9, 1895; and receipt of payment signed by Page, April 13, 1896, in Letters Received, Box 6, Ilfeld Collection.

89. Interview of grandson Charles C. Grzelachowski, May 12, 1983, author's files.

90. Interview of granddaughter Oma Gallegos, October 20, 1982; and *Las Vegas Daily Optic*, May 28, 1896.

91. Parish, "The German Jew and the Commercial Revolution," 131.

92. Klasner, *My Girlhood among Outlaws*, 281.

93. *Las Vegas Daily Optic*, May 28, 1896.

94. A Grzelachowski (per E.T. Baca) to Charles Ilfeld, Esq., January 17, 1883, Folder 3, Box 2, Ilfeld Collection.

95. *Las Vegas Daily Optic*, March 18, 1881.

96. Józef Grzelachowski to brother Alexander, March 24, 1883; and interview of Amelia's niece Oma Gallegos, October 20, 1982. As a girl Mrs. Gallegos lived with Aunt Amelia for several years.

97. Keleher, *Violence in Lincoln County*, 48. The surname Grzelachowski consists of four syllables: Grze-la-chow-ski. In the phonetic spelling that follows, the first syllable is separated into two parts for ease of pronunciation, but the first part (hard "g") and the second should be sounded almost together. The stress is on the next to the last (penultimate) syllable: thus, Gre ze la hof ski.

98. *Santa Rosa* (New Mexico) *News*, March 13 and 27, 1980; and Stanley, *Puerto de Luna Story*, 11. In 1980 a metal box was found in the old courthouse building. The box contained seventeen pages of data in Spanish that had been preserved for ninety years. These historical documents describe the establishment of Guadalupe County. The building served as a courthouse from 1893 to 1903, when the county seat was transferred to Santa Rosa. From 1904 to 1951 the building was used as a school. In 1952 it passed into private ownership, serving as a residence. In January 1981, Paul R. Kitzinger, a retired U.S. Navy captain, bought the property. Together with Richard Bailey, Kintzinger converted the building into the Karma Thegsum Choling Retreat Center, associated with Tibetan Buddhism. The old court house is again a residence (1990).

99. Records of Probate Court, Guadalupe County, for 1893 and 1894; Oaths of Office, Guadalupe County Records, 1893-1901; Index Commissioners Journal, Guadalupe County, 83; and Book No. 1, page 103, NMSRCA.

100. "A Sketch of the Dead Citizen," *Las Vegas Daily Optic*, May 28, 1896; Charles C. Grzelachowski to author, June 8, 1983, author's files;

and telephonic interview of Rev. Walter E. Cassidy, pastor of St. Rose of Lima Church, Santa Rosa, New Mexico, October 21, 1982. Father Cassidy also served as the pastor of the mission church in Puerto de Luna for many years.

101. *Las Vegas* (New Mexico) *Examiner*, May 26, 1896; and *Las Vegas Daily Optic*, May 28, 1896.

The Battle of Glorieta Pass Was the Guide Ortiz or Grzelachowski?

1. Martin Hardwick Hall, *Sibley's New Mexico Campaign* (Austin: University of Texas Press, 1960), 158.

2. William Clarke Whitford, *Colorado Volunteers in the Civil War: The New Mexico Campaign in 1862* (Denver: State Historical and Natural History Society, 1906), 122-23.

3. Hall, *Sibley's Campaign*, 140-60.

4. Hall, *Sibley's Campaign*, 159; Marc Simmons, *The Little Lion of the Southwest: A Life of Manuel Antonio Chaves* (Chicago: Swallow Press, 1973), 185; and Reginald S. Craig, *The Fighting Parson: The Biography of Colonel John M. Chivington* (Los Angeles: Westernlore Press, 1959), 125.

5. Fray Angelico Chavez, *Archives of the Archdiocese of Santa Fe, 1678-1900* (Washington, D.C.: Academy of American Franciscan History, 1957), 260-61: *The Metropolitan Catholic Almanac and Laity's Directory, 1855* (Baltimore: Lucas Brothers,

1855), 243-45; and the same directory for 1865, 182-86.

6. Telephone interview with Rev. Philip Herndon, pastor of St. Anthony's Church, Pecos, New Mexico, February 19, 1985. Father Herndon served a number of years in the Pecos area. In 1978 he was pastor of Our Lady of Guadalupe Church in Villanueva, a few miles south of San Miguel del Vado; *Catholic Almanac, 1865*, p. 183.

7. "Trouncing the Texans," [Las Vegas] *Daily Optic*, March 14, 1881: Francis C. Kajencki, "Alexander Grzelachowski: Pioneer Merchant of Puerto de Luna, New Mexico," *Arizona and the West*, 26 (Autumn 1984), 248.

8. Chaplain Alexander Grzelachowski, Second New Mexico Volunteers, to Captain Gurden Chapin, Acting Assistant Adjutant General, Department of New Mexico, August 4, 1862, microfilm F801R42 1980, reel 16, frame 0436, Register of Let-

ters Received, Headquarters, Department of New Mexico, 1854-1865, University of New Mexico Library. The author is indebted to Charles Meketa of Corrales, New Mexico, for "discovering" the letter.
9. Craig, *Fighting Parson*, 125.
10. Kajencki, "Alexander Grzelachowski," 243, 245, 256n.
11. Whitford, *Colorado Volunteers*, 122; "List of Commissioned Officers," Second Regiment, New Mexico Infantry, Description Book of Military Units, 25-26, New Mexico State Records Center and Archives, Santa Fe.

12. Charles Gardner, "The Pet Lambs of Glorieta Pass," *Civil War Times Illustrated*, 15 (November 1976), 35; Kajencki, "Alexander Grzelachowski," 244.
13. Chivington's Report, March 28, 1862, *Official Records*, Series 1, IX, 539; Colonel John M. Chivington, "The Retrospective – The Prospective," Film P-L 12, Bancroft Library, University of California – Berkeley; J. M. Chivington, "The Pet Lambs," *The Denver Republican*, April 27, 1890.

Charles Radzimiński
The United States-Mexican Boundary Survey

1. Charles Radzimiński to Adjutant General, U.S. Army, March 15. 1847, Letters Received, Records of the Adjutant General's Office, 1790s-1917, Records Group 94, National Archives.
2. Dr. Józef Kazimierski, Director of State Archives in Warsaw, to Francis Kajencki, June 6, 1989, author's files.
3. *Report of Lieut. Col. J. D. Graham, U.S. Topographical Engineers on Mason and Dixon's Line*, 2d ed. (Chicago: Steam Presses of F. Fulton & Co., 1862), 15, 54, 95, in uncatalogued box, "James D. Graham Papers," Beinecke Library, Yale University, New Haven, Connecticut.
4. Graham, *Report on Mason-Dixon's Line*, 15, 67, 94.
5. Senate Executive Document No. 119, 32d Congress, 1st Session,

"Report of the Secretary of the Interior, "Washington, D.C., July 1852, 42-43, 138; and John Russell Bartlett, *Personal Narrative of Explorations and Incidents in Texas, New Mexico, California, Sonora, and Chihuahua* (New York: D. Appleton & Company, 1854), 2 vols., I:92-93, 303.
6. William H. Emory, *Report of the United States and Mexican Boundary Survey*, 2 vols. (Washington: A.O.P. Nicholson, Printer, 1857) I:16, 18, 23: and Emory to Radziminski; Powder Horn near Indianola, September 30, 1854, Folders 67 and 68, Box 7, "William H. Emory Papers," Beinecke Library, Yale University, New Haven, Connecticut.
7. Emory, *Boundary Report*, I:16.
8. Emory to Dr. Hinckle, Washington, D.C., September 28, 1853, Box 6, Folder 55, Emory Papers.

9. William H. Goetzmann, *Army Exploration in the American West, 1803-1863* (New Haven: Yale University Press, 1959), 194. Goetzmann is a Pulitzer Prize-winning author of *Exploration and Empire* and *New Lands, New Men.* He is the Jack S. Blanton Professor of History and American Studies in the University of Texas at Austin (1990).

10. Commissioner Robert Campbell to William H. Emory, Redmonds Ranch, August 25, 1853, Box 6, Folder 54; Arthur Schott to Emory, Camp of Ringgold Barracks, Texas, October 5, 1853, Box 6, Folder 56; Radzimiński to Emory, Mouth of the Rio Grande, November 3, 1853, Box 2, Letterbook VI, 103, Emory Papers.

11. G. Clinton Gardner to Emory, Mouth of the Rio Grande, September 20, 1853, Box 6, Folder 55, Emory Papers.

12. K. Jack Bauer, *The Mexican War, 1846-48* (New York: Macmillan Publishing Co., 1974), xix.

13. James Buchanan to John B. Weller, February 13, 1849, "Report of the Secretary of the Interior in Answer to a Resolution of the Senate calling for Information in Relation to the Operation of the Commission appointed to run and mark the boundary between the United States and Mexico," Senate Exec. Doc. 34, 31st Cong. 1st sess., 4; Article V, Treaty of Guadalupe Hidalgo, February 2, 1848, in Emory, *Boundary Survey* I: xv.

14. Jerzy Jan Lerski, *A Polish Chapter in Jacksonian America* (Madi-son: University of Wisconsin Press, 1958), 94-97; Florian Stasik, *Polish Political Emigration in the United States of America, 1831-1864* (Warsaw: State Educational Publishers, 1973), 72-76, 301; Francis Bolek, ed., *Who's Who in Polish America* (New York: Harbinger House, 1943), 370.

15. William B. Chittenden to Board of Public Works, March 3, 1841, entry 84 of Board of Public Works Inventory, Box 204, Virginia State Archives, Richmond, Virginia; Oath of Office of Charles Radzimiński as second lieutenant, March 15, 1847, Records of the Adjutant General's Office, 1790s-1917, Record Group (RG) 94, National Archives, Washington, D.C.; General Orders No. 4, February 12, 1847, and General Orders No. 19, April 28, 1847, War Department, in Office of Chief of Military History, Washington, D.C.; and Francis B. Heitman, *Historical Register and Dictionary of the United States Army* (2 vols., Washing-ton, D.C.: Government Printing Office, 1903), I:80, 812.

16. Receipts of wage payments, Northeast Boundary Commission, Washington, D.C., unmarked box of miscellaneous receipts and documents, James D. Graham Papers, Americana Collection, Beinecke Library, Yale University.

17. Graham, *Report on Mason and Dixon's Line*, 7, 9, 11, 15, 54, 57, 67, 94-95.

18. Bartlett, *Personal Narrative*, I: 3, 150; William H. Emory to Thomas Ewing, August 20, 1850,

VIII: 17, and D.C. Goddard to John Russell Bartlett, October 11, 1850, VIII: 19, John Russell Bartlett Papers, 12 vols., University of Texas at El Paso Library. John Russell Bartlett was born in Providence, Rhode Island, in 1805 and became a writer, historian, ethnologist, and author. He served as corresponding secretary of the New York Historical Society, coming into contact with Albert Gallatin and other prominent individuals. He wanted to be named minister to Denmark but got the post of boundary commissioner instead. Odie B. Faulk, "Introduction," to John Russell Bartlett, *Personal Narrative* (2 vols., Chicago: Rio Grande Press, 1965).

19. Bartlett, *Personal Narrative*, I: 192-93, 303; "Report of Lieutenant Colonel James D. Graham to Colonel John J. Abert, Chief of Topographical Engineers," Senate Exec. Doc. 121, 32d Cong., 1st sess., 118.

20. Bartlett, *Personal Narrative*, I: 340-41; Odie B. Faulk, *Too Far North...Too Far South* (Los Angeles: Westernlore Press, 1967), 57-58.

21. Faulk, *Too Far North*, 74; IX: 35-37, Bartlett Papers.

22. Goetzmann, *Army Exploration*, 178; and Bartlett to Secretary of the Interior, August 7, 1851, Senate Exec. Doc. 119, 32d Cong., 1st sess., 433.

23. Bartlett, *Personal Narrative*, I: 348. Although a seasoned officer and engineer, James D. Graham behaved in an erratic, high-strung, arrogant manner while with the commission. At Santa Cruz, Mexico, Graham argued heatedly with Thomas Webb, secretary and physician of the commission. Considering his honor impugned, Graham challenged Webb to a duel, but Webb defused the issue by declining the challenge. See "Personal Journal," September 25, 1851, X: 169-71, and James D. Graham to Charles Webb, September 25, 1851, V: 105, Bartlett Papers.

24. Personal Journal, X: 143, and Radzimiński to Bartlett, August 14, 1851, V: 59, Bartlett Papers.

25. X: 143, Bartlett Papers. Radzimiński undoubtedly traveled from Santa Fe to Missouri by stage or wagon train along the Santa Fe Trail.

26. Radzimiński to Bartlett, August 30(?), 1851, V:93, Bartlett Papers. One writer refers to Radzimiński and Ambrose Burnside as "messengers," but Radzimiński served in an executive capacity. Outlining his responsibilities to the Secretary of the Interior, Bartlett wrote, "My intention was to send a competent engineer, who should be able to lay before the department the actual condition of the commission, point out its necessities, the force required to accomplish the duties assigned to it, to propose plans for bringing its expenses within the appropriation, and to hasten the completion of the boundary survey," in Bartlett to Alexander H. H. Stuart, August 16, 1851, Senate Exec. Doc. 119, 32d Cong., 1st sess., 444.

27. Henry Jacobs to Bartlett, October 10, 1851, V: 107, Bartlett

Papers; Odie B. Faulk, "The Controversial Boundary Survey and the Gadsden Treaty," *Arizona and the West*, 4 (Autumn 1962), 215. Burnside became a major general in the Civil War, commanding the Army of the Potomac at the Battle of Fredericksburg, Virginia, December 12-15, 1862.

28. Stuart to Charles M. Conrad, September 11, 1851, Senate Exec. Doc. 121, 32d Cong., 1st sess., 240-43; Bartlett, *Personal Narrative*, I: 211, 348; Faulk, *Too Far North*, 100; J.J. Abert to Graham, September 28, 1851, correspondence (August-September 1851), Graham Papers.

29. Henry B. Anthony to Bartlett, October 25, 1851, XII, Bartlett Papers; Edward S. Wallace, *The Great Reconnaissance: Soldiers, Artists, and Scientists on the Frontier, 1848-1861* (Boston: Little, Brown and Company, 1955), 9.

30. Anthony to Bartlett, October 25 and November 1, 1851, XII, Bartlett Papers.

31. Radzimiński to Bartlett, February 7, 1852, VI: 5, Bartlett Papers.

32. Radzimiński to William H. Emory, January 26, 1852, Emory to Radzimiński, January 27, 1852, Emory to O. H. Tillinghast, January 27, 1852, Emory to Stuart, February 1, 1852, all in letterbook I, box 2, William H. Emory Papers, Americana Collection, Beinecke Library, Yale University; Emory, *Boundary Survey*, I: 18-19; Emory to Bartlett, February 8, 1852, VI: 7, Bartlett Papers. Bartlett went to Sonora in search of supplies. He continued to Guaymas on the Gulf of California and from there sailed for San Diego, California, which he reached on February 9, 1852, in Bartlett, *Personal Narrative*, I: 505.

33. Radzimiński to Bartlett, February 7, 1852, VI: 5, Bartlett Papers.

34. Graham to Charles Wright, November 8, 1851, "Graham Report," Senate Exec. Doc. 121, 32d Cong., 1st sess., 198; and Emory to Bartlett, June 1, 1852, VI: 39, Bartlett Papers.

35. Emory to Radzimiński, March 27, 1852, letterbook II, box 2, Radzimiński to Emory, March 31, 1852, folder 37, box 5, Radzimiński to Emory, April 2, April 5, and May 5, 1852, letterbook II, box 2, Emory Papers.

36. Radzimiński to Emory, May 15, 1852, letterbook II, box 2, Emory Papers.

37. Emory to Radzimiński, May 9, 1852, letterbook II, box 2; Radzimiński to Emory, May 21, 1852, letterbook III, box 2, Emory Papers.

38. Radzimiński to Emory, May 23, 1852, Emory to Radzimiński, May 24 and 25, 1852, Radzimiński to Emory, May 27, 1852, and Emory to Radzimiński, May 29, 1852, letterbook III, box 2, Emory Papers.

39. Radzimiński to Emory, June 6, 1852, letterbook III, box 2, Emory Papers; and Bartlett, *Personal Narrative*, I: 196, II: 546-47.

40. Emory to Secretary of the Interior, May 2 and 17, 1852, Tillinghast to Emory, June 5 and 6, 1852, Emory to Tillinghast, June 7, 1852, Radzimiński to Emory, June 11, 1852, folders 39 and 40, box 5, Emory Papers.

James Houston mediated a similar squabble between Emory and Lieutenant W. F. Smith.
41. Emory to Bartlett, June 1, 1852, Emory to Whipple, June 11, 1852, VI: 39, 45, Bartlett Papers.
42. Bartlett, *Personal Narrative*, II: 378, 381, 396-97, 400; Radzimiński to Emory, October 5, 1852, letterbook IV, box 2, Emory Papers.
43. Emory, *Boundary Survey*, I: 13; Emory to Radzimiński, June 18 and August 28, 1852, letterbook III, box 2, Emory Papers. Emory wrote to Radzimiński in two ways, opening formally with "Sir" in official letters and informally with "Dear Radziminski" in less formal correspondence. In his informal letter of August 28, 1852, Emory explained candidly the use of maps: "In the absence of your maps, I was obliged to take the Mexican maps made by *your friend* Vandricourt, but I took as little of them as I could to settle the business."
44. Bartlett, *Personal Narrative*, II: 402, 411-14, 448-49.
45. Bartlett, *Personal Narrative*, II: 427-30. An unsigned document might explain the origin of the Condé map. The writer (possibly Graham) says Condé drew the map sometime before the joint survey and doctored the northern boundary of Chihuahua to include Santa Rita Copper Mines as part of a scheme of several Mexican entrepreneurs. The Mexican Congress, however, never approved the Condé map. In folder labeled "Undated Miscellaneous Papers," Graham Papers.

46. Goetzmann, *Army Exploration*, 188; Bartlett, *Personal Narrative*, II: 510-16, 532, 536, 538. Bartlett reached Ringgold Barracks, Texas, on December 20, 1852.
47. Emory, *Boundary Survey*, I: 15-16, 73; Henry Jacobs to Bartlett, April 14 and 28, 1853, VII: 72, 83, Bartlett Papers.
48. John H. Clarke to Bartlett, June 22, 1850, I: 50, Bartlett Papers; Emory to John Torrey, September 28, 1853, Radzimiński to Emory, November 8, 1853, letterbook VI, box 2, Emory Papers.
49. Radzimiński to Emory, October 3 and 29, 1853, letterbook VI, box 2, Emory Papers.
50. Radzimiński to Emory, July 23 and 24, 1853, letterbook VI, box 2, Radzimiński to Emory, July 31, 1853, folder 53, box 6, Emory Papers; Emory, *Boundary Survey*, I: 15-16; Radzimiński to Thomas Miller (relative of Thomas W. Jones), July 24, 1853, M. Patterson Jones to Catesby Jones (his cousin), August 2, 1853, in Robert Eden Peyton Family Papers, Virginia Historical Society, Richmond, Virginia.
51. Hamilton Prioleau to Emory, August 4, 1853, and Radzimiński to Prioleau, October 6, 1853, folders 54 and 56, box 6, Emory Papers.
52. Radzimiński to Emory, July 14, 1853, Emory to Crispin del Poso, July 16, 1853, folder 53, box 6, Emory Papers.
53. Emory to Francisco Jimenez, May 23, 1853, *Diario-Memoria de Los Trabajo Cientificos Practicados Bajo La Direccion de Francisco Jimenez, 1er Ingeniero de la*

Comision de Limites Mexicana Conforme a Las Instructiones del Senor Comisionado Don Jose Salazar Ylarrequi a Quien Se Hace Entrega de Ellos (Washington, D.C.: N.p., 1857), 233-34, 236.

54. Emory to Jimenez, August 17, 1853, Emory to Radzimiński, September 11, 1853, letterbook VI, box 2, Emory Papers; Emory, *Boundary Survey*, I: 73. Article V of the Treaty of Guadalupe Hidalgo gave the boundary commissioners treaty-making power.

55. Emory to Radzimiński, September 11, 1853, Radzimiński to Emory, October 3 and 29, November 3, 1853, Robert Campbell to Emory, November 10, 1853, letterbook VI, box 2, Emory Papers.

56. Radzimiński to Jimenez, November 14, 1853, *Diario-Memoria*, 243-47; Goetzmann, *Army Exploration*, 157. The U.S. Coast and Geodetic Survey, jointly with assistant surveyor Clinton Gardner, "sounded the mouth of the Rio Grande and carried the line the required three leagues out to sea." In Goetzmann, *Army Exploration*, 194. The original Radzimiński-Jimenez boundary agreement is found in folder 114, box 10, Emory Papers.

57. Emory, *Boundary Survey*, I: 15, 73; Radzimiński to Emory, June 9, 1854, folder 64, box 7, Emory Papers.

58. Faulk, *Too Far North*, 129, 133-38; Emory, *Boundary Survey*, I: xv.

59. Radzimiński to Robert B. Campbell, June 24, 1854, folder 64, box 7, Emory Papers; Emory, *Boundary Survey*, I: 23.

T. Frank White of Frontera, Texas, where Emory had set up an observatory, was disappointed that Graham did not receive appointment as commissioner. "As far as my knowledge extends," White wrote, "no one is pleased with the appointment of Major E. to that office." T. F. White to Graham , November 7, 1854, "Correspondence 1854," Graham Papers.

60. G. H. Crossman to Emory, August 15, 1854, Emory to Samuel Colt, August 28, 1854, Radzimiński to Lucius Campbell, September 23, 1854, Emory to Radzimiński, September 30, 1854, folders 67 and 68, box 7, Emory Papers; Emory, *Boundary Survey*, I: 24.

61. Radzimiński to Emory, October 3, 12, and 14, 1854, folders 68 and 69, box 7, Emory Papers.

62. Radzimiński to Emory, [October 14, 1854], folder 69, box 7, Emory to Robert McClelland, November 1, 1854, McClelland to Emory, November 27, 1854, folder 70, box 8, Emory Papers.

63. Radzimiński to Emory, [October 14, 1854], Emory to McClelland, October 24, 1854, folder 69, box 7, Emory Papers; Emory, *Boundary Survey*, I: 23-24. After serving with the boundary commission, Radzimiński and E. Kirby Smith joined the newly-activated Second U.S. Cavalry Regiment.

64. Emory, *Boundary Survey*, I: 26-28; E. B. Alexander to Emory, January 27, 1855, folder 72, box 8, Emory Papers.

65. Emory, *Boundary Survey*, I: 24.

66. *Ibid.*, I: 112-13.

67. *Ibid.*, I: 115-16, 118.

68. Emory to McClelland, June 20, 1855, folder 77, box 8, Emory Papers. Nathaniel Michler and Francis Patterson may have conspired to thwart Emory. Emory's decision to replace Michler could have been damaging, including loss of reputation as a surveyor and adverse impact on his army career.

69. Emory to McClelland, June 19, 1855, Emory to Radzimiński, June 20, 1855, Radzimiński to Emory, July 26, 1855, folders 77 and 78, box 8, Emory Papers.

70. Radzimiński to Colonel S. Cooper, Adjutant General, San Antonio, Texas, September 24, 1855, AGO, RG94, Letters Received, National Archives; and Samuel Cooper to Emory, January 2, 1856, folder 83, box 8, Emory Papers.

71. Emory to Radzimiński, January 4, 1856, folder 83, box 8, Emory Papers; Emory, *Boundary Survey,* I: 24.

72. Amiel W. Whipple to Graham, February 15, 1852, box marked Correspondence 1852, Graham Papers; Lenard E. Brown, *Survey of the United States-Mexican Boundary – 1849-1855* (Washington, D.C.: U.S. Department of the Interior, National Park Service, 1969), 75.

73. Emory's bare mention of Radzimiński in his published report on the survey could be attributed to Emory's intense dislike of Bartlett. Robert V. Hine writes that "Emory's attitude toward Bartlett had turned increasingly sour," and some of that hostility may have influenced Emory's attitude toward Radzimiński. Bartlett is fair to Emory in his *Personal Narrative,* but Emory could not resist derogating Bartlett in his official report. Robert V. Hine, *Bartlett's West: Drawing the Mexican Boundary* (New Haven: Yale University Press, 1968), 89.

Charles Radzimiński
in the Military Service of America

1. Colonel Francis C. Kajencki, *Star on Many a Battlefield: Brevet Brigadier General Joseph Kargé in the American Civil War* (Rutherford, New Jersey: Fairleigh Dickinson University Press, 1980), 34.

2. Francis Bolek, ed.-in-chief, *Who's Who in Polish America* (New York: Harbinger House, 1943), 370; and Emanuel Rostworowski, Redaktor Naczelny [Editor-in-Chief], *Polski Słownik Biograficzny,* Tom XXX/I, Zeszyt 124 [*Polish Biographical Dictionary,* Vol. XXX/I, Book 124] (Krakow: Wydawnictwo Polskiej Akademii Nauk [Polish Academy of Sciences, Publishers], 1987), 99-100. The name Congress Kingdom derived from the Congress of Vienna of 1815 when representatives of the European Powers met to settle the problems caused by the collapse of the Napoleonic Empire.

3. Jerzy Jan Lerski, *A Polish Chapter in Jacksonian America* (Madison:

The University of Wisconsin Press, 1958), 94-97; and Florian Stasik, *Polska Emigracja Polityczna w Stanach Zjednoczonych Ameryki, 1831-1864* [*Polish Political Emigration in the United States of America, 1831-1864*] (Warszawa: Państwowe Wydawnictwo Naukowe, 1973) [Warsaw: State Educational Publishers, 1973]), 70, 72-76, 301.

4. Stanley F. Radzyminski, "Charles Radziminski: Patriot, Exile, Pioneer," *The Chronicles of Oklahoma*, Vol. 38, No. 4 (1960-61): 356; and William B. Chittenden, Secretary of the James River and Kanawha Company, to the President and Directors of the Board of Public Works, Richmond, Virginia, March 3, 1841, Entry 84 of the Board of Public Works Inventory, Box 204, Virginia State Archives, Richmond. Radzimiński was one of twelve assistant engineers, who with six principal assistant engineers, served under a chief engineer. Radziminski was paid $2.50 per diem in 1840, and the company promised him $3.00 per diem thereafter (approximately $700 per annum based on forty-eight weeks of work per year).

5. Oath of Office of Charles Radzimiński as Second Lieutenant, U.S. Army, March 15, 1847, Records Group 94, Records of the Adjutant General's Office, 1780s-1917, National Archives; General Orders No. 4, February 12, 1847, and No. 19, April 28, 1847, War Department, in Office of Chief Military History, Washington, D.C.; Justin H. Smith, *The War with Mexico*

(New York: The Macmillan Company, 1919), II:363; and *Register of Graduates and Former Cadets, U.S. Military Academy* (West Point, New York: Association of Graduates, 1980), 218. Thomas P. Moore of Kentucky served as lieutenant colonel of the Third Dragoons. The two officers appointed as major were Lieutenant William H. Emory of the Army Topographical Engineers and Lewis Cass, Jr. of Michigan. When Emory declined the appointment, William H. Polk, brother of President James K. Polk, took his place on August 31, 1847, in Albert G. Brackett, *History of the United States Cavalry* (New York: Harper & Brothers, 1865, reprint ed., New York: Greenwood Press, Publishers, 1968), 84-85.

6. General Orders No. 8, War Department, March 4, 1847, para. 16, in Office of Chief of Military History, Washington, D.C.

7. Land Bounty Claim No. 2537 of Charles Radzimiński, Washington, D.C., November 8, 1850, Records Group 15, Records of the Veterans Administration, Bounty Land Warrant Application File, National Archives; General Orders No. 4, War Department, February 12, 1847, and Orders No. 2, Headquarters, Third Dragoons, New Orleans, April 23, 1847, Letters Received, AGO, RG 94, National Archives. The Chief Clerk at the War Department annotated Butler's order, as follows: "Col. Butler will have seen by the 'circular of the 23d ult.' that it is considered inexpe-

dient to appoint Regt. Quarter-masters for the new reg[imen]ts until they are fully organized." First and Second Lieutenants of Dragoons received $33 1/3 in pay per month plus $4 in ra-tions, in *A Compendium of the Pay of the Army from 1785 to 1888*, Thomas M. Exley, comp. (Washington: Government Printing Office, 1888), 39.

8. Colonel Edward G.W. Butler to Brigadier General Roger Jones, The Adjutant General, U.S. Army, New Orleans, Louisiana, May 20, 1847, in "Regimental Orders and Letter Book, Third U.S. Dragoons," Entry 607 (Letters Sent, April-November 1847), RG 391. Regular Army Mobile Units, 1821-1942, Na-tional Archives. The split of the Third Dragoons into two wings caused a mix-up in assignments. Captain John S. Sitgraves' Com-pany F sailed from Charleston, South Carolina by mistake to Vera Cruz, Mexico, where it was re-directed to Point Isabel, Texas. The dragoons spent forty days in transit, meanwhile com-ing down with the mumps and measles. Butler would not allow the company to enter Dragoon Camp but encamped the sick men separately and quarantined them for a time, in Butler to Lieutenant C.C. McDean, Ad-jutant of District of Lower Rio Grande, Matamoros, Mexico, July 29, 1847, Letters Sent, Third U.S. Dragoons, Entry 607, RG 391, National Ar-chives; and The Butler Family Papers, Manuscript 102 (Mex-ican War Book), The Historic New Orleans Collection

(THNOC), New Orleans, Loui-siana.

9. Returns of Third U.S. Dra-goons, May 1847-June 1848, Mi-crocopy 744, Roll No. 26, Na-tional Archives; and The Butler Family Papers, Manuscript 102, THNOC. Companies A, B, F, H, I were based in the north at Matamoros; Companies C, D, E, G, K served with General Winfield Scott's army in the south.

10. Orders No. 1, Headquarters, Cavalry Brigade, Puebla, Mex-ico, July 10, 1847, "Regimental Orders and Letter Book," Third U.S. Dragoons, Entry 607, RG 391, National Archives; and Brackett, *History of U.S. Cavalry*, 90-91.

11. George Winston Smith and Charles Judah, *Chronicles of the Gringos* (Albuquerque: Univer-sity of New Mexico Press, 1968) 29; and General Cadmus M. Wilcox, *History of the Mexican War* (Washington, D.C.: The Church News Publishing Com-pany, 1892), 620.

12. Butler to Roger Jones, Camp near Matamoros, Mexico, August 13, 1847; Butler to Cap-tain Leslie Chase, Camp near Matamoros, Mexico, August 21, 1847; and Butler to Colonel Henry Whiting, Mier, Mexico, December 29, 1847, Letters Sent, Third U.S. Dragoons, RG 391, Entry 607. The northern wing of the Third Dragoons was not supplied with horses until February 1848, in Butler to Captain Irvin McDowell (Assis-tant Adjutant General, Army of Occupation), Headquarters, District of Upper Rio Grande,

February 19, 1848, Letters Sent, RG 391, Entry 608. Other cavalry units, even those in combat around Mexico City, were also handicapped for want of animals. At the Battle of Cerro Gordo, April 17-18, 1847, the Regiment of Mounted Rifles fought on foot. Again, in the Battles of Contreras and Churubusco, August 1847, this regiment fought as infantry, in Brackett, *History of U.S. Cavalry*, 87-88, 96-97.

13. George W. Cullum, *Biographical Register of the Officers and Graduates of the U.S. Military Academy*, 3d ed. (Boston and New York: Houghton, Mifflin, and Company, 1891), 251. Radzimiński was appointed Assistant Adjutant General by Orders No. 15, Headquarters, District of Upper Rio Grande, Mier, Mexico, October 13, 1847, AGO, RG 94, National Archives. In January 1848, the District gained the post of Laredo, Texas, occupied by a company of Texas Rangers and commanded by Lieutenant H.P. Bee, in Radzimiński to Bee, District of Upper Rio Grande, January 11, 1848. Fort Bliss, Texas, was named in honor of William Wallace Smith Bliss in 1854. Irvin McDowell became a major general in the Civil War and commanded a corps in the Army of the Potomac.

14. Radzimiński to Captain John Butler, Headquarters, District of Upper Rio Grande, Mier, Mexico, October 20, 1847, Letters Sent, RG 391, Entry 608, National Archives.

15. Butler to Lieutenant Colonel J. J. Fay, commanding at Camargo,

March 11, 1848; and Butler to Irvin McDowell, March 12, 1848. Microcopy 744, Roll 26, "Returns of Third Regiment, U.S. Dragoons," National Archives.

16. Butler to General Roger Jones, December 20, 1847, and Butler to Irvin McDowell, December 25, 1847, Headquarters, District of Upper Rio Grande, Mier, Mexico, RG 391, Entry 608, National Archives.

17. Butler to General John E. Wool, January 4, 1848; Butler to General Roger Jones, February 2, 1848; Butler to Irvin McDowell, February 24, 1848; and Radzimiński to Major Ebenezer S. Sibley, June 16, 1848, Headquarters, District of Upper Rio Grande, RG 391. Entry 608. National Archives.

18. Radzimiński to Fay, January 23, 1848; Butler to Irvin McDowell, January 24, 1848; and Radzimiński to Fay, March 18, 1848, Headquarters, District of Upper Rio Grande, Mier, Mexico, Microcopy 744, Roll 26, National Archives. Colonel Fay's report of the duel seems unclear as to the identity of the dead officer. According to General Cadmus Wilcox, the victim was Captain Joshua W. Collett. Postley was the other duelist. He was later killed by a soldier on May 8, 1848, in Wilcox, *History of the Mexican War*, 642.

19. Butler to General Roger Jones, March 16, 1848; Butler to Irvin McDowell, March 18, 1848; and Regimental Orders No. 9, Headquarters, Third U.S. Dragoons, Camp Mier, Mexico, March 16, 1848, "Returns of Third Dragoons for March

1848," MF 744, Roll 26, National Archives.

20. Isabel Butler to Edward G.W. Butler, Belmont, June 3, 1848, and Frances Butler to Edward G.W. Butler, Dunboyne, June 19, 1848, in The Edward G.W. Butler Papers, THNOC; and Edward Butler to the Honorable Lewis Cass, Secretary of State, Dunboyne, Louisiana, September 17, 1858, in "Miscellaneous Letters of the Department of State," M179, Roll 165, National Archives.

21. Butler to Lieutenant C.I. Helm, Headquarters, District of Upper Rio Grande, June 15, 1848; Radzimiński to Major [E.S. Sibley], Headquarters, District of Upper Rio Grande, Camargo, Mexico, June 30, 1848, Letters Sent, Entry 608, National Archives.

22. Orders No. 14, Headquarters, Third U.S. Dragoons, Palo Alto, Texas, June 30, 1848, Manuscript 102, THNOC.

23. Francis B. Heitman, *Historical Register and Dictionary of the United States Army* (Washington, D.C.: Government Printing Office, 1903), I:80, 681; and Brackett, *History of U.S. Cavalry*, 119.

24. Receipts of wage payments, Northeast Boundary Commission, Washington, D.C., unmarked box of miscellaneous receipts and documents, James D. Graham Papers, Americana Collection, Beinecke Library, Yale University; Report of Lieutenant Colonel James D. Graham to Colonel John J. Abert, Chief of Topographical Engineers, Washington, D.C.,

in Senate Executive Document 121, 32nd Congress, 1st Session, 118; and Radzimiński to Butler, Washington, D.C., July 4, 1850. Folder 631, THNOC. In support of his application for a Regular Army commission, Radzimiński submitted letters of recommendation from Colonel Edward Butler, General Thomas S. Jesup (Army Quartermaster-General), General Georga Gibson (Army Commissary-General), and Lieutenant Colonel James D. Graham, in Radzimiński to Butler, Washington, D.C., October 3, 1850, Folder 632, THNOC.

In Washington City, Radzimiński lived with the Thomas family in the household of Mark M. Bucher, Professor in the Navy. As a resident of the First Ward, Radzimiński was a neighbor of a fellow Pole, the lawyer Gaspard Tochman, aged 43. In Tochman's household were Jan Tyssowski, 39, his wife Antoinette, 31, and their five children. Tochman lectured before American audiences on behalf of partitioned Poland for several years. In the Civil War he sided with the Confederacy, and in New Orleans he organized the Polish Brigade, composed of the 14th and 15th Louisiana Infantry Regiments. Tyssowski led the unsuccessful uprising in Kraków against Austria in 1846. Escaping to America, he settled in Washington and served as a Federal official, in Federal Census of 1850, Washington City, Wards 1-4, MF 432, Roll 56, American Genealogical Lending Library, Bountiful, Utah; and

Miecislaus Haiman, *Polish Past in America 1608-1865* (Chicago: Polish Museum of America, 1974), 81-82, 113.

25. John Russell Bartlett, *Personal Narrative of the Explorations and Incidents in Texas, New Mexico, California, Sonora, and Chihuahua*, 2 vols. (New York: D. Appleton & Company, 1854), I:3, 150; William H. Emory to Secretary of the Interior (Thomas Ewing), San Diego, California, August 20, 1850, John Russell Bartlett Papers, 12 vols., VIII:17, and D.C. Goddard, Dept. of the Interior, to John Russell Bartlett, October 11, 1850, VIII:19, MF 497 at Library of the University of Texas at El Paso.

26. Bartlett, *Personal Narrative*, I:196, II:546-47; William H. Emory, *Report of the United States and Mexican Boundary Survey* (Washington, D.C.: A.O.P. Nicholson, Printer, 1857, 2 vols., I:15-16, 24, 73; Jefferson Davis to Charles Radzimiński, War Department, June 30, 1855, AGO, Army Letters of Appointment, RG 94, National Archives; Emory to Robert McClelland, Secretary of the Interior, San Antonio, Texas, October 9, 1855; and General Samuel Cooper, The Adjutant General, to Emory, Washington, D.C., January 2, 1856, both letters in Box 8, Folders 81 and 83 respectively, William H. Emory Papers, Beinecke Library, Yale University. Camp Cooper, Texas was named in honor of the Army Adjutant General, Samuel Cooper.

27. Radzimiński's assignment to the Second U.S. Cavalry dates from June 30, 1855. The Second Cavalry was authorized by Act of Congress of March 3, 1855. During the period of recruiting, the headquarters were located at Louisville, Kentucky, and here Colonel Lee first reported on April 20, 1855. Shortly thereafter he was at Jefferson Barracks, Missouri, where the regiment was organized and trained. For most of this time, however, Lee was absent on court martial duty. Consequently, he did not accompany the regiment on its 60-day march to Texas in late 1855, in George F. Price, *Across the Continent with the Fifth Cavalry* (1883, reprint ed., New York: Antiquarian Press, Ltd., 1959), 11, 29-32, 469, 597. The Congress changed the designation of the Second Cavalry to the Fifth Cavalry in 1861.

28. Frederick Law Olmsted, *A Journey Through Texas* (New York: Burt Franklin, 1860; reprint ed., 1969), 160. While in San Antonio, Radzimiński may have met a fellow exile, Florian Liskowacki, who arrived with him in New York in 1834. Taking the name of Erasmus Andrew Florian, Liskowacki became a pioneer banker in Memphis, Tennessee, in partnership with J.C. French. Florian left Tennessee for Texas in 1853, landing at Indianola and settling in San Antonio. He became a successful businessman, public official, and philanthropist until his death in 1876, in Miecislaus Haiman, *The Poles*

in the Early History of Texas (Chicago: Polish Roman Catholic Union of America, 1936), 37.

29. Fitzhugh Lee, *General Lee* (Nashville, Tennessee: Guinn and Guinn Southwestern Publishing House, 1895), 59.

30. Stanley F. Horn, *The Army of Tennessee* (Indianapolis: The Bobbs-Merrill Company, 1941), 52-53; Carl Coke Rister, *Robert E. Lee in Texas* (Norman: University of Oklahoma Press, 1946), 17, 37-38; Price, *Fifth Cavalry*, 469, 615; and Mss 1, 15c736 (newspaper clipping), "Robert E. Lee Family Papers," Virginia Historical Society, Richmond.

31. Rister, *Lee in Texas*, 35-36; Colonel Harold B. Simpson, *Cry Comanche: The 2nd U.S. Cavalry in Texas, 1855-1861* (Hillsboro, Texas: Hill Jr. College Press, 1979), 60; and Herbert M. Hart, *Old Forts of the Southwest* (New York: Bonanza Books, 1964), 41-42. Clifford Dowdey calls Lee's assignment to Camp Cooper as the colonel's "bleakest, loneliest time" in his life. Lee had spent the past several years in the company of his family. Now, Dowdey wrote, Lee went "to his Siberia," in Clifford Dowdey, *Lee* (Boston: Little, Brown and company, 1965), 107.

32. Michael J. Krisman, ed., *Register of Graduates and Former Cadets, United States Military Academy* (West Point: New York: Association of Graduates, 1980), 229; Price, *Fifth Cavalry*, 29; Robert J. Hartje, *Van Dorn: The Life and Times of a Confederate General* (Nashville: Vanderbilt University Press, 1967), x, xii, 53;

Brackett, *History of U.S. Cavalry*, 150; and "Robert E. Lee in Texas: Letters and Diary," Colonel M.L. Crimmins, ed., *The West Texas Historical Association Year Book*, Vol. VIII (June 1932), 5.

33. Price, *Fifth Cavalry*, 29-31; and Randy Steffen, *The Horse Soldier, 1776-1943* (Norman: University of Oklahoma Press, 1978), II:35.

34. Rister, *Lee in Texas*, 40-52; Price, *Fifth Cavalry*, 45; and Crimmins, *West Texas Year Book*, 6.

35. Price, *Fifth Cavalry*, 39, 43, 52, 54-55.

36. Ray Miller, *Ray Miller's Texas Forts: A History and Guide* (Houston: Cordovan Press, 1985), 39; Hart, *Old Forts of the Southwest*, 47-48; Price, *Fifth Cavalry*, 50; and Brackett, *History of U.S. Cavalry*, 172. The Department of Texas in Special Orders No. 78, August 6, 1856, ordered Company K to displace first to Camp Colorado, located about 100 miles due south of Camp Cooper. The Company departed Camp Cooper on August 9, 1856. Four weeks later, the Department issued Special Orders No. 106, September 8, 1856, for the company to occupy Fort Inge, where Whiting's troopers arrived on September 12, Post Returns of Fort Inge, September 1856, MF 617, Roll 517, National Archives.

37. Rister, *Lee in Texas*, 64.

38. Post Returns of Fort Inge, Texas, February 1857, MF 617, Roll 517, National Archives; and Robert E. Lee to daughter Agnes Lee, San Antonio, Texas, March 11, 1857, Mss 2

L515 a161, Robert E. Lee Family Papers, Virginia Historical Society, Richmond.

39. Price, *Fifth Cavalry*, 59; Rister, *Lee in Texas*, 92; Returns of Second Cavalry, March 1855-December 1893, and Annual Return of Second Cavalry for 1857, MF 744, roll 51, National Archives; Post Returns of Fort Clark, Texas, March 1857, MF 617, Roll 213, National Archives; and *Ray Miller's Texas Forts*, 77-78. Fort Clark was located at present-day Brackettsville. Radzimiński left Company K on sick leave initially for seven days by Post Orders No. 30, Headquarters, Fort Clark, Texas, May 4, 1857, augmented by a leave of absence of two months by Special Orders No. 57, Headquarters, Department of Texas, San Antonio, April 19, 1857. The War Department extended his leave another four months by Orders No. 69, Adjutant General's Office, Washington, D.C., May 11, 1857, in Post Returns of Fort Clark, May and June 1857, MF 617, Roll 213, National Archives. It is not known where Radzimiński spent his sick leave.

40. Price, *Fifth Cavalry*, 64-66; Rister, *Lee in Texas*, 95; and Returns of Company K, Second Cavalry, April, May, June 1858, MF 744, Roll 51, National Archives.

41. Price, *Fifth Cavalry*, 66; and Returns of Second Cavalry, July and August 1858, MF 744, Roll 51, National Archives.

42. Thomas P. Shallcross to Hon. John B. Floyd, Secretary of War, Memphis, Tennessee, August 23, 1858, AGO, Letters Received, RG 94, National Archives; *The Memphis Daily Appeal*, August 19, 1858; Price, *Fifth Cavalry*, 469; and Edward G.W. Butler to Secretary of State Lewis Cass, Dunboyne, Louisiana, September 17, 1858, M179, Roll 165, National Archives.

43. Shallcross to Floyd, August 23, 1858.

44. Rister, *Lee in Texas*, 95; and Agnes Lee to brother Fitzhugh Lee, Arlington, Virginia, October 2, 1858, Mss 1 L51c 235, The Robert E. Lee Family Papers. The Ella Calvert mentioned by Agnes Lee is believed to be the daughter of Charles Benedict Calvert and Charlotte A. Norris, born at Baltimore, Maryland, on March 20, 1840, in *The Ancestry of Rosalie Morris Johnson*, R. Winder Johnson, comp. (Privately printed by Ferris & Leach, 1905), 37, 44, Virginia Historical Society. The extent of the relationship between Radzimiński and Ella Calvert is unknown. The vacancy in Company K, due to Radzimiński's death, was filled by the promotion to First Lieutenant and assignment of John Bell Hood of Kentucky.

45. Edward G.W. Butler to Lewis Cass, September 17, 1858, "Miscellaneous Letters of the Dept. of State," M179, Roll 165; Lewis Cass to Francis W. Pickins, Department of State, Washington, D.C., October 5, 1858, "Diplomatic Instructions," M77, Roll 136; and Lewis Cass to Butler, October 5, 1858, "Domestic Letters," M40, Roll 47, National Archives.

46. Price, *Fifth Cavalry*, 67-68, 82, 644; Hugh Lenox Scott, *Some Memories of a Soldier* (New York: The Century Company, 1928), 203; John W. Morris et al., *Historical Atlas of Oklahoma*, 3d ed. (Norman: University of Oklahoma Press, 1986), 27; and Muriel H. Wright, et al, *Mark of Heritage* (Oklahoma City: Oklahoma Historical Society, 1976), 30. Camp Radziminski's histori- cal marker is located on U.S. Highway 183, one mile north of Mountain Park, Kiowa County, Oklahoma.

47. Price, *Fifth Cavalry*, 81, 483.

48. Simpson, *Cry Comanche*, 21, 168-70; Price, *Fifth Cavalry*, 23-26, 28; and Richard W. Johnson, *Memoir of Maj.-Gen. George H. Thomas* (Philadelphia: J.B. Lippincott & Co., 1881), 30.

Napoleon Kościalowski
and the Santa Fe Trace Battalion

1. Miecislaus Haiman, *Polish Past in America, 1608-1865* (Chicago: Polish Museum of America, 1974), 77.

2. Louise Barry, comp., "Kansas Before 1854: A Revised Annals," *The Kansas Historical Quarterly*, Vol. 30, No. 3 (Autumn 1964): 392. Kościalowski called his company "The Kosciuszko Guards" in honor of his compatriot, American Revolutionary War General Thaddeus Kościuszko. A military engineer, Kościuszko joined the Continental Army in 1775. He selected the key site for the decisive Battle of Saratoga, fortified strategic Fortress West Point on the Hudson River, and served with General Nathanael Greene in the South. Kościuszko was among the generals at New York's Fraunces Tavern in December 1783 when George Washington bade them farewell.

3. Secretary of War William L. Marcy to General Stephen W. Kearny, Washington, D.C., September 12, 1846, 29th Congress, 2d Session, House Executive Document No. 19 (Serial 49): 13-14; and *Kansas Historical Quarterly* (Autumn 1964): 392.

4. *The Weekly Tribune* (Liberty, Missouri), September 26, 1846; and *Kansas Historical Quarterly* (Autumn 1964): 392.

5. *The Messages and Proclamations of the Governors of the State of Missouri* (Governor John Cummins Edwards), II:206-211, Missouri Historical Society, St. Louis.

6. Jerzy Jan Lerski, *A Polish Chapter in Jacksonian America* (Madison: University of Wisconsin Press, 1958). 94-97; and entries from Kościalowski Family Bible, courtesy of great granddaughter Marilyn W. Thomas of Ingram, Texas. Lerski lists Kościalowski's given name as "Jan," in *A Polish Chapter*, 174. In 1812, Kościalowski was born in the capital of the Grand Duchy of Warsaw, set up by Napoleon Bonaparte.

When his empire fell, the victorious powers met at the Congress of Vienna in 1815 to reestablish order in Europe. As a consideration to Polish nationalism, the Congress created the small kingdom of Poland, with the Russian tsar as king. Hence, the name the Congress Kingdom.

7. Ladislas John Siekaniec, *The Polish Contribution to Early American Education, 1608-1865* (San Francisco: R&E Research Associates, 1976), 96; Mrs. Isaac D. Rawlings, "Polish Exiles in Illinois," *Transactions of Illinois State Historical Society*, Vol. 13 (1927): 93-94; *Green's St. Louis Directory No. 1* (1845): 101, and *Green's Directory* (1847): 110, 115, Missouri Historical Society, St. Louis; and Kościalowski Family Bible. Kościalowski named his second son Edward Mlodzianowski, in honor of his departed friend and fellow exile. This son lived only ten years. There were six children. In addition to the four already mentioned, Mary Lenora was born in 1849 and Phillip Leon in 1851, both in Jacksonville, Illinois.

8. Floyd Calvin Shoemaker, *Missouri and Missourians*, 1943, I:712. The author is indebted to Barbara Stole, Assistant Librarian of the Missouri Historical Society, for her valuable help.

9. Thomas L. Karnes, *William Gilpin: Western Naturalist* (Austin: University of Texas Press, 1970), 190-91; and David Lavender, *Bent's Fort* (Garden City, New York: Doubleday &

Company, Inc., 1954), 298-300. William Gilpin was born in Pennsylvania on October 4, 1815. Appointed a cadet to the U.S. Military Academy in 1834, he resigned six months later. In 1836, he was commissioned a second lieutenant in the 2d U.S. Dragoons during the war with the Seminole Indians of Florida. After two years of service, he resigned and settled in St. Louis. In 1843, he joined the John C. Fremont Expedition to Oregon. He served in the War with Mexico, 1846-48. President Abraham Lincoln appointed Gilpin the first Territorial Governor of Colorado in 1861. He died in Denver, January 20, 1894.

10. *Kansas Historical Quarterly*, Vol. 30, No. 4 (Winter 1964), 543-44; and Company Muster-In Roll, Capt. Koscialowski's Co., Gilpin's Battalion, September 18, 1847, RG 94, AGO, National Archives. The election of officers in volunteer units was a common practice at the time.

11. William Gilpin to Adjutant General Roger Jones, Fort Mann, August 1, 1848, RG 94, Letters Received (Gilpin Correspondence), National Archives.

12. Gilpin to Jones, August 1, 1848.

13. Leo E. Oliva, *Soldiers on the Santa Fe Trail* (Norman: University of Oklahoma Press, 1967), 80; *The Weekly Tribune* (Liberty, Missouri), December 31, 1847; Karnes, *William Gilpin*, 192; and Gilpin to Jones, August 1, 1848.

14. William Pelzer to Gilpin, Fort Mann, November 19, 1847, RG 94, AGO, Gilpin Correspon-

dence, National Archives; St. Louis *New Era*, December 15, 1847; and Karnes, *William Gilpin*, 195.

15. Karnes, *William Gilpin*, 196, 201. The officers and men of Companies C and D forwarded a petition to Lieutenant Colonel Gilpin, recommending that he relieve Captain William Pelzer of the command of Fort Mann and of Company C. The petitioners charged that Pelzer "is not capable to sustain military Order and Discipline" and that they have lost all confidence in him. The petition contained more than 100 signatures, Petition of Companies C & D to Col. Wm. Gilpin, Fort Mann, February 22, 1848, RG 94, AGO, Gilpin Correspondence, National Archives.

16. Captain Napoleon Kościalowski to Adjutant General, War Department, Fort Mann, December 6, 1847; Brigadier General Roger Jones to Kościalowski, Washington, February 3, 1848, Letters Sent, AGO, RG 94, National Archives; and *Kansas Historical Quarterly* 31, No. 2 (Summer 1965): 140.

17. Report of Gilpin to the Adjutant General, Fort Mann, August 1, 1848. Before departing with his command for Mora, New Mexico, in early March of 1848, Gilpin received Lieutenant Phillip Stremmel's court martial charges against Captain William Pelzer. Stremmel told Gilpin that "I do not intend to serve any longer under such a man." Stremmel's charges reinforced those of Cap-

tain Paul Holzcheiter and the officers of Company D. In forwarding the charges to the Secretary of War, Gilpin reminded the Secretary of his prior recommendation (January 10, 1848) for the convening of a general court for the trial of officers and enlisted men under his command. Gilpin again recommended the discharge of Companies C and D from the service. The transmission of correspondence consumed time. Finally, the War Department appointed Colonel John Garland to investigate the charges. Because the Mexican War had ended, and the convening of a general court composed of volunteer officers was nearly impossible, Garland (among other actions) allowed Pelzer to resign from the service, in Gilpin to William L. Marcy, Camp in Bent's Fort, March 10, 1848, Gilpin Correspondence; and Karnes *William Gilpin*, 203.

18. Letter of John M. Krum, et al, St. Louis, Missouri, June 8, 1848, RG 94, AGO, Letters Received, National Archives.

19. Letter of John M. Krum, June 8, 1848.

20. Affidavit of Ceran St. Vrain and William Bent, St. Louis, Missouri, June 3, 1848; and Muster-Out Roll, Company E, Gilpin's Battalion, Missouri Infantry, RG 94, Adjutant General's Office, National Archives.

21. Muster Rolls of Company E, Santa Fe Trace Battalion, *Transactions of the Kansas State Historical Society*, 1907-1908, X:115; Frank S. Edwards, *A Campaign in New Mexico with*

Colonel Doniphan (Philadelphia: Carey and Hart, 1847; reprint ed., Readex Microprint Corporation, 1966), vii, viii, 184; and Gilpin to the Adjutant General, Fort Mann, August 1, 1848, National Archives. Edwards, who marched with Doniphan's command, tallied a total of 5,124 miles traveled from the start at St. Louis to the return at Fort Leavenworth. This distance included 2,330 miles by ship, which should be discounted. Taking the starting point of Fort Leavenworth, as for the Santa Fe Trace Battalion, Doniphan marched west to Santa Fe, south into Chihuahua, and east to Brazos Santiago on the Gulf of Mexico, where his regiment embarked for New Orleans. His total *marching* distance was 2,794 miles.

22. Roy E. Basler, ed., *The Collected Works of Abraham Lincoln*, 8 vols., (New Brunswick, New Jersey: Rutgers University Press, 1959), II:74-75.

23. Sunderine (Wilson) Temple and Wayne C. Temple, *Illinois' Fifth Capitol: The House That Lincoln Built and Caused To Be Rebuilt (1837-1865)*, (Springfield, Illinois: Phillip Brothers Printers, 1988), 106-110.

24. Enlistment Record of Napoleon Kościalowski, U.S. Marine Corps, RG 127, National Archives; U.S. Marine Corps Muster Roll of Sloop *John Adams* (1857), 227, RG 127, National Archives; Telephone interview of Mr. Pressman relating to navy training ships, Naval History Division, Washington, D.C. Navy Yard, April 26, 1989; and *Daily National Intelligencer* (Washington, D.C.), May 31, 1859, 1.

25. Florian Stasik, *Polska Emigracja Polityczna w Stanach Zjednoczonych Ameryki, 1831-1864* (Warszawa: Państwowe Wydawnictwo Naukowe, 1973) [*Polish Political Emigration in the United States of America, 1831-1864*, (Warsaw: State Educational Publishers, 1973)], 251; Rawlings, "Polish Exiles in Illinois," 93; Lerski, *A Polish Chapter*, 119, 131-32; and Mieczyslaw Haiman, *Slady Polskie w Ameryce: Szkice Historyczne* (Chicago: Drukiem Dziennika Zjednoczenia, 1938) [*Polish Traces in America: Historical Sketches* (Chicago: Daily Union Press, 1938)], 143, 148.

26. *Portrait of America: Letters of Henryk Sienkiewicz*, translated and edited by Charles Morley (New York: Columbia University Press, 1959), 92. Sienkiewicz, author of the novel *Quo Vadis?*, received the Nobel Prize for Literature in 1905.

Bibliography

I. Primary Sources

1. **Federal Census:**
   New Mexico Territory: 1860, 1870, 1880, 1885, 1900. Washington, D.C.: 1850.

2. **Government Documents** (Louis William Geck):
   Records at National Archives:
   Records Group 15, Pension, Veterans Administration.
   Records Group 94, Military Service, Adjutant General's Office.
   Records Group 109, Citizen File, War Department Collection of Confederate Records.
   "Old Timers' Stories," Interview of Caroline Geck Weir and Charles C. Geck, WPA Writers Program, 1937, NMSRCA.

3. **Government Documents** (Martin Kozlowski):
   Records at National Archives:
   Records Group 15, Pension, Veterans Administration.
   Records Group 94, Military Service, Adjutant General's Office.
   Albuquerque City Directory, 1901, University of New Mexico Library.
   Deed Book No. 4, San Miguel County Court House, Las Vegas, New Mexico.
   District Court Records, San Miguel County, New Mexico, Criminal Cases 898 and 921 (Territory of New Mexico vs. Martin Kozlowski), NMSRCA.
   House Executive Document No. 1, Part II, 34th Congress, 1st Session (Annual Report for 1855 of the Secretary of War).
   House Executive Document No. 2, Part II, 35th Congress, 1st Session (Annual Report for 1857 of the Secretary of War).

4. **Government Documents** (Alexander Grzelachowski):
   Civil Case No. 522, Alexander Grzelachowski vs. Juan A. Sarracino, Bernalillo County, Territory of New Mexico, NMSRCA.
   Deed Book No. 15, San Miguel County Court House, Las Vegas, New Mexico, Notice of Possession of A. Grzelachowski (320 acres of land at Rincon del Alamo Gordo), December 7, 1880.
   District Court Records, San Miguel County, Territory of New Mexico:
   Cause No. 724, Assumpsit, Alexander Grzelachowski vs. John S. Chisum, March 3, 1876, NMSRCA.
   Alexander Grzelachowski vs. Louis Badreaud, March 1876, NMSRCA.

House Executive Document 1, 40th Congress, 3d Session (Serial 1367),
III, Part 1, and HED, 41st Congress, 2d Session (Serial 1412), II,
Part 2, Reports of the Quartermaster General, October 20, 1868
and October 20, 1869.

Index to Real Property, Books 3, 26, 27, 30, San Miguel County Court
House, Las Vegas, New Mexico.

List of Commissioned Officers, Second Regiment, New Mexico Infantry, *Description Book of Military Units*, NMSRCA.

Records of Guadalupe County, Territory of New Mexico:
Brand Book; Probate Court Records, 1893-1894; Oaths of Office,
1893-1901; Index to Commissioners' Journal; Book I; Cause
8, *Longwill vs Grzelachowski*, Fourth District Court, April 2,
1894 (NMSRCA).

Register of Letters Received, Headquarters, Department of New Mexico,
1854-1865, Microfilm F801R42 1980, University of New Mexico
Library, Albuquerque.

5. **Government Documents** (Charles Radzimiński):
Records at National Archives:
Army Letters of Appointment, Records Group 94, Adjutant
General's Office.
Land Bounty Warrant Application, Records Group 10, Veterans
Administration.
Military Service, Records Group 94, Adjutant General's Office.
Senate Executive Documents:
No. 34, 31st Congress, 1st Session, "Report of the Secretary of the
Interior in Answer to a Resolution of the Senate Calling for
Information in Relation to the Operation of the Commission
appointed to run and mark the boundary between the
United States and Mexico."
No. 119, 32nd Congress, 1st Session, "Commissioner John Russell
Bartlett to the Secretary of the Interior," August 7, 1851.
No. 121, 32d Congress, 1st Session, "Report of Lieutenant Colo-
nel James D. Graham to Colonel John J. Abert, Chief of
Topographical Engineers."
Third Regiment, U.S. Dragoons:
Regimental Orders and Letter Book, Entry 607, Letters Sent
(April-November 1847), Records Group 391, Regular Army
Mobile Units, 1821-1942.
Returns, May 1847-June 1848, Microcopy 744, Roll No. 26.
Headquarters, District of Upper Rio Grande, Letters Sent, Entry 608,
Records Group 391, Regular Army Mobile Units, 1821-1942.
Annual Return of 2d U.S. Cavalry for 1857, MF 744, Roll 51.
Returns of Army Posts in Texas:
Camp Cooper, MF617, Roll 253.
Fort Clark, MF617, Roll 213.
Fort Inge, MF617, Roll 517.

State Department Documents:
  Domestic Letters, M40, Roll 47.
  Miscellaneous Letters, M179, Roll 165.
  Diplomatic Instructions, M77, Roll 136.
  Dispatches from Unites States Minister to Russia, M35, Roll 18.
Diario-Memoria de los Trabajo Cientificos Practicados Bajo la Direccion de Francisco Jimenez, 1er Ingeniero de la Comision de Limites Mexicana Conforme a las Instruciones del Senor Comisionado Don Jose Salazar Ylarrequi a Quien Se Hace Entrega de Ellos. Washington, D.C., 1857, University of Texas at El Paso Library.
Records of James River and Kanawha Company, Virginia State Archives, Richmond.
War Department General Orders, relating to Third U.S. Dragoons, Office of Chief of Military History and the Center of Military History, Washington, D.C.

6. **Government Documents** (Napoleon Kościalowski):
  Records Group 94, Adjutant General's Office, National Archives:
    Company Muster-In and Muster-Out Rolls, Captain Kościalowski's Company (H), 3d Regiment Missouri Infantry.
    Company Muster-In and Muster-Out Rolls, Captain Kościalowski's Company (E), Gilpin's Battalion, Missouri Infantry (Santa Fe Trace Battalion).
    William Gilpin Correspondence.
  Land Bounty Warrant Application, Records Group 10, Veterans Administration, National Archives.
  U.S. Marine Corps, Records Group 127, National Archives:
    Enlistment Papers, Marine Personnel Records.
    Muster Roll of Sloop *John Adams*, 1857.
  House Executive Document No. 19 (Serial 49), 29th Congress, 2d Session, Secretary of War to General Stephen Kearney, September 12, 1846.
  The Messages and Proclamations of the Governors of the State of Missouri (Governor John Cummins Edwards), II: 206-211, Missouri Historical Society, St. Louis.

7. **Collections**
  Charles Ilfeld Collection. University of New Mexico Library, Albuquerque, New Mexico.
  Edward G. W. Butler Family Papers. The Historic New Orleans Collection, New Orleans, Louisiana.
  James D. Graham Papers. Beinecke Rare Book and Manuscript Library, Yale University, New Haven, Connecticut.
  John Russell Bartlett Papers. John Carter Brown Library of Brown University, Providence, Rhode Island.
  Louis William Geck Papers. New Mexico Records Center and Archives, Santa Fe, New Mexico.

Robert Eden Peyton Family Papers. Virginia Historical Society, Richmond, Virginia.
Robert E. Lee Family Papers. Virginia Historical Society, Richmond, Virginia.
William H. Emory Papers. Beinecke Rare Book and Manuscript Library, Yale University, New Haven, Connecticut.

8. **Books and Articles:**
Barry, Louise, comp. "Kansas Before 1854: A Revised Annals," *The Kansas Historical Quarterly*, Vol. 30, No. 3 (Autumn 1964), No. 4 (Winter 1964), and Vol. 31, No. 2 (Summer 1965).
Bartlett, John Russell. *Personal Narrative of Explorations and Incidents in Texas, New Mexico, and California, Sonora, and Chihuahua*, 2 vols. New York: D. Appleton & Company, 1854.
Basler, Roy E., ed. *The Collected Works of Abraham Lincoln*, 8 vols. New Brunswick, New Jersey: Rutgers University Press, 1959.
"Captain Nathan Boone's Journal." *Chronicles of Oklahoma*, Vol. VII. Oklahoma Historical Society, Oklahoma City, 1929: 58-105.
Chavez, Fray Angelico, OFM. *Archives of the Archdiocese of Santa Fe, 1678-1900.* Washington, D.C.: Academy of American Franciscan History, 1957.
Chivington, John M. "The First Colorado Regiment," MF No. P-L 11. Berkeley: University of California, Bancroft Library.
_____. "Retrospective – The Prospective," MF No. P-L 12. Berkeley: University of California, Bancroft Library.
Cullum, George W. *Biographical Register of the Officers and Graduates of the U.S. Military Academy.* Boston: Houghton, Mifflin and Company, 1891.
Edwards, Frank S. *A Campaign in New Mexico with Doniphan.* Philadelphia: Carey and Hart, 1847; reprint ed., Readex Microprint Corporation, 1966.
Emory, William H. *Report of the United States and Mexican Boundary Survey*, 2 vols. Washington, D.C.: A.O.P. Nicholson Printer, 1857.
Exley, Thomas M. comp. *A Compendium of the Pay of the Army from 1775 to 1888.* Washington: Government Printing Office, 1888.
Gardner, Charles. "The Pet Lambs at Glorieta Pass," *Civil War Times Illustrated* 15 (November 1976): 30-37.
Green's St. Louis Directory for 1845 and 1847. Missouri Historical Society, St. Louis.
Heitman, Francis B. *Historical Register and Dictionary the United States Army.* Washington: Government Printing Office, 1903, Vol. 1.
Hodges, Carrie L. "Puerto de Luna," July 10, 1936, WPA Writers Program. (Museum of New Mexico, Santa Fe).
Hollister, Ovando J. *Boldly They Rode: A History of the First Colorado Regiment of Volunteers.* Lakewood, Colorado: The Golden Press, Publishers, 1949.

Inman, Colonel Henry. *The Old Santa Fe Trail*. New York: The Macmillan Company, 1898.
John Fynn Memoirs. U.S. Army Military History Institute, Carlisle Barracks, Pennsylvania.
Krisman, Michael J., ed. *Register of Graduates and Former Cadets United States Military Academy*. West Point, New York: Association of Graduates, 1980.
Lamy Memorial: Centenary of the Archdiocese of Santa Fe. 1850-1950. Santa Fe: Schifani Brothers Printing Company, 1950.
Meline, James F. *Two Thousand Miles on Horseback: Santa Fe and Back.* London: Sampson Low, and Son, and Marston, 1868.
Metropolitan Catholic Almanac and Laity's Directory, 1855 and 1865. Baltimore: Lucas Brothers.
Olmsted, Frederick Law. *A Journey Through Texas*. New York: Burt Franklin, 1860; reprint ed., 1969.
Ostrowski, Juliusz. *Księga Herbowa Rodów Polskich [Book of Polish Family Crests]*. Warszawa: Druk Józefa Sikorskiego [Józef Sikorski, Printer], 1903. [Library of Congress Call Number: CR2064.07].
Portrait of America: Letters of Henryk Sienkiewicz. Translated and edited by Charles Morley. New York: Columbia University Press, 1959.
Price, George F. *Across the Continent with the Fifth Cavalry,* 1883; reprint ed., New York: Antiquarian Press, Ltd., 1959.
Register of Baptisms and Marriages. St. Anthony's Church, Pecos, New Mexico.
Register of Baptisms, 1852. St. Michael the Archangel Church, San Miguel del Vado, New Mexico (at NMSRCA).
Report: James River and Kanawha Company, 1840/41-1844/45. Richmond, Virginia: Shepherd and Colin Printers, 1846 (Virginia State Archives).
Report of Lieut. Col. J. D. Graham, U.S. Topographical Engineers on Mason and Dixon's Line. Chicago: Steam Presses of F. Fulton & Co., 1862. (James D. Graham Papers).
Ritch, W. G., comp. *New Mexico Blue Book, 1882;* reprint ed., Albuquerque: University of New Mexico Press, 1968.
Rostworowski, Emanuel, Redaktor Naczelny [Editor-in-Chief]. *Polski Słownik Biograficzny,* Tom XXX/I, Zeszyt 124 [*Polish Biographical Dictionary,* Vol. XXX/I, Book 124]. Kraków: Wydawnictwo Polskiej Akademii Nauk [Polish Academy of Sciences, Publishers], 1987.
Scott, Hugh Lenox. *Some Memories of a Soldier*. New York: The Century Company, 1928.
War of the Rebellion: A Compilation of the Official Records of the Union and Confederate Armies, 128 vols. Washington: Government Printing Office, 1880-1901.
Who Was Who in America. Chicago: A.N. Marquis Co., 1943. (William Clarke Whitford).
WPA Writers Program. *New Mexico: A Guide to the Colorful State.* New York: Hastings House, Publishers, 1940.

9. **Newspapers**
Anthony Times (New Mexico)
Daily National Intelligencer (Washington, D.C.)
Daily New Mexican (Santa Fe)
Daily Optic (Las Vegas, New Mexico)
El Paso Times
La Voz del Pueblo (Las Vegas)
Las Animas Leader (Colorado)
Las Cruces Citizen
Las Cruces Sun-News
Las Vegas Examiner (New Mexico)
Las Vegas Gazette (New Mexico)
Memphis Daily Appeal
Rio Grande Republican (Las Cruces)
St. Louis Daily Reveille
Santa Rosa News (New Mexico)
The Denver Republican
The Mesilla Times (Arizona)
The New Era (St. Louis)
The Weekly Tribune (Liberty, Missouri)
Weekly New Mexican (Santa Fe)

II. Secondary Sources

Books and Articles

Anderson, Lillie Gerhard, and De Baca, Fabiola Cabeza. "Puerto de Luna," *New Mexico Magazine*, XXXVI (October 1958): 20-21, 43.

Bauer, K. Jack. *The Mexican War, 1846-1848*. New York: Macmillan Publishing Co., 1974.

Beck, Warren A., and Haase, Ynez D., *Historical Atlas of New Mexico*. Norman: University of Oklahoma Press, 1969.

Bolek, Rev. Francis. *Who's Who in Polish America*. New York: Harbinger House, 1943.

Brackett, Albert G. *History of the United States Cavalry*. New York: Harper & Brothers, 1865; reprint ed., New York: Greenwood Press, Publishers, 1968.

Breihan, Carl W., and Ballert, Marion. *Billy the Kid: A Date with Destiny*. Seattle, Washington: Superior Publishing Company, 1970.

Brown, Lenard E. *Survey of the United States-Mexican Boundary, 1849-1855*. Washington, D.C.: U.S. Department of the Interior, National Park Service, 1969.

Callon, Milton W. *Las Vegas, New Mexico: The Town That Wouldn't Gamble*. Las Vegas, New Mexico: Las Vegas Daily Optic, 1962.

Craig, Reginald S. *The Fighting Parson: The Biography of Colonel John M. Chivington*. Los Angeles: Westernlore Press, 1959.

Crimmins, Colonel M. L., ed. "Robert E. Lee in Texas, Letters and Diary." *The West Texas Historical Association Year Book,* Vol. VIII (June 1932): 3-24.

Day, A. Grove. *Coronado's Quest.* Berkeley: University of California Press, 1964.

Dowdey, Clifford. *Lee.* Boston: Little, Brown and Company, 1965.

Ellis, Bruce T., ed. "New Notes on Bishop Lamy's First Years in New Mexico." *El Palacio* LXV, Part 1 (February 1958) and Part II (April 1958).

Faulk, Odie B. *Too Far North...Too Far South.* Los Angeles: Westernlore Press, 1967.

_____. "The Controversial Boundary Survey and the Gadsden Treaty." *Arizona and the West* IV, No. 3 (Autumn 1962): 201-226.

Garrett, Pat F. *Authentic Life of Billy the Kid.* New York: Macmillan Company, 1927.

Goetzmann, William H. *Army Exploration in the American West, 1802-1863.* New Haven: Yale University Press, 1959.

Grigg, George. *History of the Old West.* Las Cruces, New Mexico: Bronson Printing Co., 1930.

Haggard, J. Villasana. *Handbook for Translators of Spanish Historical Documents.* Austin: The University of Texas, 1941.

Haiman, Miecislaus. *The Poles in the Early History of Texas.* Chicago: Polish Roman Catholic Union of America, 1936.

_____. *Polish Past in America, 1608-1865.* Chicago: Polish Museum of America, 1974.

_____. *Slady Polskie w Ameryce: Szkice Historyczne* [*Polish Traces in America: Historical Sketches*]. Chicago: Drukiem Dziennika Zjednoczenia [Daily Union Press], 1938.

Hall, Martin Hardwick. *Sibley' New Mexico Campaign.* Austin: University of Texas Press, 1960.

Hart, Herbert M. *Old Forts of the Far West.* New York: Bonanza Books, 1965.

_____. *Old Forts of the Southwest.* New York: Bonanza Books, 1964.

Hartje, Robert J. *Van Dorn: The Life and Times of a Confederate General.* Nashville, Tennessee: Vanderbilt University Press, 1967.

Helbock, Richard W. *Post Offices of New Mexico.* Las Cruces, New Mexico: Published by the author, 1981 (copy at NMSRCA).

Hine, Robert V. *Bartlett's West: Drawing the Mexican Boundary.* New Haven: Yale University Press, 1968.

Hinton, Harwood P. "John Simpson Chisum, 1877-84." *New Mexico Historical Review* XXXI (July 1956): 177-205.

Horgan, Paul. *Lamy of Santa Fe: His Life and Times.* New York: Farrar, Strauss and Giroux, 1975.

Horn, Stanley F. *The Army of Tennessee.* Indianapolis: The Bobbs-Merrill Company, 1941.

Howlett, Rev. W. J. *Life of the Right Reverend Joseph P. Machebeuf, D.D.* Pueblo, Colorado: n.p., 1908.

Hunt, Aurora. *Major General James Henry Carleton.* Glendale: California: The Arthur H. Clark Company, 1958.

Hunt, Frazier. *The Tragic Days of Billy the Kid.* New York: Hastings House Publishers, 1956.

Jenkins, Myra Ellen, and Schroeder, Albert H. *A Brief History of New Mexico.* Albuquerque: University of New Mexico Press, 1974.

Johnson, R. Winder, comp. *The Ancestry of Rosalie Morris Johnson.* Privately printed by Ferris & Leach, 1905. Virginia Historical Society, Richmond.

Johnson, Richard W. *Memoir of Maj. Gen. George H. Thomas.* Philadelphia: J. B. Lippincott & Co., 1881.

Kajencki, Francis C. *Star on Many a Battlefield: Brevet Brigadier General Joseph Kargé in the American Civil War.* Rutherford, New Jersey: Fairleigh Dickinson University Press, 1980.

———. "Louis William Geck: Soldier, Merchant, and Patriarch of Territorial New Mexico." *Polish American Studies* XXXIX, No. 2 (Autumn 1982): 5-23.

———. "Alexander Grzelachowski: Pioneer Merchant of Puerto de Luna, New Mexico." *Arizona and the West* 26, No. 3 (Autumn 1984): 243-260.

———. "Martin Kozlowski: Role in New Mexico History." *Polish Heritage* XXXVI, No. 4 (Winter 1986): 1, 4-6.

———. "The Battle of Glorieta Pass: Was the Guide Ortiz or Grzelachowski?" *New Mexico Historical Review* 62, No. 1 (January 1987): 47-54.

———. "Charles Radziminski and the United States Mexican Boundary Survey." *New Mexico Historical Review* 63, No. 3 (July 1988): 211-240.

Karnes, Thomas L. *William Gilpin: Western Naturalist.* Austin: University of Texas Press, 1970.

Keleher, William A. *Violence in Lincoln County.* Albuquerque: University of New Mexico Press, 1957.

———. *The Fabulous Frontier.* Albuquerque: University of New Mexico Press, 1962.

———. *Maxwell Land Grant.* New York: Argosy-Antiquarian, Ltd., 1964.

Kessell, John L. *Kiva, Cross, and Crown: The Pecos Indians and New Mexico, 1540-1840.* Washington, D.C.: National Park Service, Department of the Interior, 1979.

Klasner, Lilly. *My Girlhood among Outlaws.* Tucson: University of Arizona Press, 1972.

Lavender, David. *Bent's Fort.* Garden City, New York: Doubleday & Company, 1954.

Lee, Fitzhugh. *General Lee.* Nashville, Tennessee: Guinn and Guinn Southwestern Publishing House, 1895.

Lerski, Jerzy Jan. *A Polish Chapter in Jacksonian America.* Madison: University of Wisconsin Press, 1958.

Metz, Leon C. *The Shooters.* El Paso, Texas: Mangan Books, 1976.
———— . *Pat Garrett: The Story of a Western Lawman.* Norman: University of Oklahoma Press, 1974.
Miller, Ray. *Ray Miller's Texas Forts: A History and Guide.* Houston: Cordovan Press, 1985.
Morris, John W., et al. *Historical Atlas of Oklahoma,* 3d ed. Norman: University of Oklahoma Press, 1986.
New Mexico Historical Review 18, No. 4 (October 1943).
Newman, S. H. III. "The Las Cruces Thirty-Four Answers the School Question." *Password* 14, No. 1 (Spring 1969): 13-21.
Oliva, Leo E. *Soldiers on the Santa Fe Trail.* Norman: University of Oklahoma Press, 1967.
Parish, William J. *The Charles Ilfeld Company.* Cambridge, Massachusetts: Harvard University Press, 1961.
———— . "The German Jew and the Commercial Revolution in Territorial New Mexico, 1850-1900." *New Mexico Historical Review* 35, No. 2 (April 1960): 129-150.
Pearce, S. Grove, et al, eds. *New Mexico Newspapers: A Comprehensive Guide to Bibliographical Entries and Locations.* Albuquerque: University of New Mexico Press, 1975.
Prince, Hon. L. Bradford, comp. *The General Laws of New Mexico.* Albany, New York: W. C. Little & Company, Law Publishers, 1882.
Radzyminski, Stanley F. "Charles Radziminski: Patriot, Exile, Pioneer." *The Chronicles of Oklahoma* 38, No. 4 (1960-61): 354-368.
Rawlings, Mrs. Isaac D. "Polish Exiles in Illinois." *Transactions of Illinois State Historical Society* 13 (1927): 83-104.
Rister, Carl Coke. *Robert E. Lee in Texas.* Norman: University of Oklahoma Press, 1946.
Rodenbough, Theo. F., and Haskins, William L. *The Army of the United States.* New York: Maynard, Merrill & Co., 1896.
Shoemaker, Floyd Calvin. *Missouri and Missourians,* 1943.
Siekaniec, Rev. Ladislas John. *The Polish Contribution to Early American Education, 1608-1865.* San Francisco: R&E Research Associates, 1976.
Simmons, Marc. *The Little Lion of the Southwest: A Life of Manuel Chaves.* Chicago: Swallow Press, 1973.
Simpson, Colonel Harold B. *Cry Comanche: The 2d U.S. Cavalry in Texas, 1855-1861.* Hillsboro, Texas: Hill Jr. College Press, 1979.
Smith, George Winston, and Judah, Charles. *Chronicles of the Gringos.* Albuquerque: University of New Mexico Press, 1968.
Smith, Justin H. *The War with Mexico,* 2 vols. New York: The Macmillan Company, 1919.
Stanley, F. *The Puerto de Luna New Mexico Story.* Privately printed, 1969.
Stasik, Florian. *Polska Emigracja Polityczna w Stanach Zjednoczonych Ameryki, 1831-1864 [Polish Political Emigration in the United States of America, 1831-1865].* Warszawa: Państwowe Wydawnictwo Naukowe [State Educational Publishers], 1973.

Steffen, Randy. *The Horse Soldier, 1776-1943*, 3 vols. Norman: University of Oklahoma Press, 1978.

Stratton, Porter A. *The Territorial Press of New Mexico, 1834-1912.* Albuquerque: University of New Mexico Press, 1969.

Taylor, Morris F. *First Mail West: Stagecoach Lines on the Santa Fe Trail.* Albuquerque: University of New Mexico Press, 1971.

Temple, Sunderine (Wilson), and Temple, Wayne C. *Illinois' Fifth Capitol: The House That Lincoln Built and Caused To Be Rebuilt (1837-1865).* Springfield, Illinois: Phillips Brothers Printers, 1988.

Tevis, James H. *Arizona in the '50s.* Albuquerque: University of New Mexico Press, 1959.

Todsen, Thomas, and Dike, Sheldon. "Territorial Post Offices and Postmasters of New Mexico." Unpublished manuscript, NMSRCA.

Twitchell, Ralph Emerson. *The Leading Facts of New Mexican History*, 5 vols. Cedar Rapids, Iowa: The Torch Press, 1917.

Uruski, Hrabia [Count] Seweryn, et al., eds. *Rodzina: Herbarz Szlachty Polskiej [Family: Heraldry of Polish Gentry]*, 15 vols. Warszawa: Bookstore of Gebethner and Wolff, 1908.

Wallace, Edward S. *The Great Reconnaissance: Soldiers, Artists, and Scientists on the Frontier, 1848-1861.* Boston: Little, Brown and Company, 1955.

Wandycz, Piotr. *The Lands of Partitioned Poland, 1795-1918.* Seattle: University of Washington Press, 1974.

Warner, Louis H. *Archbishop Lamy: An Epoch Maker.* Santa Fe: Santa Fe New Mexican Publishing Company, 1936.

Westphal, David. "The Battle of Glorieta Pass: Its Importance in the Civil War." *New Mexico Historical Review* 44, No. 2 (April 1969): 137-154.

Westphal, Victor. "The Public Domain in New Mexico." *New Mexico Historical Review* 33 (April 1958): 128-143.

_____ . *The Public Domain in New Mexico, 1854-1891.* Albuquerque: University of New Mexico Press, 1965.

Whitford, William Clarke. *Colorado Volunteers in the Civil War.* Denver: The State Historical and Natural History Society, 1906.

Wilcox, General Cadmus M. *History of the Mexican War.* Washington, D.C.: The Church News Publishing Company, 1892.

Wright, Muriel H., et al. *Mark of Heritage.* Oklahoma City: Oklahoma Historical Society, 1976.

Index

About the Author

Francis Casimir Kajencki was born in Erie, Pennsylvania on November 15, 1918. A graduate of the United States Military Academy (Class of January 1943), he served his country for thirty years, retiring as colonel and Assistant Chief of Information, Department of the Army. Since then, he has pursued historical research and writing.

He was not aware until 1976 of the contribution of Poles to the history of the American Southwest. It appeared that most historians failed to include them, and this gap posed a challenge that he felt compelled to fill.

Typography and book design by Camille.
Text set in 11 point Goudy Old Style.
Jacket design and illustration
by Vicki Trego Hill.
Printing by Thomson-Shore on
60 pound Glatfelter, an acid-free paper
with an effective life of at least
three hundred years.